China, India, and Japan
The Middle Period

Edited by

WILLIAM H. McNEILL

and

JEAN W. SEDLAR

New York
OXFORD UNIVERSITY PRESS
London 1971 Toronto

Library of Congress Catalogue Card Number: 68-8409
Printed in the United States of America

Preface

This little book seeks to introduce its readers to the literary cultures of China, India, and Japan across a thousand years, A.D. 500-1500. In all three lands, Buddhism mattered; but the differences in the forms of Buddhist piety that flourished in each country were indicative of the pervasive divergences that gave each land a style of civilization unique unto itself. It therefore seemed best to treat each separately, making comparison simpler by arranging our readings under the same three heads in each case: government, religion, and society.

Both the chronological and the geographical limits of this collection of readings need brief explanation. Chronologically, we have chosen to start from the time when Indian and Chinese civilizations had attained a characteristic lasting balance, i.e. after their respective "classical" ages had passed. This of course implies that thought and letters were more strictly traditional in this "middle period" than in the ages before or after. What else could one expect when the "classical" patterns of thought available to each civilization were capable of coping with a broad range of experience and had adequate explanations for almost everything that occurred?

The terminus of 1500 was chosen to underline the novelty that presented itself to the ancient, established civilizations of Asia when European seamen first succeeded in rounding Africa and linking the Atlantic with the southern oceans. To be sure, it was the Europeans who were initially aware of the novelty; for several centuries the vast majority of Indians and Chinese were able to continue living along accustomed lines, paying little attention to the new kind of "south sea barbarians" (as the

Chinese dubbed the Europeans) who had begun to haunt their coasts. Yet in retrospect it is clear that the opening of the oceans of the world to regular shipping had fundamentally subversive consequences for the civilizations of Asia, so that the arrival of Europeans may appropriately be taken to signal the end of an era of world history.

Japan, however, was different. The Japanese islands had not become the seat of an ancient "classical" culture before A.D. 500. On the contrary, only after that date did the massive and deliberate importation of skills and knowledge from China and Korea inaugurate Japanese civilization. Equally, the arrival of the first Europeans in Japan (1540's) provoked a lively response, quite unlike the general indifference with which the Chinese and Indians reacted to the presence of these strangers.

Hence the term "middle period" does not fit Japanese patterns of development very well, unless one chooses to assign a classical Chinese heritage to the Japanese in the manner in which northern Europeans (and Americans) have commonly laid claim to the classical inheritance of the ancient Mediterranean world. As a matter of fact, the parallel is very close. For the systematic eagerness with which the Japanese apprenticed themselves to China in the seventh to ninth centuries was very like the way in which European scholars and men of taste set out to appropriate the culture of the Greeks and Romans in the twelfth to sixteenth centuries.

This, then, allows us to assign the term "middle period" to all three civilizations, despite its awkwardness. In doing so the editors deliberately eschewed the perhaps commoner term "medieval." We wished to avoid the use of nomenclature traditionally applied to European history, for most of the associations that the term "medieval" calls to mind are misleading when applied to Asian societies.

So much for chronology. Geographically, we have overlooked a number of lesser civilized societies such as those of Korea, Annam, Java, Cambodia, Tibet. In comparison with these semisatellite cultures of east Asia the primacy of China and India throughout this middle period is not seriously in question. This, together with the absence of much in the way of translated materials from the lesser Asian civilizations, perhaps justifies their exclusion from this book. Japan, at once the most successful and one of the most independent of the later blooming cultures of Asia, may perhaps serve as a kind of representative for them all.

Except peripherally in the case of India, the Islamic world is likewise not treated in this book. A separate volume in this series (Volume VI) is devoted exclusively to that civilized tradition, combining Arab, Turkish, and African materials with samplings of the Islamic experience in India, southeast Asia, and China. Islam is, however, taken for granted in some of our Indian texts, since its presence can scarcely be ignored in connection with Indian government and religion in the period following the Muslim conquests in that country.

No single, simple summary seems in the least appropriate as a characterization of Indian, Chinese, and Japanese societies and civilizations between A.D. 500-1500. The divergences between India and China, despite the link of Buddhism that ran between the two lands, were profound. Chinese concern with decorum and good government—and the various forms of rebellion against these Confucian preoccupations that can be glimpsed, for example, in the poetry of Li Po or the writings of the Taoists—stands in sharp contrast with continuing Indian interest in transcendental realities, approached (as often as not) by way of love-mysticism that sometimes took quite direct sensuous form. Krishna's dalliance with the milkmaids offers an example of how Indian tradition linked transcendentalism and sensualism, in a fashion that would have been both shocking and incomprehensible to most Chinese.

It is more tempting for Americans to lump Chinese and Japanese civilizations together; and the importance of Chinese forms for much of traditional Japanese culture gives a superficial plausibility to this confusion. Yet however faithfully the Japanese imperial court sought to duplicate the titles and rituals of China, Japan's political reality always remained far different from that prevailing on the mainland. The far greater honor paid to military prowess in Japan was one indication of the deep differences between the two societies. The importance of hereditary clans, the Shogunate, and Shinto in Japanese life had no parallels in China. Conversely, the Chinese pattern of recruitment to high office by means of examinations—a principle that inhibited the development of anything like an hereditary aristocracy in traditional China—never took root in Japan, where a military aristocracy retained its dominating role throughout the centuries we are here concerned with.

The readings assembled here ought to make these and other differences among the three Asian civilizations clear and unmistakable. The three broad topics—government, religion, and society—under which the selections are arranged may perhaps facilitate cross-cultural comparisons; on the other hand, the loose but fundamental cohesion of each civilization in all its aspects will not, I hope, be obscured by this necessarily arbitrary arrangement. For government, religion, and society—whether in Asia or in Europe, in ancient or in modern times—are no more than aspects of a single human reality; that is, the reality of a civilized style of life. Diversified, skilled, and variegated such civilized life styles certainly were; yet the lives and actions of millions upon millions of persons nevertheless fitted together in a loose but unmistakable fashion to make three separate patterns—Chinese, Indian, and Japanese—each distinctively itself.

W.H.M.

Chicago, Illinois
April 1971

Contents

I CHINA

A. GOVERNMENT

* Introductions are listed only when they pertain to more than one selection or deal with a general subject rather than a specific text.

B. RELIGION

C. SOCIETY

II INDIA

A. GOVERNMENT

B. RELIGION

C. SOCIETY

III JAPAN

A. GOVERNMENT

B. RELIGION

C. SOCIETY

Maps

Editorial Note

The present editors are responsible for all introductions and footnotes, except that footnotes reprinted verbatim (in whole or in part) are marked "(Tr.)." The texts themselves have been reproduced exactly as they stand in the sources indicated, except for the cuts made necessary by limitations of space and indicated by ellipses.

Chinese and Japanese names are given according to the custom of their countries—family name first, personal name last (except in footnotes). Indian names use the same order as in English (family name last).

Note on Pronunciation

Our spelling of Chinese terms follows the standard Wade-Giles system (see "Note on Chinese Pronunciation" at the front of Volume V of this series).

In the Japanese language, consonants are pronounced approximately as in English (with *g* always hard); the vowels as in Spanish or Italian (*a* as in f*a*ther, *e* as in *e*nd, *i* as in mach*i*ne, *o* as in *o*ld, *u* as in r*u*le).

The Sanskrit tongue has both long and short vowels (the long vowels pronounced as in Spanish or Italian); but the diacritical marks indicating this distinction have been omitted here. Consonants are ordinarily pronounced approximately as in English, except that an *h* after the letters *k*, *g*, *t*, *d*, *b*, or *p* indicates an aspirated sound (e.g. *th* resembles the English *th* in an*th*ill). The letters of the Sanskrit alphabet which are sometimes transcribed as *ś* and *ṣ* are given here simply as *sh*. The accent in Sanskrit words usually falls on the second to the last syllable.

I
China

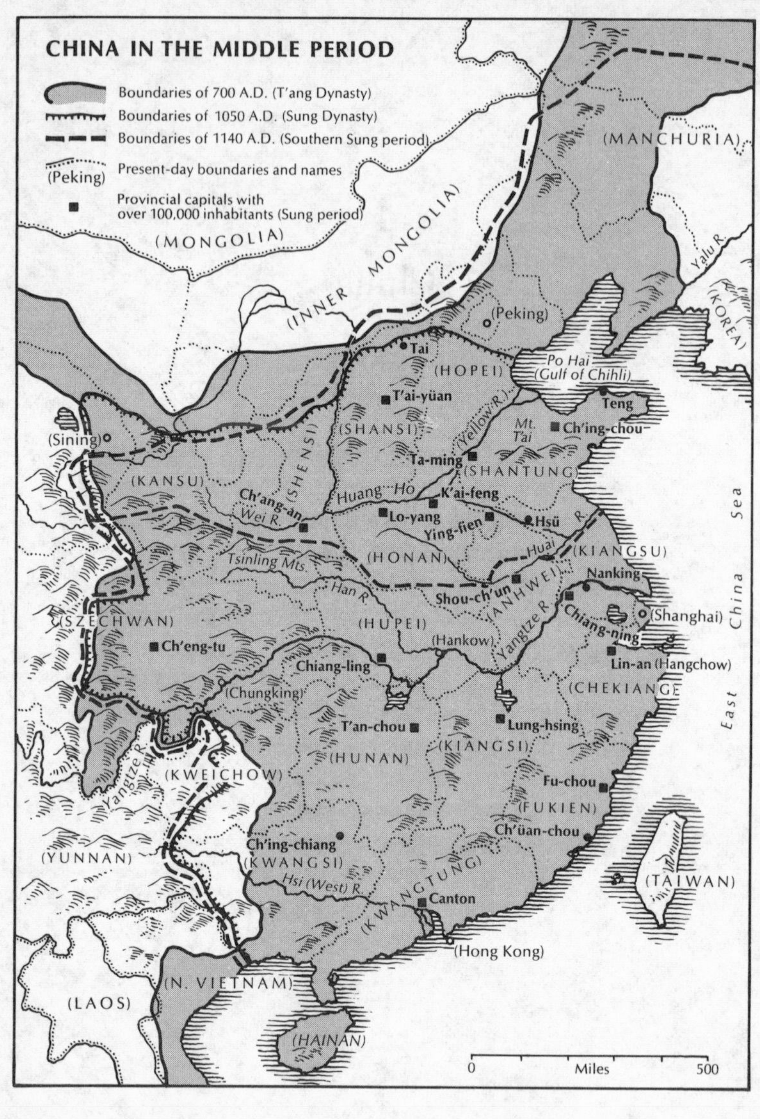

CHINA IN THE MIDDLE PERIOD
Boundaries of 700 A.D. (T'ang Dynasty)
Boundaries of 1050 A.D. (Sung Dynasty)
Boundaries of 1140 A.D. (Southern Sung period)
Present-day boundaries and names
(Peking)
Provincial capitals with over 100,000 inhabitants (Sung period)
(MONGOLIA)
(INNER MONGOLIA)
(MANCHURIA)
Yalu R.
(KOREA)
(Peking)
Tai
(HOPEI)
Po Hai
(Gulf of Chihli)
T'ai-yüan
Teng
(SHANSI)
(SHENSI)
Mt. T'ai
Ch'ing-chou
(Yellow R.)
(Sining)
Ta-ming
(SHANTUNG)
(KANSU)
Huang Ho
K'ai-feng
Ch'ang-an
Wei R.
Lo-yang
Ying-t'ien
Hsü
Huai R.
(KIANGSU)
Tsinling Mts.
(HONAN)
Nanking
Shou-ch'un
(ANHWEI)
Han R.
Yangtze R.
Chiang-ning
(Shanghai)
(SZECHWAN)
(HUPEI)
(Hankow)
Ch'eng-tu
Chiang-ling
Lin-an (Hangchow)
(Chungking)
(CHEKIANG)
East China Sea
T'an-chou
Lung-hsing
(KIANGSI)
(HUNAN)
Yangtze R.
(KWEICHOW)
Fu-chou
(FUKIEN)
Ch'ing-chiang
Ch'üan-chou
(YUNNAN)
(KWANGSI)
(KWANGTUNG)
(TAIWAN)
Hsi (West) R.
Canton
(Hong Kong)
(N. VIETNAM)
(LAOS)
(HAINAN)
0
Miles
500

Government

Land Distribution and Taxes: Introduction

A constant problem throughout the history of China has been the tendency for government expenditures to increase faster than tax revenues. An important reason for this difficulty lay in the tax system itself. Prior to the eighth century A.D., the principal source of state revenue in China was a tax assessed per head upon all free landholders, usually payable in grain, cloth, and compulsory labor. But tenant farmers paid rent to their landlords in lieu of taxes to the state; and the great estate owners frequently possessed such power and influence that they paid no taxes whatever. Moreover, in periods of internal peace the larger landowners were usually able to increase the size of their holdings, thus removing more and more free peasants from the official tax rolls. As a result, the tax burden of China as a whole became divided among fewer persons than before.

Clearly, tax rates could not be increased beyond a certain level without producing serious social dislocations—peasant revolts, vagrancy, or the widespread abandonment of agricultural holdings. Nonetheless the large estate owners resisted any attempt by the imperial authorities to curb their semi-independent, tax-exempt status. A series of Chinese governments tried in various ways to deal with this growing imbalance between revenues and expenditures. In the late fifth century A.D. the Northern Wei dynasty (which then ruled much of north China) instituted an "equal field" system of land tenure. According to this system, all land was declared to be national property subject to periodic redistribution according to the size of farmers' families, with only a small percentage of each peasant's holdings being granted in permanent (i.e. hereditary) tenure.*

* Except for this limited provision for hereditary tenure, these arrangements were modelled upon the so-called "well-field" system which supposedly had prevailed in remote antiquity. Under the "well-field" system all land was

Under the Northern Wei this system enjoyed some success, probably in part because a recent period of civil strife had reduced population to a point where considerable open land was available for distribution. Although the Wei did not disturb existing estates, and the prescribed redistributions were rarely if ever carried out, this "equal field" system nonetheless helped to stem the growth of large private landholdings and to provide a measure of fiscal stability for the Wei government.

In the time of the Sui (589-618) and early T'ang (from 618) dynasties, which ruled over a reunited China, this "equal field" system was greatly extended in scope. Although great estates still existed, they were now designated as "rank" or "office" lands—theoretically, lands held in trust for the central government according to the rank or office of their holders. Merely to maintain this system, which required an accurate, detailed census and land survey, the T'ang bureaucracy was obliged to develop complex administrative methods. Apparently little actual redistribution of land occurred; the system was applied primarily to newly opened lands or to lands which had passed out of cultivation during the wars preceding the establishment of the Sui dynasty. But despite these faults, the "equal field" system functioned with reasonable efficiency for about a century, providing the fiscal basis for the brilliant cultural achievements of the early T'ang period.

By the early eighth century, however, the "equal field" system was breaking down. A century of domestic peace had permitted the farming population to increase faster than new lands could be brought into cultivation, so that in practice most peasants tilled less than the 100 *mou*** to which they were theoretically entitled. In defiance of the laws, most agricultural land in China came to be registered as the permanent possession of its owners, and therefore not subject to redistribution at all. This failure of the "equal field" system was certainly a significant factor in the gradual decline of the authority of the T'ang government. Following the disastrous military rebellion led by An Lu-shan in A.D. 755, the "equal field" system was abandoned; and in the year 780 a variety of existing taxes on per-

national property; sections of land were divided into nine equal portions (resembling the Chinese character for "well") and redistributed periodically according to the farmers' needs. A long series of Confucian scholars, beginning with Mencius, had recommended the re-establishment of this system.

** 100 *mou* equals approximately 13.7 acres.

sons, lands, and households was abolished in favor of a single tax on land.

This so-called Twice-a-Year tax, assessed per unit of land rather than per head, marked the end of the great landowners' tax-free status. It permitted the central government to regard with comparative equanimity the existence of large private estates, which were now liable to taxes regardless of their owners' position in society. Though Confucian scholars continued to advocate some type of equal field system, the advantages of the land tax—incidentally far simpler to administer than its predecessor—proved more persuasive than ethical arguments or the example of the ancients. In practice the Twice-a-Year tax provided a fairly stable source of revenue for the imperial government; and it remained the principal tax in China down to modern times.

DECREE OF A.D. 624

Regulations for the "Equal Field" System

Five feet are to be considered one pace. Two hundred forty square paces are equal to one *mou*. One *ch'ing*[1] consists of one hundred *mou*.

Each adult male[2] is to be given one *ch'ing* of land. A person who is incurably ill or disabled will receive forty *mou* of land. Widowed wife or concubine will receive thirty *mou*. The head of a household will receive twenty *mou* in addition to his regular allotment. Of the amount of land each person receives, 20 percent is hereditary and the rest is redistributable. Upon the death of the grantee, the hereditary portion can be inherited by the head of the household next in line, while the redistributable portion is to be returned to the government for redistribution among other people.

As for the grantee's obligations towards the government, each

From Dun J. Li, ed., *The Essence of Chinese Civilization*, Princeton, N.J.: D. Van Nostrand Co., 1967, pp. 276-78. Reprinted by permission of Van Nostrand Reinhold Co.

1. About 13.7 acres.
2. The Chinese term refers to persons aged 18 years or more.

adult male is to pay two piculs[3] of grain each year as rent. Besides, there are requisitions that vary in accordance with the products of his native district. He is to deliver to the government each year two *chang*[4] of damask silk. If he chooses to pay in cloth instead of silk, the assessment will be increased by 20 percent. For a person who selects to pay in silk, he should add three ounces of floss to his payment. If he pays in cloth, he should add three catties[5] of hemp. In addition to the payments in produce, he is required to work twenty days each year for the government. He can, if he wishes to, translate his corvée obligations into payment in kind, at the rate of three feet of silk for each day of corvée service. He will be exempt from silk or cloth payment if, when the necessity arises, he is called upon to work twenty-five instead of twenty days. He is to be exempt from both grain and silk or cloth payment if he is called upon to render labor services for a period of thirty days. Under no circumstances should the corvée duties last a period longer than fifty days.

Rent is to be paid in rice in the Lingnan provinces.[6] For tax purposes all households in these provinces are to be divided into three categories: high income, medium income, and low income. Each year they are to pay 1.2, 0.8, and 0.6 piculs of rice respectively. These amounts are to be reduced by 50 percent if the taxpayers belong to the Yi or Liao minorities.[7]

As to the northern barbarians who have been Sinicized and live under Chinese jurisdiction, cash instead of produce will be accepted for tax payment. The payment is ten standard coins for a member of the high income household and five standard coins for a member of the medium income household; the members of a low income household are exempt from poll tax. However, if these barbarians have lived under Chinese jurisdiction for a period of two years or more, each of their male adults is required to deliver to the government two heads of sheep each year for

3. The picul, or Chinese bushel, was the equivalent of about three English bushels.

4. One *chang* equals ten Chinese feet.

5. A catty equals about 1⅓ lbs.

6. The southern coastal area of China (modern Kwangsi and Kwangtung).

7. These were non-Chinese peoples inhabiting the regions of present-day Kwangsi, Kweichow, and Yunnan provinces.

high income households and one head of sheep for medium income households. The tax rate for low income households is one head of sheep for every three male adults.

Taxes will be reduced in proportion to the seriousness of natural disasters, such as flood, drought, plague of locusts, and frost. If more than 40 percent of the planted crop is destroyed during a natural disaster, the affected taxpayer does not have to pay any rent. Both rent and silk or cloth obligations are cancelled if more than 60 percent of the planted crop is destroyed. All obligations towards the government, including corvée duties, cease automatically if more than 70 percent of the planted crop has been destroyed.

All households in the nation are to be divided into nine categories in accordance with the amount of properties they possess. Under the supervision of its magistrate, the grading of households in each district should be done once every three years. Such grading should be then examined, checked, and made official by the provincial authorities.

One hundred households form a hamlet, and five hamlets form a township. A neighborhood consists of four households, and a *pao* is composed of five households. Those who live in cities are organized into wards, and those in the countryside are grouped into villages. All people in each of the organizational units—village, ward, neighborhood, or hamlet—are urged to emulate one another in good behavior.[8]

The four classes of people—scholars, farmers, artisans, and merchants—earn their livelihood by engaging in their respective professions; they should not compete with people socially below them for the purpose of making profits. Artisans, merchants, and people of miscellaneous occupation are not allowed to associate themselves with scholars. . . .

Each year responsible officials should record people of different age groups in accordance with the above classifications. The registration of all households should be made once every three

8. This *pao-chia* system—whereby each member of a *pao* (group of about ten families) was held legally responsible for the others' good behavior—was a favorite device of many Chinese governments, and was used even in the twentieth century.

years. Five copies of the registration should be deposited with district and provincial authorities, and three copies should be filed with the executive branch of the central government.

Introduction to the Decrees Concerning Migrants

Chinese documents of the late seventh and of the early eighth century contain frequent references to migrants and runaways—farmers who abandoned the districts in which they were officially registered, and either disappeared altogether or settled on unoccupied land elsewhere. On the whole, these migrations proceeded from north to south. North and northeast China in this period was plagued by a series of severe floods and droughts, as well as by frequent incursions of Tartars and Turks from beyond the frontiers and by the depredations of both Chinese and barbarian armies.

The object of the following two decrees was to return the absconding peasants to the registers, so that they would again be liable for taxation, *corvée*, and military service. Evidently the earlier decree failed of its purpose; for the second takes a more conciliatory tone, and combines moral persuasion with the offer of substantial rewards for obedience. According to Chinese sources, the latter decree resulted in the reregistration of over 800,000 families.

Both decrees are issued in the name of the reigning emperor, Hsüan Tsung, who speaks in the first person. The ceremonial phrases which inevitably introduce such documents are omitted here.

DECREE OF A.D. 721

Concerning Migrants

Since, when laws are long in force they decay, and when laws decay they are infringed, to establish laws is the first requisite

This decree and the one following are from Edwin G. Pulleyblank, *The Background of the Rebellion of An Lu-shan*, London: Oxford University Press, 1955, pp. 178-80 and 181-82. Reprinted by permission of Oxford University Press.

in governing a country and to enregister the people is one's task in order to save them. Since we have been in a state of peace, people have become very indolent and dishonest. The laws of the state have sometimes become slack and frauds among the peasants have indeed multiplied. Now, wherever the calendar extends, the lands of our subjects and vassals have no beyond. Yet though the population has grown, the tax revenues show no increase. [Men] all heedlessly leave their native places and band together to wander in idleness. Sometimes powerful men provide refuge. Sometimes criminal officials make them sacks and bags [to hold their loot?]. The running away grows year by year and the corruption spreads day by day. The prefecture and county officials do not show mercy and the districts and neighborhoods suffer the harm.

In spite of my shallow virtue, the fault lies on me. It is not only that the superior officials do not exercise government and the junior officials do not keep the law. If the longer there is peace the more one relaxes, then the defences of the country will fall into ever greater disorder. Now we wish to get rid of the non-essential branches and return to the root, to block up the evil and set right the virtue, so that laws may have their establishment and men may know their direction. In these circumstances we shall have pity on the helpless and destitute, excuse unpaid debt, open the way of self-renewal [for the people] and cause the utmost benevolence to be extended.

In every prefecture the men who have run away to escape military service shall all be permitted to give themselves up within one hundred days of the day on which this decree arrives, and in accordance with the regulations shall everywhere be enrolled by households.

Those who wish to remain[1] shall be entered directly on the registers and shall be subject to taxation and other imposts according to the regulations for new registrants. In addition [the officials] shall get in touch with their native places and stop the levying [of taxes, &c., there].[2]

1. I.e., in the localities to which they have migrated.

2. To make up the loss caused by absconding taxpayers, local officials often collected additional sums from the remaining inhabitants of a district.

As for those who wish to return to their place of registration, and those who, according to the regulations, may not be enrolled [where they have settled],[3] when they have given themselves up, let a clear record be made and let their original places of registration be informed by letter without waiting until [the men themselves] are sent. Allow them to wait till after the gathering of the harvest and then be sent back.

Any who wish to return at once shall be allowed to do so. When they arrive in their native districts, this year's taxes and *corvée* shall be excused them. . . .

If any do not give themselves up within the allotted time, let them be immediately taken and sent to distant frontiers and made peasants [there]. Let the members of their families who have followed them into flight also be sent.

As for officials or private persons in the prefectures and counties who allow them to remain within the boundaries after the allotted time or in any matter do not completely [comply with this law], let the appropriate authorities make a clear prohibition against it.

As for the collection of tax arrears, of loans of food or seed grain, and of the Land Tax (*ti-shui*[4]), if demands have previously been sent but not yet paid, let everything before the twelfth month of K'ai-yüan 7 (719) be excused. Concealment and fraud by officials are excluded from the amnesty.

We shall cause all ordinances to be renewed and all lands to enjoy forgiveness; the people to return to their tasks and the officials to perfect their craft. Do all you functionaries be diligent in your offices so that the precepts of the former kings may be followed and the path of government may be made firm. Proclaim this near and far that our will may be made known.

3. The regulations forbade anyone to move from thinly populated districts to more densely populated ones, or from regions of heavy *corvée* to others with lighter *corvée,* or from the district surrounding the capital to any other place.

4. The land tax at this time was merely a small levy used to provide grain for the public granaries.

DECREE OF A.D. 724

Concerning Migrants

In recent years though there has been a certain abundance in the harvests, we still fear that land is not fully utilized and that many of the people have abandoned their occupations. The wandering beggars have not all returned; the grain-bearing fields are not uniformly cultivated. Because of this we are deeply distressed and have decided to send out commissioners to show mercy to the registered families that have run away and to inspect the extent of the wide fields.

Now this running away of the peasantry has causes of long standing. In the periods T'ien-ts'e (i.e. 695, 9th month to last month) and Shen-kung (697) the Northern Ti and Western Jung (i.e. the Khitan, Turks, and the Tibetans) made trouble. In the wakes of large armies there are always lean years. Flood and drought followed one another. Furthermore, running away was then very common and from that time became a great evil. Even to the present we suffer from it.

Now it was because they could not help it that they left their relatives and abandoned their own districts. They were in extremities and thereby looked for an escape; immediately their lands were enclosed [by landowners].[5] They not only risked punishment under the law, but also abandoned their livelihood. While they wander they are in constant fear, but if they return they have no means of support. Under this accumulation of danger and difficulty they become confirmed vagrants. Sometimes they stop under the protection of others; sometimes they hire themselves out to earn a living. Their hopes of returning home are in vain; their plans of going back to their native places are not fulfilled.

I humbly bear my great task and foster the myriad people as

5. Documents of the late seventh and of the early eighth century record many complaints about estate building. Most of it proceeded by illegal means, since under the "equal field" system the sale of land was subject to strict regulation.

my children. I have not cultivated my virtue as I ought and this evil does not mend. I have been oppressive to the people and driven [the chariot of state] with rotten reins. I am truly distressed about it. Since it is deeply to my blame, I have taken thought to lay open the road for the people to make a fresh beginning.

Now all those who have up to now run away shall be permitted to give themselves up. If they are able to apply themselves to the fields and to put their energies to ploughing and hoeing, let them till uncultivated fields wherever they are to be found. Let a fee be collected in the produce of the locality[6] but let not [the officials of] the prefectures and counties send them on military or *corvée* duty. Their regular taxes shall be entirely remitted. If they do not appear within the allotted time, or after this again run away from the customary path; or if they treat this measure as an expedient (?) and not as a fixed law; this will be to hinder our sincerity and good faith, this will be to bring into confusion the order of our state. Thereupon the appropriate authorities must apply stern punishment.

Moreover, there are many differences in the climate and soil throughout the empire. The land has not the same requirements and customs are also not the same. It is right that we command the Vice-President of the Ministry of War and Censor in Attendance Yü-wen Jung to combine [with his other offices that of] Commissioner for Encouraging Agriculture and to go about inspecting the provinces and giving comfort to the populace. Let him everywhere consult with the officials and the people. If there are any taxes, *corvée*, or other imposts which are disadvantageous for the people, let him make appropriate decisions after considering the circumstances, and thereafter report them.[7] Let him strive to gather [the people] in peacefully and not to cause any disturbance. Whenever he has to deal out rewards or punishments, let him exercise the utmost loyalty and justice. Wherever

6. Each new registrant was required to pay a fee which amounted to far less than the back taxes from which he was exempted under the decree.

7. Needless to say, the special officials sent out by this Commissioner were unpopular with the established bureaucrats—many of whom belonged to the landowning class and themselves connived at increasing their own or their relatives' estates by illegal or semi-legal means.

he goes let him show this to the people to convey our anxious concern on their behalf.

Introduction to the Twice-a-Year Tax

The Twice-a-Year tax—the new, single tax on land—was enacted in the year 780 in response to a proposal by Yang Yen, one of the Emperor's chief ministers. Actual rates of taxation were computed in 788 by adding up the various taxes to be abolished and estimating their value in money. The payment of taxes in kind was henceforth forbidden. This reform—prompted by the growth of a money economy in T'ang China together with the failure of the "equal field" system of landholding—proved to have unexpected consequences.

From the government's point of view, the shift to a money basis for tax payment marked an important step forward in the direction of greater fiscal efficiency. From the peasants' standpoint, however, the computation of taxes in monetary units meant that the amount of produce they must relinquish in order to pay taxes depended upon current market prices. The problem was complicated in the first decades after the reform by the government's failure to mint sufficient amounts of coin. The result was a sharp fall in the prices a farmer could receive for his commodities; and within a short time the rates set in 788 had become unrealistically high. Not surprisingly, the law requiring payment of taxes in money became the object of bitter criticism. In practice it was only partially enforced, and in 821 was repealed altogether, except with respect to the taxes on salt and wine.

Despite such setbacks, the reform of 780 led to a permanent increase in the use of money for taxes in China. The ninth through twelfth centuries witnessed an enormous expansion of the currency system and an ever-increasing shift toward a money economy, even including the use of paper currency. In somewhat modified form, Yang Yen's land tax remained the basis of the Chinese revenue system down to the twentieth century. As for Yang Yen himself, within a year of submitting his famous proposal he incurred the imperial displeasure, was dismissed from office, and felt impelled to save his honor by committing suicide.

OU-YANG HSIU: FROM THE NEW HISTORY OF THE T'ANG DYNASTY

On the Twice-a-Year Tax

[The circumstances which preceded enactment of the Twice-a-Year tax are discussed here in passages from an outstanding Chinese historical work, the *New History of the T'ang Dynasty* by Ou-yang Hsiu. Ou-yang (1007-72) was a leading scholar of the Sung period, a champion of orthodox Confucianism and of a natural prose style free of artificialities and conventional restraints. He was also a noted poet and a high government official.

The *New History*, though dealing only with a single dynasty, is patterned after the *Historical Records* of the great Ssu-ma Ch'ien.* Like his predecessor, Ou-yang also quotes at length from official documents. His remarks here on the difficulties of tax-collection in eighth-century China are interrupted by the text of Yang Yen's memorial proposing the Twice-a-Year tax.]

When the dynastic laws were first formulated, there was the land tax, the labor tax on able-bodied men, and the cloth tax on households. In the K'ai-yüan period [713-741] there was peace and prosperity, and the tax registers were not kept up. Enforcement of the law was lax; people migrated or died, and landed property changed hands [in violation of the ban on sale of land]. The poor rose and the rich fell. Nothing was the same as before. The Board of Revenue year after year presented out-of-date figures [on the taxable population] to the court.

[According to the regulations], those who were sent to guard the frontiers were exempted from the land tax and the labor tax for six years, after which they returned from service. Yet as Emperor Hsüan-tsung[1] was engaged in many campaigns against the barbarians, most of those sent to the frontiers died. The frontier generals, however, concealed the facts and did not report

From Wm. Theodore deBary, ed., *Sources of Chinese Tradition*, New York: Columbia University Press, 1960, pp. 419-21. Reprinted by permission of Columbia University Press.

* On Ssu-ma Ch'ien see Vol. V of this series, pp. 132-52.

1. Reigned 712-756.

their deaths. Thus their names were never removed from the tax registers. When Wang Kung held the post of Commissioner of Fiscal Census in the T'ien-pao period [742-755] he strove to increase revenue. Since these names appeared on the registers and yet the adults were missing, he concluded that they had concealed themselves to avoid paying taxes. Thereupon he examined the old registers, made allowance for the exemption [of six years] to which they were entitled, and then demanded that the households of these men pay the land and labor taxes which they would have owed the government over the previous thirty years. The people were distressed and had no place to appeal. Thus the tax system had deteriorated badly.

After the Chih-te period [756-762], there were wars all over the empire. Famine and epidemics ensued. All kinds of labor services had to be performed. The population declined and some areas were deserted. . . . There were four offices collecting taxes, and they had no control over each other, so that the system was greatly disrupted. The court had no check on the various commissioners, and the latter had no check on the local prefectures. The special tribute from all parts of the empire went into the inner treasury of the imperial palace [rather than the state treasury]. Powerful ministers and crafty officials took advantage of this and engaged in corrupt practices. The public was given to think that these were gifts to be presented to the emperor; the officials themselves thought of the tribute as so much personal loot. Often it ran into the tens of thousands. In Honan, Shantung, Chien-nan and Hsiang-chou, where large forces were stationed, the military officers all took care of themselves handsomely. Very little of the taxes which should have gone to the emperor was actually presented.

Altogether there were several hundred kinds of taxation: those which had been formally abolished were never dropped, and those which duplicated others were never eliminated. Old and new taxes piled up, and there seemed to be no limit to them. The people drained the last drop of their blood and marrow; they sold their loved ones. Month after month they were engaged in the "ten-days" of forced labor on state transport without a rest. Petty officials added to the burden, living at the people's expense.

Rich people with many able-bodied adults in their families sought to obtain exemption from labor services by having them become officials, students, Buddhist monks, and Taoist priests. The poor had nothing they could get into [to obtain such an exemption], and continued to be registered as able-bodied adults liable to labor service. The upper class had their taxes forgiven, while the lower class had their taxes increased. Thereupon the empire was ruined and in distress, and the people wandered around like vagrants. Less than four or five out of a hundred lived in their own villages and stayed on their own land.

Yang Yen was concerned over these evils, and petitioned the throne to establish the Twice-A-Year Tax in order to unify the tax system.

"The way to handle all government expenses and tax collections is first to calculate the amount needed and then to allocate the tax among the people. Thus the income of the state would be governed according to its expenses. All households would be registered in the places of their actual residence, without regard to whether they are native households or non-native. All persons should be graded according to their wealth, without regard to whether they are fully adult or only half-adult.[2] Those who do not have a permanent residence and do business as traveling merchants should be taxed in whatever prefecture or subprefecture they are located at the rate of one-thirtieth [of their capital holdings]. It is estimated that the amount taken from them will be the same as that paid by those having fixed domicile, so that they could not expect to gain from chance avoidance of the tax.

"The tax paid by residents should be collected twice a year, during the summer and autumn. All practices which cause annoyance to the people should be corrected. The separate land and labor tax, and all miscellaneous labor services should be abolished; and yet the count of the able-bodied adults should still be kept. The tax on land acreage should be based upon the amount of land cultivated in the fourteenth year of Ta-li [779], and the tax should be collected equally. The summer tax should be col-

2. According to the earlier system of census registration, persons aged sixteen to twenty were classified as "half adult," and those twenty-one or older as fully adult.

lected no later than the sixth month, and the autumn tax no later than the eleventh month. At the end of the year, local officials should be promoted or demoted according to the increase or decrease in the number of households and tax receipts. Everything should be under the control of the President of the Board of Revenue and the Commissioner of Funds."

The emperor approved of this policy and officials in the capital and the various provinces were informed of it. There were some who questioned and opposed the measure, considering that the old system of land and labor taxes had been in operation for several hundred years, and that a change should not be made precipitously. The emperor did not listen to them, however, and eventually the empire enjoyed the benefits of the measure.

PO CHÜ-I: FROM THE CH'ANG-CH'ING COLLECTION

On the Twice-a-Year Tax

[Po Chü-i (772-846), the author of this memorial, is best known as one of China's greatest poets. But like most literary men of his day, he also held a series of government appointments and wrote on political questions.]

A good tax system is one in which all forms of taxation, including land and household taxes, are paid in what the people produce. Since grain and silk are the items which the people produce, to require people to pay taxes in cash in addition to what they have already paid in produce is a violation of this principle. Where can the people obtain copper coins for the fulfillment of their tax obligations when their mulberry groves do not yield copper and when they themselves are not allowed to mint copper coins? When the tax collector presses them for the fulfillment of such obligations, they have no choice except to trade their produce for copper coins. In a bumper year when grain is

From *The Ch'ang-ch'ing Collection of Mr. Po,* reprinted in Dun J. Li, ed., *The Essence of Chinese Civilization,* Princeton, N.J.: D. Van Nostrand Co., 1967, pp. 251-52. Reprinted by permission of Van Nostrand Reinhold Co.

cheap in terms of money, they will have to sell it at half of its normal price in order to meet the tax payment; even then it is doubtful whether their produce can yield enough cash for the tax purpose. In a bad year the situation will be considerably worse. They will have to borrow money to meet their tax obligations by paying an interest of 100 percent per year; and once a debt is incurred, it is doubtful that they can ever get out of it. Thus the farmers have no hope for a better future even in good years.

The big landlords and the wealthy merchants, taking advantage of this situation, have become more and more wealthy and have bought large tracts of land. Meanwhile those who work diligently in the fields all year round have become poorer and poorer. Our social ills have become increasingly serious as the gap between the rich and the poor continues to widen.

Under these circumstances, how can we blame a farmer if he wishes to abandon farming and take up trading, or if his wife desires to stop weaving and occupy herself with a more profitable engagement such as embroidery? If a large number of farmers decide to follow his example, the fields will lie fallow and the people will become poorer. While land resources remain to be exploited, manpower continues to be wasted. The four seasons evolve in vain when they are not utilized for the raising of crops. The more carefully this problem is scrutinized, the more convincing is the conclusion that the high price of money in terms of produce is one of the most serious weaknesses of our economy.

While it is true that a high price of grain will be harmful to the consumers, it is also true that a low price will be injurious to the farmers. High price of grain will entail budgetary difficulties for those families that do not produce it; low price of grain, on the other hand, will lessen the farmers' interest in farming. An enlightened monarch, therefore, should see to it that the price of grain is neither too high nor too low, that goods circulate freely, and that all of the four classes[1] in our society will benefit from the operation of a dynamic economy. When this goal is achieved, not only can the government collect

1. I.e., scholars, farmers, artisans, and merchants.

enough revenue to meet its administrative expenses, the people will also become economically secure.

The total number of coins now in circulation has become smaller and smaller. Some of them are stored in the government's treasury while others are held by individuals. The number in circulation will be drastically reduced if the government continues to demand the payment of taxes in cash. Meanwhile, as money becomes more scarce, grain and silk will be worth less and less in terms of money. Such a development will be very harmful to farming and sericulture. If this trend continues, it is not difficult to visualize how disastrous the situation will be ten years from today.

A good tax system has two important features: first, all taxes are paid in produce and second, the amount to be paid varies with the size of the crop or the size of mulberry groves. Under this system not only will the land resources be fully developed, the harmful effects that result from the selling of produce for cash will be also eliminated. The farmers will feel economically secure in continuing farming, while those who have left farming for trade may return to their original occupation. Even the mercenaries and the professional wanderers may decide to take up farming. The first step to all of these healthy developments is an order from the government that from now on money will no longer be required for tax payments.

Introduction to Wang An-shih

Wang An-shih (1021-86), the most famous and controversial prime minister of the Sung dynasty, was born the son of a district official in Kiangsi province. A brilliant student, he received the Confucian education usual for young men of his class, and in 1042 passed the national civil service examination. A succession of official appointments followed, in the course of which Wang proved himself to be an able and conscientious administrator as well as a first-rate scholar, poet, and essayist. His obvious abilities and various unorthodox proposals for strengthening the state eventually attracted the notice of persons in high places; and Wang's reputation grew. From 1067 he held important posts at the imperial court in Ch'ang-an; and from 1070 until his resignation in 1076 (except for one brief interval) he was the chief minister of state, enjoying the emperor's full confidence.

Wang came to power at a time when the Sung dynasty had sunk to an alarming condition of military and financial weakness. Barbarian states to the north and northwest constantly threatened the frontiers, and in the previous century had overrun portions of traditionally Chinese territory. The imperial treasury showed a serious deficit every year, at the same time that increased revenues were required for military expenditures. The central government's control over the provinces was notably weaker than formerly. The young emperor Shen Tsung, ascending the throne in 1067, was ambitious to restore the power of his dynasty; and in Wang An-shih he believed he had found the man he required.

It was Wang's contention that new laws and improved administration could increase the national wealth and provide additional sources of tax revenue without thereby increasing the tax burden upon the populace. Precisely this notion was disputed by his conservative opponents within the bureaucracy, whose leader was the noted historian Ssu-ma Kuang. The conservatives regarded the economy as static and the national wealth as a fixed amount which might be re-distributed but not increased. They therefore contended that additional tax revenue could only be acquired through oppressing the common people (contrary to Confucian principles), and that a reduction in superfluous expenditures was the only possible remedy for the government's financial crisis. Moreover, they considered such mundane matters as finance and military affairs to be beneath the notice of scholars, who in their view should confine themselves to instructing the emperor in general ethical principles. According to this theory, political reform could be achieved not through active state intervention in public affairs, but only through the force of the emperor's personal moral example.

To be sure, Wang himself was thoroughly convinced of the importance of moral principles in the education of future officials—as evinced in his famous Ten-Thousand-Word Memorial.* A major stumbling-block to the success of his reforms was the provincial bureaucracy—often untrained for their specific functions and inclined

* See below, pp. 36-45.

to supplement their meager salaries through various corrupt practices. He also agreed with the conservatives as to the need for economy; after a careful inspection of the government's account-books (some of which had never before been examined) he succeeded in reducing the national budget by some 40 per cent. Nor did he neglect the old ways. Like the good Confucian that he was, he couched his reform proposals in traditional language, including the usual references to the practices of ancient kings. On the whole, his suggestions for fiscal reform were less radical than they appeared; precedents from Chinese history could be cited for most of them.

In many respects, Wang's financial policy might be said to conform to the Confucian precept that the government exists for the people's welfare. Then, as throughout much of China's history, large numbers of farmers lived in extreme poverty. While able to provide for themselves in good years, they were obliged to borrow heavily in the event of poor weather, natural disasters, military upheavals, or the ceremonial occasions considered indispensable to one's reputation in Confucian society (weddings, funerals, etc.). Owing to the borrowers' severe need and the relative scarcity of capital in a mainly agricultural society, large merchants and landowners—as the sole possessors of surplus funds—were in a position to charge exorbitant rates of interest. The result was often to reduce free peasants to tenancy or servant status; many of them never became free of debt. Similarly, when small merchants required funds they were at the mercy of the moneylenders, while frequently they could dispose of surplus merchandise only to the large merchant associations at sacrifice prices.

Wang's agricultural and trade policies were aimed at mitigating these evils, while at the same time ensuring that agricultural production and trade would not be hampered through lack of capital. The government now offered loans of money or grain to farmers at the comparatively low rate of 2 per cent per month—contrasting with the 60 or 70 per cent often charged by the moneylenders for a single growing season. To serve the small merchants, government trade bureaus were set up at various places throughout the country, empowered to offer loans at the 2 per cent rate, to purchase surplus stocks at fixed prices, and to arrange for the exchange of goods. Wang also abolished the compulsory labor service (*corvée*) which had hitherto formed part of the people's tax burden. Theoretically limited to a fixed number of days per year, in practice this labor service was often performed at the whim of local authorities, thereby providing them with fruitful opportunities for oppression and graft. Henceforth hired labor was to perform all such services, which would be financed by a special tax apportioned to fall primarily upon the wealthier classes.

Wang's radical plans and headstrong personality inevitably aroused strong opposition within the traditionalist Chinese bureaucracy—whose representatives succeeded in blackening his posthumous reputation until quite modern times. Critics contended that his New Policies oppressed the people, that their real object was merely to raise revenue for the government, that the loans were forced upon unwilling recipients, and that government interference in the market-place was undignified. Undoubtedly some of the complaints were justified. Certain over-zealous officials, anxious to impress their superiors by getting their full quota of loans subscribed, apparently forced even well-to-do people to accept them. Some of the borrowers proved unable to repay when the time came; their neighbors were then obliged to make good the deficiency. On the other hand, too few centers existed for the granting of loans; the inhabitants of country districts were often unable to utilize this service. Wang himself denied that the government derived profit from either the loan policy or the trade bureaus—a claim substantiated by the argument of the anti-reform party in 1085 that the program should be abolished precisely because of its failure to raise revenue. The market dealings of the trade bureaus tended to bring the control of prices and distribution of goods into government hands; apparently some merchants were thereby forced out of business.

Nonetheless, it is unlikely that Wang's measures were as oppressive or unpopular as his critics contended. Certainly we hear nothing of popular revolts during the entire reign of Shen Tsung, when these policies were in force. Wang's reform measures, which were designed to benefit the poorest members of society, injured just those classes which were most articulate and influential in Chinese life—the large and middle landowners, their merchant allies, and the scholar-officials, who were often of gentry origin. This fact alone accounts for much of the opposition to Wang's programs, and for the fact that virtually all of the laws he had sponsored were revoked after the death of his imperial patron, Shen Tsung, in 1085. Abolition of compulsory labor service deprived the local officials of many opportunities for intimidation and graft. Bureaucratic prejudices also played a role: the established officials were alienated by the fact that Wang had the emperor's ear and was able to bypass normal bureaucratic channels. Moreover, many officials rejected in principle the idea of active government intervention in economic life.

Recent scholarship has largely rehabilitated the reputation of Wang An-shih, recognizing his personal integrity, the breadth of his concepts, and the potentially beneficent effect of his schemes. However, given the existing conditions in eleventh-century China, it is undeniable that large-scale economic planning faced formidable obstacles. The empire was large; communications were slow and uncertain; the gentry who opposed Wang's programs remained dominant in government and society at large; and underpaid officials were prone to corruption and inaction. In the final analysis, Wang's New Policies were never fully tested. What their long-term effect might have been, and whether they might have succeeded in permanently improving the economic condition of China, must remain an open question.

DISCUSSION OF THE AGRICULTURAL LOANS MEASURE

Wang An-shih: Proposal

The stocks in the Government Granaries in all the districts amount to the value of 15,000,000 "strings."[1] The Granary Laws hitherto obtaining are being very badly administered, so that the possible advantages of the old system are not being realized. We propose that the present standards of measure be retained, that suitable arrangements be made for selling the grain when the market is high at slightly cheaper prices than those ruling outside, and that when grain is plentiful and cheap it should be purchased at a price slightly in excess of the market rate. We also suggest that the transport officers should be given liberty to demand either money or grain for the land tax according to the convenience of the people, and to exchange or dispose of stocks at will, but in all cases the grain should be valued at current rates.

Further, that after the fashion of the "Ch'ing Miao Regula-

From H. R. Williamson, *Wang An-shih, Life and Writings*, London: Arthur Probsthain, 1935, I, 146-47, 154-65. Reprinted by permission of Arthur Probsthain.

1. Strings of 1000 cash (coins).

tions" as operating in Shensi,[2] the people shall be permitted to contract loans either of money or grain, to be repaid at stipulated times, in summer and autumn, with interest at the rate of 2 per cent per month. The borrower should be free to repay either in money or grain. In cases where distress has been encountered through floods or drought, the repayment of the loan might be deferred to the next harvest. In this way not only would ample provision be made against drought, but the plutocrats would be prevented from exacting double the normal rates of interest in the intervals between the exhaustion of old stocks and the new harvest.

Under the existing Granary Regulations it has been the practice to keep in stock the grain collected at harvest season until a time of shortage and high prices comes round, when the grain would be sold out. But those who could take advantage of this were very few, being practically confined to the leisured folk of the city and environs.

The aim of the present proposal is to ensure that an adequate stock be kept in all districts, to sell when grain is dear and to buy when it is cheap. By regulating the market prices (by our own) we hope to make it possible for the farmer to get on with his work at the proper season. The plutocrats will no longer be able to take advantage of the people's extremity. This is a measure in the interests of the people, the government deriving no financial advantage therefrom. It is also in line with the ideas of the ancient rulers, who did their utmost to introduce advantageous arrangements for agriculturists.

We appeal that a number of officials be sent out to supervise the working of this measure in accordance with the needs of each particular district, and that each sub-prefecture appoint an assistant-inspector. These should be responsible for the collection, transport, and distribution services.

We propose that a beginning be made in the Circuits of Ho Pei, Ching Tung, and Huai Nan, and that later on, when the measure shall have assumed workable shape, it should be extended to all districts.

2. A program of agricultural loans which was already operative in Shensi province had proved quite successful. Wang modelled his proposals on this.

Finally we suggest that the grain in the "Charity Granary," after the needs of the aged and poor have been met, should be administered on the same lines as the stocks of the "Emergency Granary."

Letter of Wang An-shih to Ssu-ma Kuang

I acknowledge receipt of your favour. It is obvious that although we have been able to maintain friendly relations over a considerable period, we cannot reach a common mind on matters of public import, due doubtless to our different ways of viewing such things.

It would be preferable to give you a lengthy and detailed reply, but I fear that such might not receive your proper attention. Although I am conscious that this brief reply may seem to you to be lacking in courtesy, yet as it deals with the main points raised in your letter sufficiently well, in my opinion, I hope the apparent brusqueness may be overlooked.

One of the great aims of the Confucian scholar is to ensure that whatever statement he makes shall be representative of the actual facts. If that can be attained, then nothing else matters.

I gather that you think I have trespassed upon the authority of other officials, that I am out to make trouble, that my sole concern is to make revenue for the government, that I resent criticism, and that I have incurred the resentment of the whole empire in consequence.

On the contrary I think I have done nothing but what the Emperor has commanded me to do, that all of my proposals for the revision of the existing regulations have been discussed in the open forum of the Court before being proceeded with, and that the actual execution of such measures of a new character as have been approved has been delegated to the proper authorities. That cannot surely be interpreted as an infringement upon the authority of others.

I also consider that I have adopted the government method of the ancient rulers with the one object of relieving the people of their economic distresses and the eradication of certain great public evils. Such surely cannot be interpreted as the act of a trouble maker.

My proposals for financial reform are in the interests of the empire as a whole (not only in the interests of the government but also of the people). That surely cannot be termed the policy of a "tax-gatherer" actuated by considerations of financial gain alone.

I regard myself as an exposer of fallacious arguments and the foe of specious talkers. But that is not being "resentful of criticism."

And as regards the fact that critics and slanderers are numerous, I knew long ago that this was bound to come.

The governing class has been addicted to a policy of laissez-faire too long. The great scholars and officials for the most part do not give much thought to matters of state, regarding the status quo and the good opinion of the majority as the highest good. But the Emperor is desirous of altering all this, and as for myself I am determined to render him any assistance in my power regardless of the number of my enemies. . . .

I will admit that if you mean that during my term of office I have been unable to carry through any project of great benefit to the people that your criticism is just. But I cannot admit the cogency of your contention that a policy of quiescence and conservatism is what the country needs to-day.

With my regrets that I cannot see you personally, and assuring you of my sincere regard, I remain . . .

Han Ch'i: Memorial concerning the Agricultural Loans

I note that in accordance with the Imperial decree recently promulgated in connection with the Agricultural Loans, that great stress is laid upon the benefits which this measure will bring to the common people. It also emphasizes the fact that it will prevent the rich from taking advantage of the extremity of the poor to exact heavy rates of interest. It also claims that the government will not benefit financially from it.

But according to the regulations now in force, farmers and merchants alike are ordered to borrow 1,000 "cash" and repay 1,300. This is surely a case of the officials lending out money on interest, and therefore the original purpose of the measure is being contravened.[3] I know that according to the provisions of

3. Wang had never intended to lend out money free of interest.

the measure compulsion of any sort is supposed to be prohibited, but the fact remains that unless compulsion is exercised none but the poorer classes will take the loans, and they will find it very difficult to repay. As time goes on it will be found necessary for the general community to assume responsibility for the repayment.

All that is necessary to ease the financial situation is that your Majesty should exercise strict economy, for then the people will follow your example. There is absolutely no need to send out these revenue-seeking officials into the whole country, for they only disturb the people. I implore you to recall those who have been specially appointed to supervise this new measure, and to instruct the Circuit superintendents of justice to put the old Granary-laws once more into effect.

Reply of Wang An-shih

If we were acting like Sang Hung Yang, whose sole object was to fill the private purse of the emperor, we might justly be termed "profiteering officials." But the fact is that in reviving this measure as handed down from the Duke of Chou we are solely concerned with the relief of the poor and the repression of the rich. The enrichment of the national coffers has not entered into our calculations, so it is quite unreasonable to brand this as a profiteering measure.

Ssu-ma Kuang's Memorial Refusing High Office

Your Majesty should find out whether a man is loyal or not, and what contribution he has to make to the government before appointing him. If you give him position and emoluments simply out of personal favour, and make no use of his advice, that is simply abusing the government system. From the standpoint of the official concerned, to take position and emoluments in such circumstances is simply robbing the government treasury, for it means that one will be given no real opportunity to save the people from their distresses. I should be grateful if your Majesty would abolish the Financial Reorganization Bureau,[4] recall the officials who have been specially appointed to supervise the new measures, and revoke the Agricultural Loans measure. If that is done I care not whether you use me in office or not.

4. I.e., the agency set up by Wang to administer the loans.

In distributing the loans in connection with this measure, the officials, in their fear lest the money should never be repaid, compel the poor to seek guarantors amongst the rich. When the poor find themselves unable to repay they disappear, while the rich, who cannot abscond, are called upon to pay for them. If this is allowed to continue, after the lapse of ten years or so the resources of the poor will be exhausted and the rich will have become poor. The ordinary methods of grain distribution will have become non-operative. There are the dire possibilities of war to be faced, with consequent famine. The result will be that the fields will be full of the corpses of the poor, and the more sturdy elements will overrun the country as bandits. Such, as I see it, will be the outcome of this measure.

Wang An-shih: Letter to Tseng Kung Li

You have written me about the Agricultural Loans Measure. I would begin by making the general remark that it is not in the interests of the wicked to see good government prevailing. So the moment they see that something opposed to good government is mooted, they support it blindly. Their interest is not in the law.

The hatred of Mencius of those who discussed "profit" was directed against those who planned to get revenue for the government, either without any consideration for the people or for their own personal gain.

My critics' particular type of "government" waits until conditions have become so serious that animals are fed with food which the people need, or deaths have occurred from famine, before taking any steps to relieve the situation.

True "government" is concerned, and concerned most intimately, with matters of finance, and it is one's bounden duty to engage in work of this kind. More than half of the *Rituals of Chou* (*Chou Li*)[5] is connected with finance, but the Duke of Chou[6] was surely not a "profiteer"?

5. The *Rituals of Chou* is an ancient text which attributes to the early Chou rulers a variety of positive actions on behalf of the people. Wang's opponents cited against it the *Spring and Autumn Annals*, which takes a more moralistic approach to the art of governing.

6. Statesman of the early Chou dynasty famed for his ability and uprightness.

Evil-minded folk compose their plausible arguments to confuse the issue, deceiving both small and great. But what can they do against the clearly expressed willingness of the people for the promulgation of this measure? It was said at first that the people would not ask for the loans. But we cannot cope with the demand. Then it was said they would not repay. But so far there has been no difficulty on that score either. The reason is to be found in the fact that the people naturally find the measure to their interest.

Of course, I quite see that it would be better if we could reduce the interest to one per cent per month, or even lend the money without interest at all. It would be better still perhaps to give the people the grain outright, and not regard it as a loan. Why, then, is two per cent necessary and regarded as the only alternative to free relief? Simply because the work is to be continued in the future, for failure to make such a good work permanent would show faulty thinking somewhere. If we failed there, we should hardly get the credit of "being benevolent without waste." It is therefore necessary to have a loan system of some kind.

There are the salaries of the officials concerned to be paid; transport charges must be met; we must prepare for some losses through people leaving their homes in times of drought or flood; there will be losses from rats and birds. We must also plan for the exigencies of famine years, when free relief will have to be administered. The question is whether this can be done on anything less than the two per cent basis.

This basis of two per cent per month was considered all right in connection with the Granary Laws, so that there should be no objection to our adopting this basis in connection with the new measure.

If you will take the opportunity to discuss again this matter with those who are thoroughly conversant with the principles on which it has been framed, you will find that all I have said above is in strict accordance with regular law, and that the conventional critics are not worth the time you would have to spend on them in eliciting their point of view.

Government Service: Introduction

All major Chinese dynasties since Han times have recognized the importance of a well-organized, reasonably efficient civil administration in holding together so large and geographically diverse a country as China. Indeed, the extraordinary duration and stability of the Chinese empire over a period of more than two millennia must be ascribed in large part to the quality of its civil service. Recruited at least partly through a series of periodic examinations designed to secure the best possible talent in government, it was the practical application of Confucian political theory. Although China never developed democratic institutions in the Western sense, its civil service embodied a basically egalitarian ideal, according to which the humblest citizen might conceivably rise to the highest positions of honor and influence.

The system of civil service examinations reached maturity in the first century of the Sung dynasty (from A.D. 960); but its beginnings go back to the Former Han (206 B.C.-A.D. 8). As early as 165 B.C., the Han emperor Wen Ti required candidates for certain high offices to answer questions in writing. This became a regular practice under Wu Ti (r. 141-87), who appointed official "Scholars of Wide Learning" to conduct the examinations and to rank the candidates according to their answers. From these rather simple beginnings, the examination procedure became gradually more complex. In Sung times, preliminary examinations were held in local districts (prefectures); successful candidates then went on to a further test at the capital. Under the Ming (1368-1644) and Ch'ing (1644-1912) dynasties, the examinations were given at three levels: district, provincial, and national. The importance of the candidate's actual performance in determining the results of the examinations also increased with time. Under the Han and early T'ang, the "selection system" prevailed: candidates for office were nominated by their local governments, by high officials, or by persons influential at the imperial court. The actual examinations only confirmed such nominations; in many cases the rank of the candidates was determined in advance. But by the eighth century the concept of a merit bureaucracy had taken firm hold; and under the Sung dynasty the examinations were by far the most important means of entrance into the civil service.

The content of the examinations varied at different periods; but those exams which led to the higher ranks of the service invariably required a thorough grounding in Confucianism. In T'ang times the candidates could choose between degrees in Classics and in General Literature. The former included tests upon five Classics and depended largely upon pure memory; the latter demanded a thorough mastery of only one Classic, but required original compositions in both prose and poetry. Candidates for both degrees wrote essays upon general ethical questions and upon current administrative problems. Under the Ming dynasty the examinations were based upon the so-called Four Books,[1] which were now regarded as embodying the essence of Confucianism, and upon the Five Classics[2] as interpreted by the Neo-Confucian school of Chu Hsi. After 1487 the famous "eight-legged" essay was added—a highly restricted literary form requiring the treatment of a classical theme under eight main headings, employing no more than 700 characters. At all periods subsidiary examinations were given also in law, mathematics, and calligraphy; but these subjects were regarded merely as technical skills leading to low-ranking positions.

From the mid-T'ang period onward, the scholar-officials—those who had passed the examinations and received official appointment—constituted the highest social class in China. They were a very select group: it has been estimated that in Sung times only between 1 and 10 per cent of the candidates passed the prefectural examinations; and 90 per cent of these were eliminated at the national level. The status of the scholar-officials derived both from the power and perquisites of office and from the traditional prestige of scholarship. Moreover, in pre-industrial China political office was the only occupation granting both power and prestige; and for most persons the examinations provided the sole possible route to office. The rewards for success were thus immense; and unsuccessful candidates frequently attempted the examinations many times over, even in middle and old age.

The Chinese system contained various safeguards intended to ensure not only the admission of the best men to office, but also the

1. The *Analects*, the *Mencius*, the "Great Learning" and the "Doctrine of the Mean" (chapters of the *Book of Rites*).

2. The *Book of History*, *Book of Songs*, *Book of Changes*, *Book of Rites*, and the *Spring and Autumn Annals*.

promotion within the service of those who demonstrated real competence. The examiners, specially appointed for each occasion, were supposed to be officials of the highest rank and reputation. At the examinations themselves, identifying numbers were substituted for the candidates' names, while clerks copied all papers in case the examiners might recognize a candidate's handwriting. The promotion of junior officials was based partly upon personal recommendations, but also upon such objective criteria as the increase or decrease of population or tax revenues within the official's district. Superior officials who recommended a junior were held legally as well as morally accountable for the conduct of their protégés. Moreover, the Confucian education which was indispensable for success at the examinations ensured that all who entered the civil service by this route would be imbued with high standards of uprightness, responsibility for the public welfare, and loyalty to the existing order.

An important safeguard which existed within the civil service itself was the Censorate. The purpose of this remarkable institution was not only to point out defects in day-to-day administration and expose corrupt practices, but also to criticize the highest acts of state policy. The chief censors enjoyed direct access to the emperor. Each government department had its own censorial staff; censors were periodically sent into the provinces to report on conditions there. In theory, and often in practice also, only men of proven ability, courage, and honesty could be appointed as censors. In principle they enjoyed immunity from punishment for any criticism they saw fit to make; and this immunity was protected by public opinion. Many instances might be cited where Chinese emperors not only tolerated, but even rewarded the most outspoken criticism of their policies or personal morals. On the other hand, like all other civil officials in China, the censors served at the emperor's pleasure; and on occasion they were dismissed, demoted, or even executed for their frankness.

From the eighth century until the twentieth—except for relatively brief intervals—the majority of high civil officials in China were men who had first passed the national examinations. But at no time did the examination system provide the only means of entrance into official life. Under every dynasty, office and rank could be purchased, though the extent to which this was actually done has not been determined. The relatives of high officials were sometimes admitted to office without examination, and allowed to circumvent the regular bureaucratic channels. Chinese emperors also developed the habit of employing eunuchs at court. Originally used to guard the imperial harem, some of the eunuchs came to occupy the highest posts in both civil and military administration. Eunuchs were in theory house-slaves, usually acquired by capture from the border peoples; emperors came to rely upon them because their low social origin and lack of descendants generally made them totally loyal to the monarch's interests. The ordinary civil servants despised the eunuchs as men of little education and as rivals for power; conflict was endemic between the two groups—the "without" and the "within," as the Chinese phrased it. Chinese historians likewise have usually painted eunuchs in the most unfavorable colors, though at least some of them apparently filled their posts with distinction. But the most serious omission from the regular civil service system was the military establishment. By the middle of the T'ang dynasty the Chinese had come to despise the art of war. Soldiering was regarded as a career fit only for the dregs of society, or for barbarians in Chinese service. Thus even the highest officers of the army lacked the traditions and education of the civilian bureaucracy, and in times of political weakness were able to threaten the dynasty's very existence.

Certainly the merits of the Chinese civil administration were impressive. Those who entered via the examination route were necessarily men of superior ability; indeed, the best minds of the nation were attracted to government service. The examination system tended to produce a homogeneous ruling class, because those who sought official careers were led to seek a uniform type of education. The educated classes became the strongest supporters of the existing regime, instead of its sharpest critics; and even the lower ranks of society had a stake in maintaining the status quo. While success at the examinations demanded a long and careful education which normally only the landed gentry could provide for its sons, even the poorest and humblest men were not excluded *per se* from the system. On the other hand, by rewarding an orthodox brand of Confucianism the examinations tended to stifle original thought; and studies in the ancient Classics were not necessarily the best preparation for politics. The traditionalism and immobility of the bureaucracy had both positive and negative aspects—positive in its contribution to the long stability of Chinese government; negative in its inability to respond effectively to changed conditions. On balance, however, the merits of the civil service system certainly outweighed its defects. It was the supreme achievement of Chinese political thought, and provided the Chinese empire with a degree of administrative competence probably unequaled elsewhere in the world before the nineteenth century.

Introduction to the Letter to Ch'en Ching

The civil service examinations were in theory scrupulously fair; but until the late T'ang period, political favoritism often played a role in determining the results. Knowing this, the candidates sought if possible to improve their chances by the aid of persons in high places. In advance of the examinations, they circulated samples of their literary work, and paid courtesy calls upon important officials or courtiers who were in a position to influence the examiners.

The poet Po Chü-i penned the following letter in A.D. 800, while at Ch'ang-an waiting to take the national examination. The recipient, Ch'en Ching, was an elder statesman known as an authority on imperial tombs. Despite Po's assertions to the contrary, the letter was almost certainly intended to attract favorable attention to his candidacy. History has not recorded whether Ch'en Ching interceded on Po's behalf; but it so happened that the chief examiner in that year was a man of scrupulous honesty and independent judgment. For whatever reason, the name of Po Chü-i subsequently appeared on the list of successful candidates.

PO CHÜ-I: LETTER TO CH'EN CHING

On this New Year's day Po Chü-i, a candidate sent up by his home-town for examination, respectfully sends his page-boy with a letter to your Excellency the Supervising Censor. I know that your Excellency's doors are thronged not only by would-be visitors, but also by the bearers of innumerable letters. But the

From Arthur Waley, *The Life and Times of Po Chü-i*, London: George Allen & Unwin, Ltd., 1949, pp. 18-19. Reprinted by permission of George Allen & Unwin, Ltd.

purpose of those who thus obtrude themselves upon you, numerous though they are, is I believe in every case the same. Their one and only aim is to obtain your Excellency's commendation and patronage. My object is a very different one. The reason that I do not attempt to see you in person and instead am sending you this letter is that I merely wish to furnish you with evidence upon which you may decide for me a point about which I am in doubt. . . .

The ambition of a candidate who has decided to take the Literary Examination, whatever his merits, is naturally to pass successfully and make a name for himself. In this respect I cannot claim to be any exception and for that very reason I have devoted myself unreservedly to the most painstaking study of literature for ten years, and was at last sent up by my hometown for examination.

Among those in like case there are some who have obtained their degree at the first attempt, and their example stirs my ambition and encourages me to push on. But I see that there are others who fail even at a tenth attempt; and this makes me wonder whether I can stay the course and had not better give up. . . . Your Excellency! Everywhere under Heaven literature owes much to you, and in our own day there is no finer critic. That is why, without regard for my humble position and origin, I make bold to open my heart to you. I am a man of undistinguished birth. At Court I have no powerful connections to help me on; at home I have no influential friends to commend me. Why then have I come to the Capital? In the hope that my powers as a writer will serve me. I am dependent therefore on fair treatment by my examiner. Fortunately Kao Ying, of the Board of Rites, is to be the examiner, and there is no juster man than he. But is my talent for literature of a kind to justify me in taking this examination? I have not the least idea, and it is this question that I want your Excellency to decide. Can your Excellency refuse? . . .

I am sending you herewith twenty pieces of miscellaneous prose and a hundred poems. I entreat you to recognize the sincerity of my request. The matter is trivial and I am myself of no account. Do not for that reason ignore it, but in a moment of leisure from public business cast a critical eye on these writings. If they justify me in going forward, I beg for one word to that effect; in which case I shall make every effort to polish my dull wits, whip up my nag and forge ahead. If on the other hand you tell me not to stand, then I will give up my plans, retrace my steps and content myself with a life of obscurity.

For days past this conflict has been warring in my breast. I beg for a single word to resolve it. I shall hope for an answer within ten days. If I hear that you have deigned to glance at my shabby productions, I shall be as one "robbed of breath and ravished of his soul." But I must be brief. Chü-i respectfully twice prostrates himself.

WANG AN-SHIH: FROM THE TEN-THOUSAND-WORD MEMORIAL*

[The following memorial—which a modern Chinese scholar[1] has termed "the greatest document on government since the times of Ch'in and Han"—outlines some of the difficulties which compromised the practical effectiveness of the civil service system. The author is the same Wang An-shih who would later become the most famous prime minister of the Sung dynasty,[2] though at the time of writing (1058) he was no more than an important provincial official. Both as a preview of Wang's later reforms and as a description of current administrative practice in China, the memorial is of unusual interest. It is in fact prophetic of the fate of those reforms, which were subsequently mismanaged through some of the same official incompetence which he criticizes here.]

I, your Majesty's ignorant and incapable servant, have been honoured with your commission to take a part in the administra-

From H. R. Williamson, *Wang An-shih, Life and Writings*, London: Arthur Probsthain, 1935, I, 48, 52, 54-67, 69-70, 73-75. Reprinted by permission of Arthur Probsthain.

* This title originated with the authors of the *Sung Dynastic History*, who were impressed by the memorial's unusual length. The actual number of words is 8,565.

1. Liang Ch'i Ch'ao (1873-1929), himself a well-known political reformer, was the first important Chinese thinker to attempt the rehabilitation of Wang's posthumous reputation.

2. See above, pp. 19-29.

tion of one of the circuits.[1] I feel it to be my duty, now that I am called to Court to report on conditions in my district, to bring to your attention certain matters affecting the Government. I presume to do this on the ground of the experience gained during my period of official service, and regardless of my own inability. I shall consider it most fortunate if my suggestions receive your careful attention, and if you can see your way to adopt such as seem in your opinion to be of a reasonable character.

To my mind the greatest need of the time is the securing of capable officials. We should ensure that an increasing number of these should be made available for the services of the State, so that from this larger group we shall be able to select a sufficient number for our purpose, and secure the possibility of getting men into their right positions. Although the modern Empire is the same as that ruled by the ancients, there is this scarcity of capable men in the government services, while in their day such men were numerous. How are we to account for that? I believe it is due to our not having the right method of producing them.

The number of capable men available depends upon the ruler taking such a course as shall develop useful gifts in the people, and on making it possible for such to bring their natural gifts to fruition. By this I mean that a proper method should be devised whereby such men can be trained, maintained, selected and appointed.

Firstly, what is the proper method of instructing these men?

The ancient rulers had a graded system of schools ranging from the National University to the district and village schools. For the control and development of these, a considerable number of educational officers and teachers were appointed, who had been selected with the greatest care. The conduct of Court ceremonies, music, and Government administration were all part of the recognized curriculum. So that the model held up before the student, and in which he gradually became well versed, was the example, precept, and fundamental principles of government observed by the ancient rulers. The students trained under this

1. The circuits (*tao*) were administrative districts superior to the prefectures. They were first established under the T'ang dynasty.

system were found to be of such ability and character as the Government required and could use. No student was received into the schools who had not shown promise of developing such a capacity. But all who demonstrated that they possessed this potentiality were without exception received.

This I consider to be the right method of training these men.

It is true that nowadays each "chou" and "hsien"[2] is supposed to have schools. In reality, however, these schools are just so much "bricks and mortar." For there are no teachers or real training carried on in them. It is true there are instructors in the National University, but these are not selected with any care. Court ceremonies, music and government administration have no place in the curriculum. I admit that the students have a vague idea that these things form part of the responsibility of those in public office, but they do not apprehend that these are the very things with which they ought to make themselves fully acquainted.

In the main the instruction they receive consists of explanations of the texts of the Classics, analysed into sections and sentences. That, however, was not the ancient method.

More recently a new method of instructing students to prepare for the official tests by writing essays has come into existence. This method, however, calls for the recitation and memorizing of an enormous amount of literature, and the candidate must devote himself strenuously to this task the whole day long if he is to achieve success. But even if success in this matter is gained, it does not qualify the best student for the ruler's position, or the less successful for the other public services. So that even if they should go on learning in these schools until their hair turned grey, and give themselves the whole day long to the attempt to conform to the requirements of their superiors, they would have only the vaguest notion of what to do when they were appointed to actual office.

The students of the present day ought to study methods of practical administration. But either no instruction at all is given, or they have to exhaust themselves in strenuous cultivation of the art of essay writing. The ancients gave their time and energy

2. Prefecture and district.

specifically to the study of practical administration, and yet not all developed equal ability for the same. But nowadays the time and energy of students is diverted into quite other channels, and they give themselves to useless studies. It is not to be wondered at that when such men are given government appointment very few find themselves capable of discharging their duties.

Further, in the times of the ancient rulers, the students were given instruction in both civil and military subjects. In connection with the Military services, none who had not been specially trained in such matters were given positions, though those who had received such training were all given positions according to their ability. The better qualified were appointed to the chief civil posts during peace, or to the chief military posts in a time of border trouble or war. Those of lesser qualifications were appointed to the headship of the various civil groups, or to the command of the different military units. In this way the big garrison posts, and the important Circuit positions were all filled by great men, who were at one and the same time both scholars and generals.

Nowadays great emphasis is laid upon the distinction between civil and military matters by the students. The rule is that they confess to knowing nothing about military matters, being solely concerned with the civil services. So it comes about that important military positions are left to those who are termed "military men." These are often promoted from the hired levies, who in the main are the good-for-nothings of the country-side. For any who have the ability to maintain themselves alive in their own village are unwilling to offer themselves to the army. But these garrison posts and other military commands are of the most vital importance to the country, and the selection of the right men for these positions ought to have the serious attention of the ruler.

Nowadays, however, this most important responsibility, which should be carried by men selected with the greatest care, is thrust upon the shoulders of "good-for-nothings" who have been unable to maintain themselves in a bare livelihood in their own villages. That accounts for the fact that we have this constant anxiety about the situation on the borders, and explains why we are so concerned about the reliability of the regular army if the State should be endangered.

The main contributing factor to this is the way in which present-day students regard the carrying of weapons as a disgrace, so amongst them we find none who are able to ride, shoot, or take part in any military manœuvers. This leaves us with no alternative but to depend upon the hired forces for the protection of the country.

Further, the reason why the carrying of arms is regarded as a disgrace by the students, is because no proper instruction in military matters is given in the schools, and because no proper care is given to the selection of men for the military positions.

This is an illustration of our not having the right method of instruction.

Secondly, what is the proper method of maintaining capable men?

In a word, they should be given adequate financial provision; they should be taught the restraints of propriety, and controlled by adequate laws and regulations.

The rate of salaries paid nowadays to officials is too low. With the exception of the very highly placed officials in the Court circle, all who have large families to support engage either in agriculture or trade to eke out. Those in the lower positions like district officials are at the most in receipt of 8,000 or 9,000 "cash,"[3] while many only get as much as 4,000 or 5,000 a month. When the time during which they have to wait for appointments, and the intervals between appointments are taken into account, say over a period of six or seven years, we find that they only receive the equivalent of three years' allowances. So that they draw in actual cash an average of less than 4,000 or 5,000 "cash" a month. From this they have to provide the wages of a servant, and make provision for the support of their parents; and funeral and wedding expenses.

It may be urged that a man of superior character will maintain his integrity and good name, even though he should be in

3. The "cash" was a small, round copper coin with a hole in the center for stringing purposes. It was the standard Chinese coin from the Chou era until the end of the nineteenth century.

very poor circumstances financially. It is also commonly said that a man of inferior moral character will remain mean even though he should become rich. But the mediocre man does not come within these general rules. In this case poverty induces moral degradation, and wealth helps him to maintain his good name. If we consider for a moment the whole of the educated class in the country, not more than one per cent may be classed as either superior or inferior men. Practically all are of the mediocre class, in whom, as I have just said, poverty induces moral degradation, and wealth helps to maintain their good name.

With the present scale of salaries, however, it is impossible for the ordinary man to be honest and self-respecting, and it is useless to expect that he should. So we find that the big officials both offer and receive bribes and presents, and carry on private business, thinking nothing of being regarded as "corrupt." The smaller fry of the official world practice all manner of device for making money, not only engaging in trade and barter, but even descending to begging. Once the officials have earned the reputation of being corrupt, they become negligent, caring for nothing but the holding of their positions. Real earnestness and devotion to the public cause become unknown. With official duties neglected in this fashion, it is of course impossible for government to make any sound progress. But when bribery is added, and intimidation with a view to "mulcting" the people, we see the implication of the statement that we are not providing our officials with sufficient financial help.

The ancient rulers drew up a series of regulations regarding weddings, funerals, sacrifices, support of the aged, banquets, presents, dress, food, utensils, etc., etc. Expenditure on these things was to be regulated according to the rank and grade of official. The aim was to adjust their financial outlay in an equitable manner, having due regard to their varying circumstances. A man might have a certain rank, which, if that alone was considered, would demand the expenditure of considerable sums on such things. But he might not possess the means to do the thing in the style which his rank required. The regulations provided for this contingency and he was not expected to conduct such matters in the lavish way that his rank alone would call for. But supposing a man had the means to meet all the requirements of high official rank on such occasions, but lacked the necessary rank which entitled him to make such a display, the regulations forbade him to do so, prohibiting the addition of the smallest fraction to the standard he was entitled to observe under them.

[Nowadays,] seeing that there are no regulations controlling expenditure on weddings, funerals, support of parents, clothes, food, and the appurtenances of life, everyone comes to regard extravagance as admirable, and economy as disgraceful. If a man has wealth he does everything in the most lavish style, merely following the line of his own fancy. As this is in no way prohibited by the authorities, the people begin to look upon it as the right thing to do. A man who is of straitened means, and who cannot live up to this conventional standard of doing things, constantly offends his relatives in such matters as weddings and funerals. So men are led to regard economy as something to be ashamed of. The wealthy seek for more wealth and become completely addicted to the lust for money, while the poor with their limited means exhaust their resources in the attempt to "keep up" with them. It thus becomes doubly difficult for an official to be honest.

Thirdly, what is the correct method of selecting officials?

I propose that those whom you have already found by experience to be of good character and great ability, and to whom you have committed important responsibilities, should be entrusted with the task of selecting men of like qualifications. Also that these should be given an adequate period of probation in official life, after which they too should be allowed to make recommendations to the throne. When this has been done, and when the men recommended have been found to be worthy, rank, emoluments, and promotion should be conferred by way of reward.

The present method of selecting officials is as follows:— If a man has a colossal memory, can repeat extensive portions of the classics, and has some skill at composition, he is termed specially brilliant or worthy, and chosen for the highest grades of State ministers. Those who are not possessed of such retentive memories, or of such wide recitative powers, and yet have some skill in composition, showing their gifts of poesy and rhyming, are granted the "Chin Shih"[4] degree, the highest of which are also eligible to be appointed to the high positions. It should need no discussion to show that the knowledge and skill which these men display in no sense of itself fits them for such places of authority and distinction. It is, however, the prevailing opinion, that this method which has been used so long has been proved capable of producing men suitable for these posts. It is then urged that it is quite unnecessary to alter the regulations, or to seek to follow the ancient practice in the matter. That I contend is faulty reasoning.

It is of course reasonable to assume that some men of literary ability should prove themselves equal to carrying the responsibilities of high office, but mere literary skill should not be the only factor to be taken into account, for on that score unworthy men might also be elected to these responsible positions. As a matter of fact nine out of every ten who are capable of administering the duties of these high positions have spent their lives in subordinate posts in the provinces, just because they did not possess the necessary literary ability, which as I have said, is of itself no real help to a man occupying an administrative position.

Fourthly, what is the right method to be adopted regarding the appointment of officials?

The ancient rulers were cognizant of the fact that men differ in character, and their ability for actual work. They recognized that they were specially suited for certain definite tasks, and could not be reasonably expected to take up any and every kind of work indiscriminately.

They further recognized the fact that it is only after a prolonged period in any one appointment, allowing one's superior sufficient time to learn of his real capacity and attainments, and for the people under him to become truly subservient and happy under his control, that the really worthy have the chance to display their worth, and on the other hand that the evil-minded may have their wickedness exposed.

4. Or: Doctor of Literature.

I have already indicated that the current method of selecting officials is wrong in principle. I have now to add that in the actual appointing of a man to office, no enquiry is made as to his real capability for the particular post to which he is allocated. All that is considered is his year of graduation, or his particular position in the examination lists. Or again instead of investigating his suitability for a certain position, regard is paid only to the number of years he has been engaged in the government service.

On the basis of possessing literary ability a man may be appointed to a financial post, then he may be transferred to a legal position, or again to an office connected with the Board of Rites. One cannot expect anything else than that he finds it difficult to fill any office in any satisfactory manner, seeing that he is required to be ready to fill any position whatsoever. It is only natural in such circumstances to find very few who can fulfil their obligations in any one position. That has led in its turn to their falling into the habit of doing nothing at all. If a man receives an appointment to the Board of Rites, he is in nowise concerned about his utter ignorance of Rites, for the simple reason that he knows that those in the Rites department have never received any instruction in the business of their office. The same holds true with regard to those appointed to the legal positions.

Then I must refer to the current practice of frequent transfer of officials from one place to another. The fact that men are not allowed to remain in one office for any length of time prevents their superiors from getting to know them or their ability in any real sense. Again, those in inferior positions, because they have not had time to learn to respect superiors, are mostly unwilling to obey them. A worthy man has not sufficient time to bring his plans to fruition, and an unworthy man does not remain long enough in any one post for his evil disposition to manifest itself. There are other evils attendant upon this system, such as the burden which devolves upon the local population in the constant receptions of new officials, and the farewells to old occupants of the positions. There are too many defects in accounting and the keeping of records for which these constant changes are responsible. These are among the minor evils attendant upon this system.

It ought to be a rule that appointments should be made for a protracted period, relatively longer periods being allowed to those who have control of greater areas, or particularly heavy responsibilities. Only in that case can we expect a man to make some really valuable and constructive contribution to the state. But the current practice is of a contrary type, many officials being transferred after only a few days in one post.

Another defect I must now stress is that after they are appointed to office, they are not trusted to carry out their duties. An official is hedged about by a multitude of minute prohibitions and hindrances, so that he simply cannot carry out any ideas he may chance to have. This is one of the great reasons why those now in the government service are mainly unsuited for their positions. Since you have the wrong men in office I realize that unless you should hedge them about in this way, they would proceed to all manner of lawlessness if given the slightest liberty. That may be true. But what I wish particularly now to emphasize is that history proves it to be impossible to secure proper government by merely relying on the power of the law to control officials when the latter are not the right men for their job. It is equally futile to expect efficient government if, having the right men in their proper positions, you hedge them about by a multitude of minute and harassing prohibitions.

Seeing that all the evils outlined above do exist, even though worthy and able men should find their way into the government service, it is just as if they were unworthy and incapable.

FROM THE WORKS OF SHUI-HSIN (YEH SHIH)

[In the following memorial Yeh Shih (Yeh Shui-hsin), a well-known scholar-official of the twelfth century, suggests an additional defect inherent in the system of civil service examinations.]

From Dun J. Li, ed., *The Essence of Chinese Civilization*, Princeton, N.J.: D. Van Nostrand Co., 1967, pp. 167-68. Reprinted by permission of Van Nostrand Reinhold Co.

Civil Service Examinations

Formerly, a successful candidate of the civil service examination was a person who had established a name for himself in the literary circle or had achieved some well-known deeds prior to his participation in the examination. The situation today is entirely different. The candidates who pass the examination are not necessarily those who deserve to pass, and the man who scores the highest often becomes the target of ridicule. Meanwhile even the least talented in the countryside and the most mediocre in a family are busying themselves in books, reciting and memorizing, for the sole purpose of passing the examinations.

A father urges his son to study not because he believes that books are important in themselves but because they are keys whereby his son can open the door to officialdom. While the government attaches great importance to the examination system, the people view it as merely a means to a worldly end. What they like about a successful candidate is not the character of the candidate as a person; rather, it is his writings that they appreciate. In fact, they know nothing about the candidate himself because a man's writings are not necessarily indicative of his person. It is not surprising that our examination system today does not produce men who command esteem, since it has become a vehicle whereby men of dubious motives ride to officialdom. Yet it is the major instrument whereby scholars are transformed into officials from whom ministers of great responsibilities will eventually emerge. Is it not contradictory that a man who is despised on account of his selfish motives when entering the civil service examinations will be relied upon by the nation to shoulder great responsibilities?

A harmful corollary of using the examination to select governmental personnel is to convert all scholars to aspirants for governmental positions. A healthy society cannot come about when people study not for the purpose of gaining wisdom and knowledge but for the purpose of becoming government officials. A person who seeks knowledge will know what "righteousness" means, and a man of righteousness does not need a salary to become rich and a title to become honorable. The outward things that other people envy and seek after will not in any way affect his determination to preserve his own integrity.

Nowadays the situation is different. Beginning with childhood, all of a man's study is centered on one aim alone: to emerge successfully from the three days' examinations, and all he has in his mind is what success can bring to him in terms of power, influence, and prestige. His father and elder brothers push him towards this goal, and so do the best of his friends, because all of them, like him, believe that this is the only proper path to follow. The old concept of studying for the refinement of one's character and for the acquirement of the sense of righteousness is painfully noteworthy because of its absence. How can one sincerely believe that a system which produces persons of this type as government officials can also generate men of talent eager and able to shoulder great responsibilities? . . .

OU-YANG HSIU: FROM HIS BIOGRAPHIES OF EUNUCHS*

Eunuchs come about because of a monarch's love of sexual indulgence. Yet the harms they cause to a nation are much more serious than those resulting from sexual indulgence. This has been true throughout history.

There are numerous ways in which eunuchs can bring harm to a nation. As they are close to and on familiar terms with a monarch, they have an advantage which no one else possesses. They can afford to be harsh and dictatorial. They do small favors to please and keep their promises in nonessential matters so as to win trust from others. However, once a monarch trusts them and takes them into his confidence, they manipulate or sometimes control him through a simple device: they remind

From Dun J. Li, ed., *The Essence of Chinese Civilization*, Princeton, N.J.: D. Van Nostrand Co., 1967, pp. 148-49. Reprinted by permission of Van Nostrand Reinhold Co.

* From his *New History of the Five Dynasties*. On Ou-yang Hsiu see also pp. 14-17 above.

him of the evil consequences that might ensue if he does not listen to their advice. Even though there are loyal scholar-ministers in the court, the monarch will not trust them because, in his judgement, they are too remote and unfamiliar and are not so reliable as those who are around him every day from morning to night.

As the monarch draws closer and closer to the persons surrounding him, his alienation from his scholar-ministers also becomes greater and greater. Meanwhile he becomes more and more isolated from the outside world. The more isolated he is, the more fearful he becomes; the more fearful he becomes; the the greater will he be subject to the eunuch's control. Eventually even his life is at the mercy of his nominal servants who decide whether he should live or die in accordance with their whims: danger has thus lurked behind every door or curtain in his imperial palace. The persons whom he thought he could trust have now become a source of danger to him.

Once the danger becomes too obvious, the monarch will doubtless try to make an alliance with his hitherto alienated ministers for the purpose of eliminating the very persons who until then have been his closest allies. If for some reason he and his ministers decide to wait for a propitious moment to take such a drastic step, the danger to his life will continue to deepen. If on the other hand they decide to take immediate action, the eunuchs, being close by, can hold the monarch as hostage. In view of this situation, it is extremely difficult for the ministers to initiate an alliance with the monarch against the eunuchs, however capable the ministers happen to be. Even if such an alliance can be formed, it is unlikely that it will be followed by concrete action. Even if action can be taken, it is doubtful that it can really achieve its purpose, because in the end an action of this sort will bring about damage and defeat to the allies as well as the eunuchs. It may cause the monarch to lose his kingdom. Even if the dynasty does manage to survive, the monarch himself may be killed. This in turn will give some strong but unprincipled man the needed excuse to kill all eunuchs so as to allay the anger of all people in the nation. Instances of this description appear time and again in recorded history, and it is clear that the eunuch curse is not confined to a particular generation or period.

No monarch wishes to cultivate danger to himself within his palace ground or to alienate his loyal scholar-ministers deliberately. Nevertheless, the danger comes about because, given the situation described above, it slowly but inevitably feeds itself until it becomes a reality too large to be ignored. In the case of sexual indulgence, a monarch will of course suffer evil consequences if he remains unaware of the danger he is in. However, once he becomes aware of it, he can easily eliminate that danger by dismissing the women who have hitherto surrounded him. The eunuch danger, on the other hand, cannot be easily eliminated even after the danger has been recognized. . . . This is what I mean when I say that the evils caused by eunuchs are much more serious than those resulting from a monarch's sexual indulgence. How can future monarchs afford not to be alert to this danger?

SU SHIH: FROM HIS LETTER TO THE EMPEROR SHEN TSUNG

Concerning the Censorate

[The following letter was written in the year 1070 by an official named Su Shih, better known as the poet Su Tung-p'o. In it Su defends the principle of the Censorate and objects to the recent dismissal of several censors who had criticized the economic reform policies of Wang An-shih.]

Now I am well aware that so humble a servant as I cannot fully appreciate or comprehend the deep-laid and farsighted plans of emperors of the past; but the single example of the power delegated to the censors seems to me a preventive measure of supreme wisdom. Though several hundred men from the Ch'in and Han down to the Five Dynasties paid for their criticism with their lives, since the beginning of our [Sung] dynasty no

Translated by J. K. Rideout in Cyril Birch, ed., *Anthology of Chinese Literature*, New York: Grove Press, 1965, pp. 377-78. Reprinted by permission of Audrey J. Rideout.

man has ever suffered for a single word. On the contrary the slightest criticism has won for the censors immediate promotion. Permission has been given them to lay anonymous charges against officers of the highest rank; no man however great or however humble is safe from their denunciations. Even the Son of Heaven has changed countenance when their remonstrances have been directed against his person; even the chancellor has awaited punishment.

A lesser age [such as this] cannot be expected to appreciate the profound wisdom of the sages; but merely because not all the censors selected have been good, nor all their criticisms justified, there is no reason to condemn as futile the practice of giving great power [of criticism] to men of acute perception. Its justification is that by breaking the first shoots of ministerial dishonesty, it guards against the evil of too great a concentration of power [at the center]. For though the censor's criticism is enough to break the first beginnings of ministerial dishonesty, even armed force cannot remove it once it has spread. Now, I know, the laws are scrupulously administered, the court is sincerely honest, and there could be no possible ground for the rise of what I call ministerial dishonesty. None the less cats are kept to get rid of mice, and freedom from mice is no excuse for keeping a cat that could not catch one; dogs are there to keep away thieves, and the absence of thieves is no reason for keeping a dog that will not bark. The emperors of the past established the office of censor as a protection for their descendants for all time; can Your Majesty afford to ignore the motives of the one or the needs of the other? Can [imperial] court discipline ever have any stronger support?

Judging from notes made when I was young, and from what I heard my elders say, the criticisms made by the censors always followed public opinion, upholding what the people approved, and condemning what they attacked . . . But now[1] when the whole air is charged with criticism, indignation is encountered on every side, and the trends of public opinion are plain for all to see, the censors look at one another and utter not a word, and the hopes of all are dashed to the ground. For even the most

1. I.e., since Wang An-shih assumed office.

moderate will rouse themselves if wrong is successfully denounced by the censors; but let [the censors] once lose their authority, and even the boldest [citizens] will be impotent. What I fear is that the subservience of censors, once established as a habit, will become widespread, that they will degenerate into the personal tools of the powerful, and that the emperor will thus be completely isolated. For who knows what may not happen once their corrective influence is lost?

Religion

Chinese Buddhism in the Middle Period: Introduction

The first two centuries of the T'ang dynasty (618-907) mark the apogee of Buddhism in China, both in the extent of its influence on society and in intellectual and artistic creativity. At the top of the social pyramid, emperors and nobles kept company with Buddhist monks and gave generously to Buddhist institutions, while Buddhist ritual formed an important part of imperial court ceremonies. A career in religion became attractive even to the children of the gentry class; and the number of monks and nuns increased enormously. Among the populace, Buddhist holidays were the occasions of great public festivals, at which large crowds gathered to honor the Buddhist saints, hear readings of the Sutras, or listen to a preacher expound some point of doctrine. Buddhism also provided the principal outlet for the creative talents of the age. Gifted artists and architects worked to build and adorn magnificent temples and monasteries, while outstanding scholars turned their minds to the elaboration of Buddhist doctrine. All the famous T'ang poets and essayists were affected to some degree by Buddhist notions. Buddhist institutions became ever wealthier, enriched not only by imperial patronage but by private gifts; for it was believed that pious donations would wipe out some of the evil *karma* which the giver had accumulated in previous lives upon earth. Often the Buddhist monasteries became important elements in the rural economy, owning extensive tracts of land and accumulating the capital with which to engage in commerce.

Owing to its wide acceptance among all classes of society, Buddhism was a unifying force within the Chinese state; and the governments of the T'ang and Sung periods generally regarded it as an ally. On the whole, the Buddhist religion was apolitical. Its thinkers never developed any comprehensive political theory; and Buddhist monks were not usually inclined to seek political power for themselves. On the contrary, they emphasized private meditation, withdrawal from secular activities, and the search for personal Enlightenment (Nirvana) or salvation after death. Buddhist notions of the afterlife, in fact, proved useful to the Chinese military establishment. Whereas Confucians believed that the only immortality a man could expect was the reverence paid him by his descendants at the family shrine, the popular Buddhist sects taught another sort of immortality in one of the many heavens presided over by the Buddhas and Bodhisattvas. To die without sons in a faraway place was thus a far less frightening prospect to the Buddhist than to the Confucian; and the government recognized this fact by erecting Buddhist temples at the sites of major battles and endowing perpetual services for the souls of the war dead. Inevitably, Buddhist ideas also had their effect upon government policies. Buddhist insistence upon the virtue of compassion was probably responsible for mitigating the harshness of the penalties for certain crimes; and the government itself, especially under the Sung dynasty, undertook to support various charitable institutions.

Some Buddhist ideas, however, were potentially subversive of government. All Buddhists accepted the Indian theory of the ages of the world, according to which the present era was one of decay in which no conceivable government could enjoy the respect and loyalty of true believers. In particular the adherents of Maitreya, the future Buddha, contended that the end of the world was imminent and that Maitreya would soon descend to earth to inaugurate a new age. A variety of rebel movements and secret societies in Sui and T'ang times employed such theories as their intellectual justification. Partly for this reason, Chinese governments always took care to retain a controlling influence over Buddhist activities. A government bureau was created in order to supervise the clergy. To prevent undue proliferation of monks and nuns, the bureau insisted that aspirants to clerical status be properly examined and ordained, and once ordained, that they obey their own monastic rules. Each temple and monastery was required to hold a government charter; and new ones could be built only with official permission.

Chinese Buddhism under the Sui and T'ang dynasties exhibited an enormous intellectual creativity. Whereas in the Six Dynasties period (A.D. 222-589) Buddhists had attempted primarily to assimilate Indian ideas, the sects which now arose provided distinctively Chinese interpretations of doctrine. With a few notable exceptions (e.g., the pilgrim Hsüan Tsang), the original thinkers of Chinese Buddhism in this period could not read any Indian languages; and they expressed Indian abstractions in Chinese terms which often bore connotations quite different from the Indian originals. The two Buddhist sects which lasted longest and ultimately proved most influential in China—the Ch'an and the Pure Land—first came to prominence in this period; and both were greatly affected by indigenous Chinese modes of thought.

Ch'an Buddhism (in Japanese: Zen) lays prime stress upon individual meditation and introspection. Its central doctrine is that a single essence—the Buddha-nature—is immanent in all created beings. Discovery of this Buddha-nature within oneself constitutes Enlightenment—a mystic state described as the ultimate degree of knowledge and bliss. In many respects, Ch'an Buddhism continues the tradition of philosophic Taoism. Like Taoism, it distrusts books and learning, and advocates a life close to nature; its literature contains a rich store of paradox and concrete metaphor. Long after Buddhism as a whole had declined in China, the Ch'an philosophy of Enlightenment through introspection and intuition continued to appeal to educated people, especially artists and writers. Ch'an ultimately divided into two branches: one which held that Enlightenment could be attained only by gradual stages; the other insisting that it occurs in a single instant of sudden illumination. The latter branch was responsible for a characteristic Ch'an literary form: the paradoxical tale in which the obscure, apparently nonsensical utterance of a teacher or fellow monk stimulates the aspirant to awareness of ultimate Truth. But though this final Enlightenment might occur instantly and unexpectedly, even the advocates of sudden illumination agreed that years might be spent in searching for it.

The Pure Land sect—so named from the heaven of the Buddha Amitabha[1]—was only one of a number of Buddhist groups which believed in salvation through faith in one of the Buddhist deities. Mahayana Buddhism in India had already produced a vast literature describing the marvelous deeds of innumerable Buddhas and Bodhisattvas; and many Chinese sects addressed their devotions to one of these. The salvation-sects denied that a long preparatory period of study and spiritual discipline was prerequisite to salvation. They taught that anyone at all—even if illiterate and ignorant of doctrine—might be saved through a simple act of faith. In place of the traditional Buddhist goal of Enlightenment (i.e., Nirvana), which is a state of being rather than a place, these sects taught that the believer would be transported after death to one of the many Buddhist heavens. Devotees of Amitabha could thus look forward to

1. In Chinese: O-mi-t'o-fo; in Japanese: Amida.

residence in the Pure Land (also called the Western Paradise). One form of Amitabha-worship went so far as to declare that a single repetition of Amitabha's name, if accompanied by sincere faith, is sufficient to ensure rebirth in the Pure Land.

The efflorescence of Chinese Buddhism in the seventh and eighth centuries was followed by a gradual decline in the ninth. The latter part of the eighth century witnessed prolonged disorders following the abortive rebellion led by An Lu-shan (A.D. 755); perhaps this time of troubles gave rise to a kind of cultural defensiveness. In any event, many of the old objections to Buddhism—first heard at the time of its introduction into China—began to be revived. Critics pointed out that Buddhism was of foreign origin; that it taught a universalistic ethic contrary to the traditional Chinese distinctions of superior and inferior; that its temples were extravagant and the clergy often idle and unproductive; and that its lands and clergy, being tax-free, constituted a drain upon the treasury. This criticism bore fruit in the extensive Buddhist persecutions of the years 842-845. By the emperor's command, Buddhist temples and monasteries throughout the country were destroyed and their lands confiscated; many monks and nuns were forced back into lay life.

Chinese Buddhism never fully recovered from this disaster. Many of the destroyed edifices were never rebuilt; and the monastic orders never again enjoyed their former prosperity. The Ch'an school suffered least, probably in part because its monasteries were located in out-of-the-way places rather than in cities. Under the Sung dynasty occurred that return to native Chinese traditions which is known as Neo-Confucianism; and from that time onward the intellectual orientation of the upper classes was Confucian rather than Buddhist. Though Buddhism continued to exist in China until the twentieth century, its old prestige was gone, and it had ceased to attract the best talents within Chinese society.

Introduction to Hsüan Tsang

Hsüan Tsang (A.D. 603-664) is probably the most famous Buddhist pilgrim, diarist, and translator in the history of East Asia. Born in Honan province, at age thirteen he entered a monastery at Loyang, where his elder brother had preceded him, and at twenty was ordained a monk. Subsequently he traveled widely within China seeking further instruction in Buddhist doctrine. Presumably he was dissatisfied with the answers which his questions elicited, for in A.D. 629 he defied an imperial prohibition against foreign travel and set out for India—the Buddhist Holy Land.

In the fifteen years he spent in India, Hsüan Tsang visited all the major regions of that country, studying with noted Buddhist teachers and touring the holy places connected with the Buddha's life. He was received with honor by a variety of Indian kings; even the great Emperor Harsha bowed down before him. Returning to India in 645, Hsüan Tsang brought with him a large collection of Buddhist relics, statues, and holy books, carried on the backs of twenty-two horses. The remainder of his life he spent in lecturing on Buddhist doctrine and, with the aid of a staff of scholars, in translating Buddhist books from Sanskrit into Chinese. His *Records of the Western World* (i.e., of the countries west of China) is the diary of his adventures and observations in India, and incidentally the principal extant source for that period of Indian history.

The following preface to the *Records*, while written by an admirer in the flowery style typical of such panegyrics, nonetheless indicates the enormous respect and affection which was felt for Hsüan Tsang throughout the Buddhist world.

FROM THE PREFACE TO HSÜAN TSANG'S RECORDS OF THE WESTERN WORLD

There was in the temple of "great benevolence" a doctor of the three Pitakas[1] called Hsüan Tsang . . . In him were joined sweetness and virtue. These roots, combined and deeply planted, produced their fruits rapidly. The source of his wisdom was deep, and wonderfully it increased. At his opening life he was rosy as the evening vapours and (round) as the rising moon. As a boy he was sweet as the odour of cinnamon or the vanilla tree. When he grew up he thoroughly mastered the ancient

From Samuel Beal, trans., *Buddhist Records of the Western World,* London: Kegan Paul, Trench, Trübner & Co., Ltd., 1914, pp. 2-6. Reprinted by permission of Routledge & Kegan Paul, Ltd.

1. The three divisions ("baskets") of the Buddhist canon.

Chinese books; the nine borders were filled with his renown, the five prefectures together resounded his praise.

At early dawn he studied the true and the false, and through the night shone forth his goodness; the mirror of his wisdom, fixed on the true receptacle, remained stationary. He considered the limits of life, and was permanently at rest (in the persuasion that) the vermilion ribbon and the violet silken tassels[2] are the pleasing bonds that keep one attached to the world; but the precious car and the red pillow,[3] these are the means of crossing the ford and escaping the world. Wherefore he put away from him the pleasures of sense, and spoke of finding refuge in some hermit retreat. His noble brother Chang-hsi was a Master of the Law, a pillar and support of the school of Buddha. He [Hsüan Tsang] was as a dragon or an elephant in his own generation, and, as a falcon or a crane, he mounted above those to come. In the court and the wilderness was his fame exalted; within and without was his renown spread. Being deeply affectionate, [the brothers] loved one another, and so fulfilled the harmony of mutual relationship. The Master of the Law [Hsüan Tsang] was diligent in his labour as a student; he lost not a moment of time, and by his studies he rendered his teachers illustrious, and was an ornament to his place of study. His virtuous qualities were rightly balanced, and he caused the perfume of his fame to extend through the home of his adoption. Whip raised, he travelled on his even way; he mastered the nine divisions of the books, and acquired a vast erudition; he worked his paddles across the dark ford; he gave his attention to the four Vedas, whilst finding [his own country] small.[4]

From this time he travelled forth and frequented places of discussion, and so passed many years, his merit completed, even as his ability was perfected . . .

With all the fame of these acquirements, he yet embarked in

2. Emblems of official rank.

3. Buddhist symbols.

4. This is an allusion to a passage in the *Mencius*: "Confucius mounted on the mountain of the East, and found that the king of Lu (i.e., of his own country) was small." The meaning here seems to be that Hsüan Tsang found his previous studies to be limited in scope, and therefore also examined the Vedas.

the boat of humility and departed alone . . . Men near and afar beheld him with admiration . . . The Master of the Law [Hsüan Tsang], from his early days till he grew up, pondered in heart the mysterious principles (of religion). His fame spread wide among eminent men.

At this time the schools were mutually contentious; they hastened to grasp the end without regarding the beginning; they seized the flower and rejected the reality; so there followed the contradictory teaching of the North and South,[5] and the confused sounds of "Yes" and "No," perpetual words! On this he was afflicted at heart, and fearing lest he should be unable to find out completely the errors of translations, he purposed to examine thoroughly the (best) literature . . .

With a virtue of unequalled character, and at a time favourable in its indications, he took his staff, dusted his clothes, and set off for distant regions. On this he left behind him the dark waters of the Pa river;[6] he bent his gaze forwards; he then advanced right on to the Tsinling mountains.[7] In following the courses of rivers and crossing the plains he encountered constant dangers. Compared with him [the general] Po-wang[8] went but a little way, and the journey of [the pilgrim] Fa-hsien[9] was short indeed. In all the districts through which he journeyed he learnt thoroughly the dialects; he investigated throughout the deep secrets (of religion) and penetrated to the very source of the stream. Thus he was able to correct the books and transcend (the writers of) India. The texts being transcribed on palm leaves, he then returned to China.

The Emperor T'ai Tsung, who held the golden wheel[10] and was seated royally on the throne, waited with impatience for that eminent man. He summoned him therefore to the green

5. Reference to the divergent interpretations of Buddhism in North and South China during the Six Dynasties period.

6. In Shensi province (northwestern China).

7. The Tsinling range divides Shensi from Szechwan province to the south; it is an extension of the K'un-lun mountains of northern Tibet.

8. General Po-wang (Chang Ch'ien) was the first Chinese to reach as far west as Turkestan, where he was sent in 139 B.C. to negotiate a treaty with the Yüeh-chih nomads.

9. Fa-hsien was a Buddhist pilgrim who resided in India A.D. 399-414.

10. Symbol of the Buddhist Law (*Dharma*).

enclosure (surrounding the imperial seat), and, impressed by his past acquirements, he knelt before him in the yellow palace. With his hand he wrote proclamations full of affectionate sentiments; the officers of the interior attended him constantly; condescending to exhibit his illustrious thoughts, he wrote a preface to the sacred doctrine of the Tripitaka, consisting of 780 words. The present emperor (Kao Tsung) had composed in the spring pavilion a sacred record consisting of 579 words, in which he sounded to the bottom the stream of deep mystery and expressed himself in lofty utterances. But now, if he (Hsüan Tsang) had not displayed his wisdom in the wood of the cock (near Pataliputra), nor scattered his brightness on the peak of the vulture near Rajagriha,[11] how could the emperor have been able to abase his sacred composition in the praise of the ornament of his time?

In virtue of a royal mandate, (Hsüan Tsang) translated 657 works from the original Sanskrit. Having thoroughly examined the different manners of distant countries, the diverse customs of separate people, the various products of the soil and the class divisions of the people, the regions where the [Chinese] royal calendar is received[12] and where the sounds of moral instruction have come, he has composed (a work) in twelve books. Herein he has collected and written down the most secret principles of the religion of Buddha, couched in language plain and precise. It may be said, indeed, of him, that his works perish not.

11. Pataliputra and Rajagriha were places associated with the life of Guatama, the Buddha.

12. This calendar, containing various information about the seasons, was distributed annually throughout the Chinese empire.

Introduction to the Platform Sutra[1]

As the school of thought known as Ch'an began to evolve into an independent Buddhist sect, its followers increasingly felt the need for a historical tradition linking the founders of the sect with the Indian Buddha. Drawing on old legends, and sometimes inventing new ones, rival Ch'an Masters of the eighth century created and promoted differing versions of their sect's history. In particular, the identity of the patriarchs—the transmitters of the true Law (*Dharma*)—became a subject of much dispute. By the beginning of the ninth century, however, most Ch'an Buddhists agreed that the *Dharma* had reached China directly through a series of twenty-nine Indian and six Chinese patriarchs. Of these latter six the first was declared to be Bodhidharma, an Indian Brahmin who preached in south China between *c.* 520 and 534; the sixth was Hui-neng, who lived from 638 to 713. The *Platform Sutra* (*T'an Ching*) attributed to Hui-neng is an exposition of Ch'an doctrine allegedly spoken by him, though the work assumed its present form only between about 780 and 800. Subsequently it became one of the most popular of all Ch'an writings; and as a result Hui-neng is the best-known Ch'an Master in Chinese history.

The autobiography of Hui-neng which appears in sections 2-11 of the *Sutra* is evidently heavily overlaid with fiction; for it is not corroborated by any other historical source. It records how Hui-neng, then an unlearned layman, joined the monastic community on the East Mountain (in present-day Hupeh) headed by Hung-jen, the fifth patriarch. Hung-jen soon recognized Hui-neng as the disciple who most perfectly comprehended his teaching, and designated him as the next patriarch. Ch'an Buddhists subsequently laid great stress upon Hui-neng's alleged illiteracy to make the point that Ch'an is a silent transmission of the truth from "mind to mind" which need not depend upon the written word. His autobiography thereby demonstrates that the highest spiritual understanding is not

1. The name apparently refers to the platform from which sermons were preached. In traditional Buddhist terminology, however, a *sutra* records the words of the Buddha himself. The *Platform Sutra* is the earliest known instance in which a composition dealing merely with the career and opinions of a Master of the Law is given that title.

limited to literati and/or monks. In the *Sutra* itself, Hui-neng is represented as preaching the doctrine to a mixed audience of monks and laymen at the request of a high government official.

Many of the ideas set forth in the *Platform Sutra* are not unique to Ch'an, but belong to the general store of Mahayana Buddhist ideas —e.g., the concept of the Buddha's threefold nature, the four vows of a Bodhisattva, the importance of meditation, and the striving for Enlightenment. Within Ch'an itself, the *Sutra* defends the doctrine of sudden illumination as against the exponents of gradualism. It rejects the premises of Pure Land and the other salvation schools that the goal of the religious life is residence in heaven, attainable through faith; it likewise condemns the notion that good works can influence final salvation. To the Ch'an sect all merit, like all reality, is in the mind; and only through rigorous discipline and self-examination can the final Enlightenment be obtained.

FROM THE PLATFORM SUTRA OF THE SIXTH PATRIARCH

1. The Master Hui-neng ascended the high seat at the lecture hall of the Ta-fan Temple and expounded the Dharma of the Great Perfection of Wisdom, and transmitted the precepts of formlessness.[1] At that time over ten thousand monks, nuns, and lay followers sat before him. The prefect of Shao-chou,[2] Wei Ch'ü, some thirty officials from various departments, and some thirty Confucian scholars all begged the Master to preach on the Dharma of the Great Perfection of Wisdom. The prefect then had the monk-disciple Fa-hai record his words so that they might become known to later generations and be of benefit to students of the Way, in order that they might receive the pivot of the teaching and transmit it among themselves, taking these words as their authority.

12. [The Master Hui-neng said:] "I was predestined to come

From Philip B. Yampolsky, *The Platform Sutra of the Sixth Patriarch*, New York: Columbia University Press, 1967, pp. 125-26, 134-37, 139-44, 151-52. Reprinted by permission of Columbia University Press.

1. Formlessness is an attribute (characteristic) of the ultimate Wisdom, which cannot be compressed into any shape or form.

2. District in modern Kwangtung, where the Ta-fan Temple apparently was located.

to live here and to preach to you officials, monks, and laymen. My teaching has been handed down from the sages of the past; it is not my own personal knowledge. If you wish to hear the teachings of the sages of the past, each of you must quiet his mind and hear me to the end. Please cast aside your own delusions; then you will be no different from the sages of the past. (What follows below is the Dharma)."

The Master Hui-neng called, saying: "Good friends, enlightenment (*bodhi*) and intuitive wisdom (*prajna*)[3] are from the outset possessed by men of this world themselves. It is just because the mind is deluded that men cannot attain awakening to themselves. They must seek a good teacher to show them how to see into their own natures. Good friends, if you meet awakening, [Buddha]-wisdom will be achieved.

13. "Good friends, my teaching of the Dharma takes meditation and wisdom as its basis. Never under any circumstances say mistakenly that meditation and wisdom are different; they are a unity, not two things. Meditation itself is the substance of wisdom; wisdom itself is the function of meditation.[4] At the very moment when there is wisdom, then meditation exists in wisdom; at the very moment when there is meditation, then wisdom exists in meditation. Good friends, this means that meditation and wisdom are alike. Students, be careful not to say that meditation gives rise to wisdom, or that wisdom gives rise to meditation, or that meditation and wisdom are different from each other. To hold this view implies that things have duality—if good is spoken while the mind is not good, meditation and wisdom will not be alike. If mind and speech are both good, then the internal and the external are the same and meditation and wisdom are alike. The practice of self-awakening does not lie in verbal arguments. If you argue which comes first, meditation or wisdom, you are deluded people. You won't be able to settle the argument and instead will cling to objective things, and will never escape from the four states of phenomena.[5]

3. These two terms (*bodhi* and *prajna*) are ordinarily interchangeable, though *prajna* has more the connotation of "reason," *bodhi* of "wisdom."

4. This asserted unity of meditation and wisdom is a characteristic Ch'an doctrine.

5. Birth, being, change, and death.

15. "Good friends, how then are meditation and wisdom alike? They are like the lamp and the light it gives forth. If there is a lamp there is light; if there is no lamp there is no light. The lamp is the substance of light; the light is the function of the lamp. Thus, although they have two names, in substance they are not two. Meditation and wisdom are also like this.

16. "Good friends, in the Dharma there is no sudden or gradual, but among people some are keen and others dull. The deluded recommend the gradual method, the enlightened practice the sudden teaching. To understand the original mind of yourself is to see into your own original nature. Once enlightened, there is from the outset no distinction between these two methods; those who are not enlightened will for long kalpas[6] be caught in the cycle of transmigration.

18. "Good friends, if someone speaks of 'viewing purity,' [then I would say] that man's nature is of itself pure, but because of false thoughts True Reality is obscured. If you exclude delusions then the original nature reveals its purity. If you activate your mind to view purity without realizing that your own nature is originally pure, delusions of purity will be produced. Since this delusion has no place to exist, then you know that whatever you see[7] is nothing but delusion. Purity has no form, but, nonetheless, some people try to postulate the form of purity and consider this to be Ch'an practice. People who hold this view obstruct their own original natures . . .

19. "Now that we know that this is so, what is it in this teaching that we call 'sitting in meditation'? In this teaching 'sitting' means without any obstruction anywhere, outwardly and under all circumstances, not to activate thoughts. 'Meditation' is internally to see the original nature and not become confused.

"And what do we call Ch'an meditation? Outwardly to exclude form is 'ch'an'; inwardly to be unconfused is meditation. Even though there is form on the outside, when internally the nature is not confused, then, from the outset, you are of yourself pure and of yourself in meditation. The very contact with cir-

6. The *kalpa* is the basic time-cycle in Indian cosmology, equivalent to 320 million earthly years.

7. Including mental states as well as tangible objects.

cumstances itself causes confusion. Separation from form on the outside is 'ch'an'; being untouched on the inside is meditation. Being 'ch'an' externally and meditation internally, it is known as ch'an meditation . . .

"Good friends, see for yourselves the purity of your own natures, practice and accomplish for yourselves. Your own nature is the *Dharmakaya*[8] and self-practice is the practice of Buddha; by self-accomplishment you may achieve the Buddha Way for yourselves.

20. "Good friends, you must all with your own bodies receive the precepts of formlessness and recite in unison what I am about to say. It will make you see the threefold body of the Buddha in your own selves. 'I take refuge in the pure *Dharmakaya* Buddha[9] in my own physical body. I take refuge in the ten thousand hundred billion *Nirmanakaya* Buddhas[10] in my own physical body. I take refuge in the future perfect *Sambhogakaya* Buddha[11] in my own physical body.' (Recite the above three times). The physical body is your own home; you cannot speak of turning to it. The threefold body which I just mentioned is within your own self-natures. Everyone in the world possesses it, but being deluded, he cannot see it and seeks the threefold body of the Tathagata[12] on the outside. Thus he cannot find the threefold Buddha body in his own physical body.

"Good friends, listen! I shall make you see that there is a threefold Buddha body of your own self-natures in your own physical bodies. The threefold Buddha body is produced from your own natures.

"What is the pure *Dharmakaya* Buddha? Good friends, although the nature of people in this world is from the outset pure

8. The "body of the Law," or system of the universe.
9. The Buddha in his nature as the essence of the universe.
10. Or "body of transformation": the Buddha-nature as manifested in all the phenomena of this world. Guatama Shakyamuni (the Buddha who lived and preached in sixth-century India) is an example of the *Nirmanakaya* Buddha—the Buddha-nature in human form.
11. Or "body of bliss": the Buddha in his spiritual aspect, possessing all wisdom and psychic powers.
12. Name for the Buddha as a spiritual principle rather than a historical personality.

in itself, the ten thousand things are all within their own natures. If people think of all the evil things, then they will practice evil; if they think of all the good things, then they will practice good. Thus it is clear that in this way all the *dharmas*[13] are within your own natures, yet your own natures are always pure. The sun and the moon are always bright, yet if they are covered by clouds, although above they are bright, below they are darkened, and the sun, moon, stars, and planets cannot be seen clearly. But if suddenly the wind of wisdom should blow and roll away the clouds and mists, all forms in the universe appear at once. The purity of the nature of man in this world is like the blue sky; wisdom is like the sun, knowledge like the moon. Although knowledge and wisdom are always clear, if you cling to external environments, the floating clouds of false thoughts will create a cover, and your own natures cannot become clear. Therefore, if you meet a good teacher, open up the true Dharma, and waft aside your delusions and errors; inside and outside will become clear. Within your own natures the ten thousand things will all appear, for all things of themselves are within your own natures. Given a name, this is the pure *Dharmakaya* Buddha. Taking refuge in oneself is to cast aside all actions that are not good; this is known as taking refuge.[14]

"What are the ten thousand hundred billion *Nirmanakaya* Buddhas? If you do not think, then your nature is empty;[15] if you do think, then you yourself will change. If you think of evil things then you will change and enter hell; if you think of good things then you will change and enter heaven. [If you think of] harm you will change and become a beast; [If you think of] compassion you will change and become a Bodhisattva. [If you think of] intuitive wisdom you will change and enter the upper realms; [if you think of] ignorance you will change and enter the lower quarters. The changes of your own natures are ex-

13. In Buddhist philosophy, *dharmas* are the innumerable, infinitesimal energy-points of which all phenomena are composed. Each *dharma* exists for only an instant and then passes away.

14. Compare the vows of the Buddhist monk: "I take refuge in [i.e., place my trust in] the Buddha; I take refuge in the Dharma; I take refuge in the Order [of monks]."

15. "Emptiness" or the "Void" are Buddhist equivalents for ultimate Truth, which is necessarily without specific attributes.

treme, yet the deluded person is not himself conscious of this. [Successive thoughts give rise to evil and evil ways are always practiced]. But if a single thought of good evolves, intuitive wisdom is born. [This is called the *Nirmanakaya* Buddha of your own nature. What is the perfect *Sambhogakaya* Buddha?] As one lamp serves to dispel a thousand years of darkness, so one flash of wisdom destroys ten thousand years of ignorance. Do not think of the past; always think of the future; if your future thoughts are always good, you may be called the *Sambhogakaya* Buddha. An instant of thought of evil will result in the destruction of good which has continued a thousand years; an instant of thought of good compensates for a thousand years of evil and destruction. If from the timeless beginning future thoughts have always been good, you may be called the *Sambhogakaya* Buddha . . .

21. "Now that you have already taken refuge in the threefold body of Buddha, I shall expound to you the four great vows [of a Bodhisattva]. Good friends, recite in unison what I say: 'I vow to save all sentient beings everywhere. I vow to cut off all the passions everywhere. I vow to study all the Buddhist teachings everywhere. I vow to achieve the unsurpassed Buddha Way.' (Recite three times.)

"Good friends, when I say 'I vow to save all sentient beings everywhere,' it is not that I will save you, but that sentient beings, each with their own natures, must save themselves. What is meant by 'saving yourselves with your own natures'? Despite heterodox views, passions, ignorance, and delusions, in your own physical bodies you have in yourselves the attributes of inherent enlightenment, so that with correct views you can be saved. If you are awakened to correct views, the wisdom of *prajna* will wipe away ignorance and delusion, and you all will save yourselves. If false views come, with correct views you will be saved; if delusion comes, with awakening you will be saved; if ignorance comes, with wisdom you will be saved; if evil comes, with good you will be saved; if the passions come, with *bodhi* [wisdom] you will be saved. Being saved in this way is known as true salvation.

" 'I vow to cut off all the passions everywhere' is, with your own minds to cast aside the unreal and the false. 'I vow to study all the Buddhist teachings everywhere' is to study the unsurpassed true Dharma. 'I vow to achieve the unsurpassed Buddha Way' is always to act humbly, to practice reverence for all things, to separate oneself from erroneous attachments, and to awaken to the wisdom of *prajna*. When delusions are cast aside you are self-enlightened, achieve the Buddha Way, and put into practice the power of the vows.

31. "Good friends, when I was at Priest[16] [Hung-]jen's place, hearing [the Diamond Sutra] just once, I immediately gained the great awakening and saw suddenly that True Reality was my original nature. Therefore, I have taken this teaching and, passing it on to later generations, shall make you students of the Way suddenly awaken to enlightenment, and let each of you see into your own minds, and suddenly awaken to your own original natures. If you cannot gain enlightenment for yourselves, you must seek a great teacher to show you the way to see into your own self-natures. What is a great teacher? He is a man who understands at once that the Dharma of the Supreme Vehicle[17] is indeed the correct path. This is a great teacher. This is the great causal event, the so-called conversion which will enable you to see Buddha. All the good *dharmas* are activated by a great teacher. Therefore, although the Buddhas of the three worlds and all the twelve divisions of the canon are from the beginning within the nature of man, if he cannot gain awakening with his own nature, he must obtain a good teacher to show him how to see into his own self-nature. But if you awaken by yourself, do not rely on teachers outside. If you try to seek a teacher outside and hope to obtain deliverance, you will find it impossible. If you have recognized the good teacher within your own mind, you have already obtained deliverance. If you are deluded in your own mind and harbor erroneous thoughts and contrary concepts, even though you go to an outside teacher [you will not be able to obtain salvation].

. . . .

16. In contrast to Christianity, Buddhism does not distinguish between monks and priests; the same term may thus be translated either way.

17. I.e., the Mahayana, known as the "Great Vehicle" in contrast to the Hinayana or "Small Vehicle."

Introduction to Han Yü

The foremost opponent of Buddhism under the T'ang dynasty was Han Yü (786-824), a government official who was also an eminent poet and essayist. In literary matters as well as in politics, he advocated a return to the ancient Confucian traditions. His poetry was noted for its serious tone; his essays were composed in a simple and rather archaic style, contrasting sharply with the elaborate and somewhat artificial rhetoric which was then fashionable. Han Yü argued endlessly for a return to the traditional Confucian code of the gentleman, based upon humanity (*jen*), righteousness (*li*), and proper relations within family and state. While the literati of the T'ang period generally proclaimed that Confucianism, Taoism, and Buddhism were essentially harmonious, Han Yü insisted that Confucianism was both separate and superior to the others. He disliked foreignness—a highly unusual standpoint for this period; part of his opposition to Buddhism was based upon its Indian origin. He composed various polemics against the foreign religion, one of which—the "Memorial on the Bone of Buddha"—resulted in his exile to the far southern borderlands.

Han Yü enjoyed very little influence among his own contemporaries, most of whom considered him an extremist and something of an eccentric. But in Sung times he was rediscovered. The leaders of the new Confucian revival studied his ideas, imitated his literary style, and assigned him the place of honor he has since held in Chinese intellectual history as the first of the Neo-Confucianists.

HAN YÜ: FROM AN INQUIRY ON THE WAY

Humanity and righteousness are definite values, whereas the [Taoist] Way and virtue have no substance in themselves [but depend on humanity and righteousness for it]. Thus we have the Way of the superior man[1] [as in Confucianism] and the

From Wing-tsit Chan, *A Source Book in Chinese Philosophy*, Princeton, N.J.: Princeton University Press, 1963, pp. 454-56. Reprinted by permission of Princeton University Press.

1. I.e., the gentleman (*chün tzu*).

Way of the inferior man [as in Taoism], and there are the inauspicious virtue [as in Taoism] and auspicious virtue [as in Confucianism]. Lao Tzu[2] belittled humanity and righteousness not because he destroyed them but because his viewpoint was small. If a man sits at the bottom of a well, looks up at the sky, and says, "The sky is small," it does not mean that the sky is really small. Lao Tzu considered little acts [of kindness] as humanity and isolated deeds [of good] as righteousness. It is no wonder that he belittled them. . . .

Now the method [of the Taoists and Buddhists] is to insist on discarding the relationship between ruler and ministers, doing away with the relationship between father and son, and stopping the process of sustaining and supporting the life of one another, in order to seek for what they call silence and annihilation. . . . The Classic says, "The ancients who wished to manifest their clear character to the world would first bring order to their states. Those who wished to bring order to their states would first regulate their families. Those who wished to regulate their families would first cultivate their personal lives. Those who wished to cultivate their personal lives would first rectify their minds. Those who wished to rectify their minds would first make their wills sincere."[3] Thus what the ancients meant by rectifying the mind and making the will sincere was to engage in activity [as against the inaction of the Taoists and Buddhists]. But now [the Taoists and Buddhists] seek to govern their hearts by escaping from the world, the state, and the family. They destroy the natural principles of human relations so that the son does not regard his father as a father, the minister does not regard his ruler as a ruler, and the people do not attend to their work. . . . Now, they take the ways of barbarism and elevate them above the teachings of our ancient kings. Does this not almost make all of us barbarians?

What were the teachings of our ancient kings? Universal love[4] is called humanity. To practice this in the proper manner

2. Supposed author of the *Tao-te-Ching* and founder of philosophic Taoism. On Lao Tzu see Vol. V of this series, pp. 184-94.

3. Quoted from the "Great Learning," a chapter of the *Book of Rites*. See Vol. V, pp. 44-49.

4. Here Han Yü takes care to avoid both the Mohist term for "universal love" and the Buddhist term for "compassion."

is called righteousness. To proceed according to these is called the Way. To be sufficient in oneself without depending on anything outside is called virtue. Their literature comprised the Books of *Odes*, *History*, *Changes*, and the *Spring and Autumn Annals*. Their methods consisted of rules of propriety, music, laws, and governmental measures. Their people were the four classes of scholars, farmers, artisans, and merchants.[5] Their relationships were those between ruler and minister, father and son, teacher and friend, guest and host,[6] elder and younger brother, and husband and wife. Their clothing was hemp and silk. Their dwellings were halls and houses.[7] Their food consisted of grain and rice, fruit and vegetables, fish and meat.[8] As methods theirs were easy to understand and as teachings theirs were easy to practice. Employed to conduct oneself, they brought harmony and blessing, and employed to deal with others, love and impartiality. Employed to cultivate the mind, they gave peace and harmony, and employed to deal with the world, the state, and the family, they are always fitting no matter where they were applied. Consequently, in life people were able to express their feelings, and at death the eternal relations between them and their descendants were fulfilled [by the latter]. They offered sacrifices to Heaven and the gods came to receive them. They offered sacrifices to their ancestors and the ancestors enjoyed them. What Way is this? I say: This is what I call the Way, and not what the Taoists and the Buddhists called the Way. . . .

5. I.e., neither monks nor nuns, Taoist recluses, etc.
6. The usual enumeration of the Confucian relationships substitutes "friend and friend" for Han Yü's "teacher and friend," "guest and host."
7. I.e., not monasteries or temples.
8. As opposed to the vegetarian diet of the Buddhists.

From Wm. Theodore deBary, ed., *Sources of Chinese Tradition*, New York: Columbia University Press, 1960, pp. 427-29. Reprinted by permission of Columbia University Press.

1. I.e., Han Yü.

HAN YÜ: FROM HIS MEMORIAL ON THE BONE OF BUDDHA

Your servant[1] begs leave to say that Buddhism is no more than a cult of the barbarian peoples which spread to China in the time of the Latter Han.[2] It did not exist here in ancient times. . . . When Emperor Kao-tsu [founder of the T'ang] received the throne from the House of Sui, he deliberated upon the suppression of Buddhism. But at that time the various officials, being of small worth and knowledge, were unable fully to comprehend the ways of the ancient kings and the exigencies of past and present, and so could not implement the wisdom of the emperor and rescue the age from corruption. Thus the matter came to nought, to your servant's constant regret.

Now Your Majesty, wise in the arts of peace and war, unparalleled in divine glory from countless ages past, upon your accession prohibited men and women from taking Buddhist orders and forbade the erection of temples and monasteries, and your servant believed that at Your Majesty's hand the will of Kao-tsu would be carried out. Even if the suppression of Buddhism should be as yet impossible, your servant hardly thought that Your Majesty would encourage it and on the contrary cause it to spread. Yet now your servant hears that Your Majesty has ordered the community of monks to go to Feng-hsiang to greet the bone of Buddha,[3] that Your Majesty will ascend a tower to watch as it is brought into the palace, and that the various temples have been commanded to welcome and worship it in turn. Though your servant is abundantly ignorant, he understands that Your Majesty is not so misled by Buddhism as to honor it thus in hopes of receiving some blessing or reward, but only that, the year being one of plenty and the people joyful, Your Majesty would accord with the hearts of the multitude in setting forth for the officials and citizens of the capital some curious show and toy for their amusement. How could it be, indeed, that with such sagely wisdom Your Majesty should in truth give credence to these affairs? But the common people are ignorant and dull, easily misled and hard to enlighten, and should they see their emperor do these things, they might say that Your Majesty was serving Buddhism with a true heart. "The Son of Heaven is a Great Sage," they would cry, "and yet he reverences and believes with all his heart! How should we,

2. A.D. 25-220.
3. A relic supposed to be part of the Buddha's finger-bone.

the common people, then begrudge our bodies and our lives?" Then would they set about singeing their heads and scorching their fingers,[4] binding together in groups of ten and a hundred, doffing their common clothes and scattering their money, from morning to evening urging each other on lest one be slow, till old and young alike had abandoned their occupations to follow [Buddhism]. If this is not checked and the bone is carried from one temple to another, there will be those who will cut off their arms and mutilate their flesh in offering [to the Buddha]. Then will our old ways be corrupted, our customs violated, and the tale will spread to make us the mockery of the world. This is no trifling matter!

Now Buddha was a man of the barbarians who did not speak the language of China and wore clothes of a different fashion. His sayings did not concern the ways of our ancient kings, nor did his manner of dress conform to their laws. He understood neither the duties that bind sovereign and subject, nor the affections of father and son. If he were still alive today and came to our court by order of his ruler, Your Majesty might condescend to receive him, but it would amount to no more than one audience in the Hsüan-cheng Hall, a banquet by the Office for Receiving Guests, the presentation of a suit of clothes, and he would then be escorted to the borders of the nation, dismissed, and not allowed to delude the masses. How then, when he has long been dead, could his rotten bones, the foul and unlucky remains of his body, be rightly admitted to the palace? Confucius said: "Respect ghosts and spirits, but keep them at a distance!"[5] So when the princes of ancient times went to pay their condolences at a funeral within the state, they sent exorcists in advance with peach wands to drive out evil, and only then would they advance. Now without reason Your Majesty has caused this loathsome thing to be brought in and would personally go to view it. No exorcists have been sent ahead, no peach wands employed. The host of officials have not spoken out against this wrong, and the censors have failed to note its im-

4. Acts symbolic of a person's renunciation of the world upon entering Buddhist orders. (Tr.)
5. *Analects* VI, 20.

propriety. Your servant is deeply shamed and begs that this bone be given to the proper authorities to be cast into fire and water, that this evil may be rooted out, the world freed from its error, and later generations spared this delusion. Then may all men know how the acts of their wise sovereign transcend the commonplace a thousandfold. Would this not be glorious? Would it not be joyful?

Should the Buddha indeed have supernatural power to send down curses and calamities, may they fall only upon the person of your servant, who calls upon High Heaven to witness that he does not regret his words. With all gratitude and sincerity your servant presents this memorial for consideration, being filled with respect and awe.

EMPEROR WU TSUNG: EDICT AGAINST BUDDHISM

[The most severe religious persecutions in Chinese history occurred during the reign of Wu Tsung (r. 838-846), a half-insane emperor who was personally obsessed with the search for Taoist immortality. The following edict makes clear, however, that the prime motive for the persecutions was financial.]

We have heard that previous to the Three Dynasties (A.D. 221-265) the name of Buddha was unknown. It was from the time of the Han and the Wei[1] [dynasties] that his images and his doctrines became familiar institutions in the land. The strength of man was lavished over his shrines; the wealth of man diverted to their costly adornment with gold and jewels. Unsurpassed was the injury to public morals: unsurpassed the injury to the welfare of the people!

A man who does not work, suffers bitter consequences in cold and hunger. But these priests and priestesses of Buddha, they

From Herbert A. Giles, trans., *Gems of Chinese Literature—Prose*, London: Bernard Quaritch Ltd., 1923, pp. 153-54.

1. The Wei dynasty ruled most of north China from the fall of the Han (A.D. 220) until A.D. 264.

consume food and raiment without contributing to the production of either. Their handsome temples reach up to the clouds and vie with the palaces of kings. The vice, the corruption, of those dynasties which followed upon the Three Kingdoms, can be attributed to no other source.

The founders of the House of T'ang put down disorder by *might*; and then proceeded to govern by *right*. With these two engines of power, they succeeded in establishing their rule;—shall, then, some paltry creed from the West be allowed to dispute with Us the sovereign power?

At the beginning of the present dynasty, efforts were made to get rid of this pest; but its extermination was not complete, and the faith became rampant once more. Now We, having extensively studied the wisdom of the ancients, and guided moreover by public opinion, have no hesitation in saying that this evil can be rooted out. Do you, loyal officers of the State, only aid me in carrying out my great project by enforcing the laws,—and the thing is done. Already, more than 4,600 monasteries have been destroyed; and their inmates, to the number of 265,000 persons of both sexes, have been compelled to return to the world. Of temples and shrines, more than 40,000 have likewise been demolished; while many thousand acres of fat soil have been added to the wealth of the people. The work which my predecessors left undone, I have been able to accomplish. Let us then seize this favourable hour, and from the four quarters of the earth lead back the black-haired people once again into the Imperial fold!

And should there be any to whom Our action in this matter may not be clear, do you officers of government enlighten them on the subject.

Introduction to Neo-Confucianism

Confucianism as an all-inclusive philosophy of life, touching upon every aspect of human existence, was eclipsed by both Buddhism and Taoism in the centuries following the fall of the Han dynasty (A.D. 220). With the reunification of China under the Sui (589-907) and T'ang (618-907), it returned partially to favor; but its importance was chiefly in the realm of government. As the only available body of political theory and concrete ethical prescriptions, it became officially established as the subject matter of the civil service examinations; and its ancient rituals were revived to give the imperial house an aura of legitimacy. Nonetheless, under the Sui and T'ang the best creative talent of China was channeled toward Buddhism, which now developed its own, uniquely Chinese modes of thought. Confucianism in that period was largely antiquarian in outlook, stereotyped in its interpretations, and studied mainly as a means to official advancement through the examination system.

Under the Sung dynasty (960-1279), however, Confucianism acquired a new lease on life. A series of major philosophers, culminating in the great synthesizer, Chu Hsi (1130-1200), redefined and transformed the ancient Confucian principles to create the system of thought usually known in the West as Neo-Confucianism. Especially in the areas of metaphysics, cosmology, and psychology, the Neo-Confucians owed a great debt to Buddhism and Taoism. But they were bitterly opposed to what they considered their rivals' anti-social and individualistic attitude. Both Buddhism and Taoism tended to regard earthly activities as insignificant compared to the private realization of supreme Truth. The Neo-Confucians, by contrast, reaffirmed the traditional Confucian insistence upon ethics and upon the ultimate meaningfulness of human existence.

From the twelfth to the twentieth century, Confucianism as interpreted by the followers of Chu Hsi remained the dominant intellectual influence in China. In fact, the Chinese term for philosophy itself (*hsing li*) has Neo-Confucian connotations, meaning "the principles of Nature." "Nature" in Neo-Confucianism is a key term, denoting mental and spiritual as well as physical phenomena. It combines the ethical universalism of Mahayana Buddhism, which recognizes no distinctions of class, race, or family, with the ancient Confucian notion of harmony and the reconciliation of differences. Everything that exists partakes of a single Nature, which means that the same principles apply equally to mankind and to all other animate and inanimate beings. The task of philosophy is "the investigation of things" (a phrase borrowed from the "Great Learning"). Nonetheless, the Neo-Confucians were primarily oriented toward human rather than physical Nature; and they never succeeded in developing a true scientific method.

In the attempt to give their ideas a solid basis in tradition, the Neo-Confucianists inevitably turned to the *Book of Changes* (*I Ching*)—the only one of the Five Classics[1] which lends itself to a metaphysical interpretation. The *Changes* is in fact a hand-book for soothsayers, the oldest part of which probably dates back to the early Chou dynasty.[2] The core of the book consists of sixty-four hexagrams which together represent all the possible combinations of six solid and broken lines. Associated with each hexagram is a cryptic prophecy of very ancient date, traditionally attributed to the Duke of Chou.[3] The underlying idea of the *Changes* is that everything in the universe exists in a state of flux, alternating between activity (*yang*) and passivity (*yin*). Through a prescribed method of sorting a pile of yarrow stalks (or sometimes, the tossing of coins) a hexagram was obtained and the corresponding prophecy applied, which allegedly revealed the direction of future events. In Han times the *Book of Changes* was enlarged through a series of appendices, or "Wings," which provide orthodox Confucian interpretations for the generally obscure ancient prophecies.

The Neo-Confucianists made much of a passage in the Third Appendix to the *Changes* which speaks of something called the "Great Ultimate" (*T'ai Chi*). Mentioned only briefly in the Appendix, where its meaning is unclear, this Great Ultimate came to be accepted as the fundamental principle of Neo-Confucianism. Chou Tun-i (1017-73), the first of the "Great Five" Neo-Confucian philosophers,[4] regarded it as the single source of all the phenomena of the

1. For Introduction to the Five Classics see Vol. V of this series, pp. 42-43.
2. Traditionally beginning in the late twelfth century B.C.
3. One of Confucius' heroes: the brother of the first Chou king and a man famous for his ability and uprightness.
4. The others are Chang Tsai, the two brothers Ch'eng (Ch'eng Hao and Ch'eng I), and Chu Hsi.

universe. Resembling the Buddhist Void or the Tao of the Taoists in its all-encompassing character, the Great Ultimate is the infinite, unlimited, absolute Truth which is immanent in all beings. For Chang Tsai (1021-77), author of the famous "Western Inscription," this concept of the Great Ultimate becomes the basis of ethics. According to Chang, the fact that the universe is One means also that the wise man should love everyone and everything within it.

This ethical orientation of Neo-Confucianism is seen also in the doctrine, first propounded by Ch'eng I (1033-1107) but greatly elaborated by Chu Hsi, that the basic Oneness of the universe may be differentiated into principle (*li*) and material-force (*ch'i*). The word for "principle" is the same which Confucius had employed in the sense of "decorum" or "propriety." For the Neo-Confucianists, *li* signified the eternal laws which direct the movement of the universe. *Ch'i*, on the other hand, denoted the fundamental material from which everything is made. According to Chu Hsi, *ch'i* through a process of integration forms all the things of this world; through disintegration it causes them to decay and die. But while principle and material force are always found together, principle is the higher of the two—the power which regulates the transformation of material force.

The followers of Chu Hsi thus stressed the ultimate rationality of the universe, which they thought could be comprehended through a slow accumulation of knowledge leading to moral perfection. But a rival group, known as the "school of mind" (or "intuition"), thought that an understanding of the universe could only come through meditation on the Reality within onself. The affinity of this idea to Buddhist (especially Ch'an) contemplative practice is obvious. Though some of the doctrines of the "school of mind" are foreshadowed in the writings of Ch'eng Hao (1032-85), one of the original "Great Five," this school found its most effective spokesman in Wang Yang-ming (1472-1529). Wang regarded mind (or intuition) as being the embodiment of principle. On the deepest level, the mind of each human being is thus identical with the mind of Heaven (or of the universe as a whole). Through innate knowledge (i.e., intuition) a person may become conscious of this fundamental identity. The old Confucian notion of "humanity" or "goodness" (*jen*)[5] is now redefined as the realization of each individual's unity with the governing principles of the universe.

In contrast to traditional Confucianism, the "school of mind" did

5. On *jen* in its earlier meaning see Vol. V, p. 8, "On Goodness."

not regard education, study, and "investigation of things" as the prerequisites for wisdom. In obvious analogy to the Ch'an doctrine of instant illumination, Wang Yang-ming contended that Truth could break in suddenly upon a person. Thus even an unlettered (but spiritually talented) peasant might conceivably become a sage in a single moment merely by following his intuition; the chief obstacle to such enlightenment (just as in Buddhism) is selfish desire. But despite its strong affinities to Buddhism and Taoism, the "'school of mind" retained the typically Confucian emphasis upon action. Its representatives felt that the attainment of Truth should result not only in personal tranquility, wisdom, or salvation after death, but also in positive ethical action in this present world.

CHANG TSAI: FROM THE WESTERN INSCRIPTION

[The following short essay acquired its name from the fact that Chang Tsai had it inscribed on the western wall of his study. It later came to be regarded as a fundamental statement of Neo-Confucian doctrine.]

Heaven is my father and earth is my mother, and even such a small creature as I finds an intimate place in their midst.

Therefore that which extends throughout the universe I regard as my body and that which directs the universe I consider as my nature.

All people are my brothers and sisters, and all things are my companions.

The great ruler [the emperor] is the eldest son of my parents [Heaven and earth], and the great ministers are his stewards. Respect the aged—this is the way to treat them as elders should be treated. Show affection toward the orphaned and the weak—this is the way to treat them as the young should be treated. The sage identifies his character with that of Heaven and earth, and the virtuous man is the best [among the children of Heaven and earth]. Even those who are tired and infirm, crippled or sick, those who have no brothers or children, wives or husbands,

From Wm. Theodore deBary, ed., *Sources of Chinese Tradition*, New York: Columbia University Press, 1960, pp. 524-25. Reprinted by permission of Columbia University Press.

are all my brothers who are in distress and have no one to turn to.

When the time comes, to keep himself from harm—this is the care of a son. To rejoice in Heaven and have no anxiety—this is filial piety at its purest.

He who disobeys [the principle of Heaven] violates virtue. He who destroys humanity (*jen*) is a robber. He who promotes evil lacks [moral] capacity. But he who puts his moral nature into practice and brings his physical existence to complete fulfillment can match [Heaven and earth].

He who knows the principles of transformation will skillfully carry forward the undertakings [of Heaven and earth], and he who penetrates spirit to the highest degree will skillfully carry out their will.

Do nothing shameful even in the recesses of your own house and thus bring no dishonor to them. Preserve the mind and nourish the nature and thus [serve them] with untiring effort. . . .

Wealth, honor, blessing, and benefit are meant for the enrichment of my life, while poverty, humble station, care, and sorrow will be my helpmates to fulfillment.

In life I follow and serve [Heaven and earth]. In death I will be at peace.

CHU HSI: FROM HIS WORKS

Principle and Material-Force

In the universe there has never been any material-force (*ch'i*) without principle (*li*) or principle without material-force.

Question: Which exists first, principle or material-force?

Answer: Principle has never been separated from material-force. However, principle is above the realm of corporeality

From Wm. Theodore deBary, ed., *Sources of Chinese Tradition,* New York: Columbia University Press, 1960, pp. 536-44. Reprinted by permission of Columbia University Press.

Numbers in square brackets refer to chapter and paragraph divisions in the original Chinese text.

whereas material-force is within the realm of corporeality. Hence when spoken of as being above or within the realm of corporeality, is there not a difference of priority and posteriority? Principle has no corporeal form, but material-force is coarse and contains impurities. [49: 1a-b]

Fundamentally principle and material-force cannot be spoken of as prior or posterior. But if we must trace their origin, we are obliged to say that principle is prior. However, principle is not a separate entity. It exists right in material-force. Without material-force, principle would have nothing to adhere to. Material-force consists of the five agents of metal, wood, water, fire, and earth, while principle contains humanity, righteousness, propriety, and wisdom. [49: 1b]

Question about the relation between principle and material-force.

Answer: Ch'eng I expressed it very well when he said that principle is one but its manifestations are many. When Heaven, earth, and the myriad things are spoken of together, there is only one principle. As applied to man, however, there is in each individual a particular principle. [49:1b]

Question: What are the evidences that principle is in material-force?

Answer: For example, there is order in the complicated interfusion of the yin and the yang and the five agents. This is [an evidence of] principle [in material-force]. If material-force did not consolidate and integrate, principle would have nothing to attach itself to. [49: 2b]

Question: May we say that before Heaven and earth existed there was first of all principle?

Answer: Before Heaven and earth existed, there was certainly only principle. As there is this principle, therefore there are Heaven and earth. If there were no principle, there would also be no Heaven and earth, no man, no things, and in fact, no containing or sustaining [of things by Heaven and earth] to speak of. As there is principle, there is therefore material-force, which operates everywhere and nourishes and develops all things.

Question: Is it principle that nourishes and develops all things?

Answer: As there is this principle, therefore there is this material-force operating, nourishing, and developing. Principle itself has neither corporeal form nor body. [49:3a-b]

K'o-chi asked: When the creative process disposes of things, is it the end once a thing is gone, or is there a principle by which a thing that is gone may return?[1]

Answer: It is the end once a thing is gone. How can there be material-force that has disintegrated and yet integrates once more? [49:3b-4a]

Question: "The Lord-on-High has conferred even on the inferior people a moral sense." "When Heaven is about to confer a great responsibility on any man." "Heaven, to protect the common people, made for them rulers.". . .[2] In passages like these, does it mean that there is really a master doing all this up in the blue sky or does it mean that Heaven has no personal consciousness and the passages are merely deductions from principle?

Answer: These passages have the same meaning. It is simply that principle operates this way. [49:4a]

Throughout the universe there are both principle and material-force. Principle refers to the Way [Tao], which is above the realm of corporeality and is the source from which all things are produced. Material-force refers to material objects, which are within the realm of corporeality; it is the instrument by which things are produced. Therefore in the production of man and things, they must be endowed with principle before they have their material force, and they must be endowed with material-force before they have corporeal form. [49:5b]

The Great Ultimate

Question: The Great Ultimate is not a thing existing in a chaotic state before the formation of Heaven and earth, but a general name for the principles of Heaven and earth and the myriad things. Is that correct?

Answer: The Great Ultimate is merely the principle of

1. Apparent reference to the Buddhist doctrine of transmigration of souls.
2. Quotations from the *Book of History*.

Heaven and earth and the myriad things. With respect to Heaven and earth, there is the Great Ultimate in them. With respect to the myriad things, there is the Great Ultimate in each and every one of them. Before Heaven and earth existed, there was assuredly this principle. It is the principle that through movement generates the yang. It is also this principle that through tranquillity generates the yin. [49:8b-9a]

Question: [In one of your works], you said: "Principle is a single, concrete entity, and the myriad things partake of it as their reality. Hence each of the myriad things possesses in it a Great Ultimate." According to this theory, does the Great Ultimate not split up into parts?

Answer: Fundamentally there is only one Great Ultimate, yet each of the myriad things has been endowed with it and each in itself possesses the Great Ultimate in its entirety. This is similar to the fact that there is only one moon in the sky but when its light is scattered upon rivers and lakes, it can be seen everywhere. It cannot be said that the moon has been split. [49:10b-11a]

Someone asked about the Great Ultimate.

Answer: The Great Ultimate is simply the principle of the highest good. Each and every person has in him the Great Ultimate and each and every thing has in it the Great Ultimate. What Master Chou [Tun-i] called the Great Ultimate is an appellation for all virtues and the highest good in Heaven and earth, man and things. [49:11b]

The Great Ultimate is similar to the top of a house or the zenith of the sky, beyond which point there is no more. It is the ultimate of principle. Yang is active and yin is tranquil. In these it is not the Great Ultimate that acts or remains tranquil. It is simply that there are the principles of activity and tranquillity. Principle is not visible; it becomes visible through yin and yang. Principle attaches itself to yin and yang as a man sits astride a horse. As soon as yin and yang produce the five agents,[3] they are confined and fixed by physical nature and are thus differentiated into individual things each with its nature. But the Great Ultimate is in all of them. [49:13a]

3. Wood, metal, fire, water, and earth—supposedly the five basic elements.

Heaven and Earth

In the beginning of the universe there was only material-force [*ch'i*] consisting of yin and yang. This force moved and circulated, turning this way and that. As this movement gained speed, a mass of sediment was pushed together and, since there was no outlet for this, it consolidated to form the earth in the center of the universe. The clear part of material-force formed the sky, the sun and moon, and the stars and zodiacal spaces. It is only on the outside that the encircling movement perpetually goes on. The earth exists motionless in the center of the system, not at the bottom. [49: 19a]

In the beginning of the universe, when it was still in a state of undifferentiated chaos, I imagine there were only water and fire. The sediment from water formed the earth. If today we climb the high mountains and look around, we will see ranges of mountains in the shape of waves. This is because the water formed them like this, though we do not know at what period they solidified. This solidification was at first very soft, but in time it became hard.

Question: I imagine it is like the tide rushing upon and making waves in the sand. [Is that right?]

Answer: Yes. The most turbid water formed the earth and the purest fire became wind, thunder, lightning, stars, and the like. [49: 19b-20a]

Further Question: Can the universe be destroyed?

Answer: It is indestructible. But in time man will lose all moral principles and everything will be thrown together in a chaos. Man and things will all die out, and then there will be a new beginning.

Further Question: How was the first man created?

Answer: Through the transformation of material-force. When the essence of yin and yang and the five agents are united, man's corporeal form is established. This is what the Buddhists call production by transformation. [49: 20a]

WANG YANG-MING: FROM INQUIRY ON THE GREAT LEARNING

Question: The *Great Learning* was considered by a former scholar [Chu Hsi] to be the learning of the great man. I venture to ask why the learning of the great man should consist in "manifesting the clear character"?[1]

Master Wang said: The great man regards Heaven and earth and the myriad things as one body. He regards the world as one family and the country as one person. As to those who make a cleavage between objects and distinguish between the self and others, they are small men. That the great man can regard Heaven, earth, and the myriad things as one body is not because he deliberately wants to do so, but because it is natural with the humane nature of his mind that he should form a unity with Heaven, earth, and the myriad things. This is true not only of the great man. Even the mind of the small man is no different. Only he himself makes it small. Therefore when he sees a child about to fall into a well, he cannot help a feeling of alarm and commiseration. This shows that his humanity (*jen*) forms one body with the child. It may be objected that the child belongs to the same species [as he]. Yet when he observes the pitiful cries and frightened appearance of birds and animals [about to be slaughtered], he cannot help feeling an "inability to bear" their suffering. This shows that his humanity forms one body with birds and animals. It may be objected that birds and animals are sentient beings [as he is]. But when he sees plants broken and destroyed, he cannot help a feeling of pity. This shows that his humanity forms one body with plants. It may be said that plants are living things [as he is]. Yet even when he sees tiles and stones shattered and crushed he cannot help a feeling of regret. This shows that his humanity forms one body with tiles and stones. This means that even the mind of the small

From Wm. Theodore deBary, ed., *Sources of Chinese Tradition,* New York: Columbia University Press, 1960, pp. 571-74. Reprinted by permission of Columbia University Press.

1. Quotation from the "Great Learning."

man necessarily has the humanity that forms one body with all. Such a mind is rooted in his Heaven-endowed nature, and is naturally intelligent, clear, and not obscured. For this reason it is called the "clear character."

Although the mind of the small man is divided and narrow, yet his humanity that forms a unity can remain free from darkness like this. This is due to the fact that his mind has not yet been aroused by desires and blinded by selfishness. When it is aroused by desires and blinded by selfishness, compelled by the greed for gain and fear of harm, and stirred by anger, he will destroy things, kill members of his own species, and will do everything to the extreme, even to the slaughtering of his own brothers, and the humanity that forms a unity will disappear completely. Hence if it is not blinded by selfish desires, even the mind of the small man has the humanity that forms a unity with all as does the mind of the great man. As soon as it is obscured by selfish desires, even the mind of the great man will be divided and narrow, like that of the small man. Thus the learning of the great man consists entirely in getting rid of the blindness of selfish desires in order by one's own efforts to make manifest his clear character, so that the original condition of the unity of Heaven, earth, and the myriad things may be restored, that is all. Nothing can be added to this original nature from outside.

Question: Why, then, does the learning of the great man consist also in loving the people?

Answer: To manifest the clear character is to bring about the substance of the unity of Heaven, earth, and the myriad things, whereas loving the people is to put into universal operation the function of that unity. Hence manifesting the clear character must lie in loving the people, and loving the people is the way to manifest the clear character. Therefore, only when I love my father, the fathers of others, and the fathers of all men, can my humanity really form one body with my father, the fathers of others, and the fathers of all men. When it truly forms one body with them, then the clear character of filial piety will be manifested. Only when I love my brother, the brothers of others, and the brothers of all men can my humanity really form one body with my brother, the brothers of others, and the brothers of all men. When it truly forms one body with them, then the clear character of brotherly respect will be manifested. Everything from ruler, minister, husband, wife, and friends to mountains, rivers, heavenly and earthly spirits, birds, animals, and plants, all should be truly loved in order to realize my humanity that forms a unity, and then my clear character will be completely manifested, and I will really form one body with Heaven, earth, and the myriad things. This is what is meant by "manifesting the clear character throughout the empire." This is what is meant by "regulating the family," "ordering the state," and "pacifying the world." This is what is meant by "fully developing one's nature."

Question: Then why does the learning of the great man consist in "abiding in the highest good"?

Answer: The highest good is the ultimate principle of manifesting character and loving people. The nature endowed in us by Heaven is pure and perfect. The fact that it is intelligent, clear, and not obscured is evidence of the emanation and revelation of the highest good. It is the original nature of the clear character which is called innate knowledge [of the good]. As the highest good emanates and reveals itself, one will consider right as right and wrong as wrong. Things of greater or less importance and situations of grave or light character will be responded to as they act upon us. In all our changes and activities, we will entertain no preconceived attitude; in all this we will do nothing that is not natural. This is the normal nature of man and the principle of things. . . . Later generations fail to realize that the highest good is inherent in their own minds, but each in accordance with his own ideas gropes for it outside the mind, believing that every event and every object has its own definite principle. For this reason the law of right and wrong is obscured; the mind becomes concerned with fragmentary and isolated details, the desires of man become rampant and the principle of Heaven is at an end. And thus the education for manifesting character and loving people is everywhere thrown into confusion.

In the past there have been people who wanted to manifest their clear character, of course. But simply because they did not know how to abide in the highest good, but instead drove their own minds toward something too lofty, they thereby lost them in illusions, emptiness, and quietude, having nothing to do with the work of the family, the country, and the world. Such are the followers of Buddhism and Taoism. There have been those who wanted to love their people, of course. But simply because they did not know how to abide in the highest good, but instead sank their own minds in base and trifling things, they thereby lost them in scheming strategy and tricks, having neither the sincerity of humanity nor that of commiseration. Such are the followers of the Five Overlords [as opposed to true kings] and the pursuers of profit and gain. All of these are due to a failure to know how to abide in the highest good. Therefore abiding in the highest good is to manifesting character and loving people as the carpenter's square and compass are to the square and the circle, or rule and measure to length, or balances and scales to weight. If the square and the circle do not abide by the compass and the carpenter's square, their standard will be wrong; if length does not abide by the rule and measure, its adjustment will be lost; if the weight does not abide by the balances, its exactness will be gone; and if manifesting clear character and loving people do not abide by the highest good, their foundation will disappear. Therefore, abiding in the highest good so as to love people and manifest the clear character is what is meant by the learning of the great man.

Chinese Popular Religion: Introduction

The three principal thought-forms of ancient China—Confucianism, Taoism, and Buddhism—were all based upon sophisticated and complex philosophies incomprehensible to ordinary people. Confucianism, with its stress upon scholarship, history, and the Classics, was by definition a doctrine for the educated. Philosophic Taoism was the mysticism of an educated gentry weary of the world which sought a return to naturalness and the ultimate sources of life.

Buddhism possessed a highly complex theology; its many schools disputed about the subtlest of doctrinal distinctions. Even those sects which taught sudden illumination or salvation through faith encouraged reading or hearing of the sutras; and the founders of such sects had themselves devoted long years to studying Buddhist doctrine.

At all periods of Chinese history, however, simpler forms of faith prevailed among the peasant masses. Varying somewhat from district to district, these faiths included a confusing selection of notions derived from Buddhism, Taoism, and Confucianism together with the worship of local nature-deities. In the popular mind, the abstract Supreme Being (Ti) of Confucianism became a world-governor who was said to reside near the remote K'un-lun range; popular mythology described him as neither omniscient nor omnipotent. The political orientation of Confucianism is reflected in the curious notion that the spirits of dead persons become officials and bureaucrats in the afterworld, holding positions similar to those they occupied in life. Taoism degenerated into a system of magic, exorcism, divination, and spirit-worship; while Taoist "sages" studied alchemy with the object of discovering an elixir of life. The Buddhist doctrine of transmigration of souls became confused with the Taoist notion that the spirits of the dead inhabit a variety of animate and inanimate objects. While Confucians believed that the ten souls in each human body (the three *hun* and seven *p'o*) are dissipated after the person's death, Taoists thought that they become spirits or demons who roam the earth or reside in the underworld; Buddhists believed in a single soul within each living being which will be reincarnated through a succession of earthly lives. The Buddhas and Bodhisattvas became transformed in the popular imagination into the patrons of various earthly activities. Local nature divinities were worshipped under Buddhist names; Buddhist shrines were often located in spots which formerly had been the centers of nature-cults. Relics of Buddhist saints were enshrined in temples and worshipped; and it was popularly believed that the invocation or recitation of one of the holy texts—particularly the *Lotus Sutra* or the *Diamond Sutra*—would ensure one's admission to paradise.

FROM THE T'ANG COLLECTION OF REPRINTS

[The following tales, which appear in an anthology of Chinese prose literature known as the *T'ang Collection of Reprints*, exemplify a wide variety of popular religious beliefs. Though the anthology itself is of uncertain date, the stories it contains are for the most part attributable to known literary figures of the T'ang period—men whose chief activity was serious scholarship. Such persons wrote in the popular vein only for their own amusement, to draw attention to their "serious" writings, or to satisfy the popular demand for entertainment. But while some of the tales in the *T'ang Collection* may be deliberate inventions, in style and content they are typical of the myths popular with the common people. In fact, most of them appear to be genuine folk-legends put into scholarly language.]

A Rural Official Becomes a God

Chiang Tzu-wen, a native of Kuang-ling, was a wild and dissolute young man, addicted to wine and women. He used to say that his bones were so light that he would die young and be transformed into a god.

During the disturbances at the end of the Han dynasty, Chiang, then a junior military officer stationed at Mo-ling, successfully drove back the insurgents as far as the foot of Mount Chung, but was wounded in the forehead during the engagement. In consequence of this he resigned his post and shortly afterwards he died.

Some years later, a junior officer who had served under him during the wars, met his old leader with a white feather in his hand, riding on a white horse, and followed by his retinue just as in life. The terrified officer fled, but Chiang quickly overtook him.

"I am now the god of this district, appointed to look after the well-being of the people," he declared. "Proclaim this among them and let a temple be erected to me. Otherwise heavy punishment will follow."

That summer the district was swept by an epidemic so severe that people were afraid of one another. Many therefore believed and sacrificed to Chiang in secret.

In a second message sent through a magician, the god threat-

From E. D. Edwards, *Chinese Prose Literature of the T'ang Period,* London: Arthur Probsthain, 1938, II, 52-53, 230-31, 232-33 & 241, 254-56, 279, 317-19, 385-86 & 389-90. Reprinted by permission of Arthur Probsthain.

Titles of the selections have been supplied by the editors.

ened to send a plague of insects unless his new dignity was officially recognized. Before long the threat was fulfilled. Small insects resembling deer-gadflies crept into men's ears and killed them, doctors being powerless to save them. The hearts of the people melted within them, but the magistrate, still incredulous, refused to take action.

Once more the warning came.

"If a temple is not built for me I will send fire upon you."

During that year fires broke out everywhere, sometimes in ten different places in a day. Finally, when his own palace caught fire, the magistrate became alarmed. His advisers expressed the view that a spirit was at work. They believed, however, that it was not malignant, and thought that something ought to be done to appease it. Envoys, armed with the necessary decree, were sent to appoint Chiang Marquis of Ch'ung-tu, and present him with the seals of his office. His younger brother was also appointed to a post. A temple was built in Chiang's honour and the name of Mount Chung was changed to Mount Chiang. After that the fires ceased.

The Magical Arrow

On the 9th day of the 9th moon of the year A.D. 754 the emperor was hunting in the Imperial Park [in Shensi province] when he saw a solitary crane flapping leisurely along among the clouds. He shot and wounded it, and the bird began to fall towards the earth with the arrow still in it. However, as the emperor and his attendants waited, expecting the thud of its fall, it suddenly made a great effort and soared away towards the south-west. The hunters stood looking after it until it disappeared.

Near I-chou in Szechwan the Bright Moon monastery stands in deep solitude among pine and cassia trees on a hillside by the river. . . . The rooms on the east side, which are even more secluded than the rest of the place, were the favourite lodging of Hsü Tso-ch'ing, an old man who called himself the Taoist of Ch'ing ch'eng.[1] He would stay a week or ten days, and then say he was going back to Ch'ing-ch'eng. He was held in high esteem by other Taoists.

1. A famous mountain in Szechwan province.

One day he arrived unexpectedly and seemed put out.

"I was in the mountains," he said, "and was struck by an arrow. It did not hurt me, but as it is not an ordinary arrow I shall hang it here on the wall. Its owner will come the year after next and it must be returned to him, so take care that it is not lost."

He wrote on the wall: "This arrow was hung on the 9th day of the 9th month, of the 13th year."

When the emperor fled into Szechwan he passed that way, and entranced by the beauty of the temple, turned aside to visit it. Entering the hall, he saw the arrow and had it brought for his inspection. He was astonished to find it was an imperial arrow, and asked the Taoists how it came into their possession. They repeated the story Hsü had told them two years earlier. It was the arrow the emperor had shot in the imperial hunting-park in Shensi, and the solitary crane his arrow had struck was Hsü, who had hung it up in the temple in Szechwan on the very day on which he was shot with it.

Wondering greatly, the emperor took the arrow and kept it carefully. The old Taoist was never seen again in Szechwan.

Magic Discredited

Hsiao Ying-shih of Lan-ling was travelling to the south by river. One day he observed two of his boatmen staring at him.

"This man is very like So-and-So," one said to the other, mentioning Hsiao's great-grandfather.

A little later they told Hsiao that they were acquainted with an ancestor of his. He said nothing till they reached the end of their journey, and as soon as he began to question them the two men ran away.

"If they aren't immortals they must be spirits," he thought to himself, and decided not to pursue the matter any further.

A year later, on his way north again, he happened to reach the *yamen*[2] in a certain city just when a party of graverobbers were brought in. Bound hand and foot, they were made to kneel in the presence of the magistrate. Presently Hsiao, running his eye over them, was astounded to see the two boatmen who had puzzled him so much the year before.

2. A government office.

"If they are not immortals they are spirits," he said to himself again, and told the magistrate his story. The two prisoners were then interrogated apart, and ordered to explain their uncanny recognition of Hsiao.

"Nothing could be simpler," they declared. "From time to time we have robbed the imperial graves in P'o-yang, where rich stores of gold and jade are buried. In one grave we found an official, his complexion as fresh as if he were still alive, and his hair streaked with grey, lying on a stone couch. Master Hsiao here is so like him that when we saw him on the boat we were surprised into giving ourselves away by remarking on the likeness. As for there being anything uncanny about our recognizing him, that's all nonsense."

. . . .

From a Taoist monastery noted for its ascetic rule one priest disappeared annually on a certain night and was believed to become immortal. On that night all doors were left open and each priest shunned the company of his fellows.

After many years a sceptical person sent two braves on the auspicious night to keep watch. In due course a black tiger entered the monastery and soon reappeared carrying a priest. The watchers promptly shot at it but missed, and dropping its burden, it made off.

When morning came and the priests found their numbers still complete, they blamed the sceptic, who, however, organized a hunt in the course of which several tigers were killed, and piles of human bones discovered, the remains of the unfortunate Taoists who had "become immortal."

A Spirit Foretells the Future

Early in the ninth century a high official named Tse Lu, having been impeached, was allowed to commit suicide at K'ang-chou.

In A.D. 825 Li Hsiang, sailing home after a term of service as governor of Meng-chou, went ashore one day to consult a witch.

"I can foretell the future and call up spirits," said the wise woman, "but there are two classes of spirits, the meritorious, able to converse directly with mortals from time to time, and the inferior, with weaker vitality, who speak through me, and I can never guarantee which kind will appear."

"But how do we find a spirit to question?" Li asked.

"Under a tree outside this house is a person wearing purple with a fish at his girdle, who calls himself Tse Lu. Come and pay your respects and consult him."

Accompanied by the witch, Li went into the courtyard and bowed towards the tree.

"His Excellency, Tse Lu, has returned your bow," announced the witch. Then a voice spoke from the air.

"I died in this hall, strangled by a bow-string, and I still hate the things," it said. "I beg therefore that you will be kind enough to lay aside your bow."

Li did so, and there being nothing visible except a fan fluttering beside a flight of steps, he forgot that he was in the presence of the spirit of a person of importance and moved to sit down.

"Where are your manners?" cried the witch. "His Excellency is a high official! Why don't you wait to be invited to sit in his presence? Now you have angered him by your lack of ceremony and he has gone."

After repeated bowings and abject apologies from Li the spirit was at length persuaded to return, and the séance proceeded, Li standing with folded hands.

"His Excellency has mounted the steps," the witch announced, and then: "His Excellency is seated."

Li sat down and waited.

"What is it you want to know?" inquired the voice.

"I am an official returning to Court from a distant post," Li replied, "and I am very anxious to know if my career will be successful. I know Your Excellency is supernaturally perspicacious, and entreat you to give me a hint as to my future."

"In a month from the time you reach the city," the voice replied, "you will become magistrate of Wu-chou." To this it would add nothing further.

Li's anxiety about his own affairs relieved, he became curious concerning the spirit.

"You have been dead a long time, Your Excellency," he remarked. "Why don't you return to the world of mortals instead of continuing among the shades?"

"What an idea!" the other exclaimed. "Man's life is toil, anxiety, and vexation. Mortals struggle and hurry after fame and fortune like moths round a lamp till melancholy overtakes them; their hair turns white, their minds fail, and their bodies become feeble; within the limits of a square inch they cover ten thousand yards; they envy, they steal, they are fiercer than beasts. Hence the Buddhists speak of the world as a fiery furnace, while the Taoists regard the body as a misfortune. Having already escaped from the scorching fire on which I look down, why should I wish to lie in it again? . . . The ruler of a kingdom of ten thousand chariots is not my equal, how much less, therefore, are ordinary persons?"

After refusing either to explain the mystic processes by which he had attained his condition, or to add anything to his statement about Li, the spirit took his departure.

The fact that Li died during his term of office in Wu-chou sufficiently explained why the spirit was unwilling to divulge more.

Transmigration of a Soul

Mr. Ch'ien and Mr. P'ei were neighbours and good friends. Mr. Ch'ien was taken ill and died, but before long was restored to life and told his experiences to his wife.

"First," he said, "I heard a voice calling me by name. "Your destiny has run its course," it announced, "but since you have lived an innocent life you are to be reborn as a male child."

I then went to the house of a shop-keeper in the market looking for a body to put my soul into. The house was quite unpretentious to look at, but it was very comfortable and well-furnished inside, and the shop-keeper's wife was expecting a baby in about a month. But suddenly a messenger came running after me.

"There has been a mistake," he cried. "You are to go to Mr. P'ei's for your body, and be born a son of the house of P'ei. You've come to the wrong house."

So I followed the messenger to Mr. P'ei's house, and saw his wife. But since her child will not be born for some time yet, they told me to come home and wait for forty days."

When the time was up Mr. Ch'ien died again and on the very same day Mr. P'ei's wife gave birth to a child who closely resembled their deceased friend. What Mr. Ch'ien had said about the shop-keeper's wife was verified by subsequent events.

Return from the Underworld

About A.D. 753 a judge named Wang Lun died while on circuit a long way from home. In the judgment-hall of the nether regions he met a number of officials like himself, among them his elder brother, who had died a few years earlier.

"You have no business to have died yet," his brother said when they met, "and if you can obtain thirty thousand strings of cash you will be restored to life."

Remembering how far he was from home, Lun looked round hopelessly. But catching sight of a high mountain with a little path leading over it he set off on his quest and in due time reached home. He went in and told his wife that he was dead but would be able to revive if she could provide him with the required number of strings of cash. He waited a little in order to find out whether his message was understood. Presently the dog barked, and he heard his wife weeping and saying that she had dreamed that her husband was dead and in want of money. Sending quickly for a witch, they set to work to cut out the necessary quantity of paper cash and burnt it. Lun received it and could not tell it from the money he had used when he was alive.

Now in the region of darkness there is neither day nor night, but always a dimness like the gloom of winter during a period of snow. The king of the spirits wears a purple robe and metes out punishment and happiness, with several scores of judges assisting. Heartlessness is adjudged the worst of all crimes. The majority of those being judged were priests, nuns, and gentry.

Lun had committed only one sin—he had always eaten meat.

"Although this man has been a meat-eater, he has never killed wilfully," an officer now announced.

Before his illness Lun had spent time and effort on copying the whole of a sutra,[3] and had rolled and wrapped it and placed

3. Any one of a number of Buddhist scriptures.

it with his own hands in a Buddhist temple. It was because of this one good deed he was to be able to visit the king of the underworld in the land of shades, and afterwards return to life. He was shown the sutra, and it was the actual copy he had written.

Now the king and the judges, though they had all been friends in life, did not discuss the past, nor, when their relatives and acquaintances came and bowed before them, did they ask them how they fared, but treated them as strangers. Nor, when brothers met, was there any sign of brotherly feeling, except indeed, in the case of Lun, whose brother looked on him with kindly eyes; but that was only because he was so recently dead.

Presently an attendant approached Lun.

"You will enjoy emolument and long life," he told him, "but do not let to-day's affair leak out." As he spoke he disappeared, and Lun found himself once more alive.

The Efficacy of the Diamond Sutra

Early in the ninth century an official named Wang, a devout reader of the *Diamond Sutra*, was travelling to a new post when his boat sprang a leak and he and four others were thrown into the river. It seemed to him that someone pushed a bamboo pole into his hands, so that, rising and falling with the waves, he was able to keep himself afloat, and eventually he came to shore a hundred miles downstream.

As he stood dripping on the bank he glanced down at the pole in his hands. It was his scroll of the *Diamond Sutra*.

. . . .

There once lived a priest in Chiang-ling who thrice a day recited the *Diamond Sutra* seven times. He was taken ill and died, and was conducted to Hades, where he was led into the presence of a person of kingly mien seated on a dais.

"What merit have you accumulated during your life?" inquired this person.

"I have recited the *Diamond Sutra* regularly," replied the priest, bowing.

He was immediately invited to ascend the dais and sit down.

Then he was told to read the *Sutra* through seven times. All present listened in perfect silence and when the reading was over a satellite was deputed to escort him back to earth. The king came down the steps and took leave of him, telling him that he had been granted a further thirty years of life.

"But do not fail to continue to read the *Sutra*," he added. They parted and the priest followed his guide a few paces till they came to a great pit, into which he fell as through space.

A week intervened between his death and his return to life. Throughout that time a slight warmth was noticeable in his face. He lived till he was over eighty, and another priest of the same place who knew him personally told this tale.

. . . .

In the year A.D. 765, a Chinese dealer went to trade in horses on the border of Tibet. For a time all went well, but eventually he fell into the hands of the Tibetans. For many months he existed entirely on scraps of food and dregs of wine. But one day he refused food altogether and sat in his corner weeping.

"Why are you crying?" asked the captain of his guards.

"I have an old mother," he replied, "and I've seen her in a dream."

Now the captain was a good-hearted man, and that night he called the prisoner into his tent.

"Our Tibetan laws are very strict," he said, "and there is no possible chance of your being liberated and sent home. But I have two horses of yours which are very fast. If you take them and follow a road I will point out you can escape. But whatever you do, don't let anyone know I helped you to get away."

As soon as ever he got his horses, the dealer escaped and rode day and night towards the border. After some days he developed boils on his leg and was unable to go further, so he rested for a while hidden in a gully. As he sat there, a piece of cloth was blown by the wind across his path. Thankfully he bound up his leg and started off once more.

It was not long before he realized that the pain in the injured leg had disappeared, and he was able to push on at a smart pace. He reached home without encountering any further difficulty, to find his mother still alive.

"Ever since I lost you," cried the old lady joyfully, "I have been reciting the *Diamond Sutra*, hardly stopping for a bite of food or a wink of sleep! And now here you are!"

Gratefully she lifted down her sutra and opened it to recite a prayer of thanks for her son's safe return. Several leaves, she found to her astonishment, were missing. She hunted high and low for them, till at last, to distract her attention, her son began to tell her about his boils and about the piece of cloth that had so fortunately been blown in his way. Full of concern, his mother insisted on looking at the leg. It was quite healed, and the so timely bandage, to their amazement, was the lost portion of the old lady's *Diamond Sutra*.

Society

T'ang and Sung Poetry: Introduction

Poets and poetry-writing occupy a central place in traditional Chinese culture to a degree scarcely imaginable in Western countries. At least until recently the truly well-educated Chinese, by definition, was not only proficient in the Confucian Classics; he could also write respectable verse. The speech and writing of the literati was liberally adorned with quotations from famous poems; and poetry often served as a medium of communication between friends, acquaintances, or lovers. So widespread was the art of versification that literally thousands of poets' names, and hundreds of thousands of verses, have been preserved from the T'ang and Sung periods alone. Of the three major T'ang poets, over 1000 poems are extant by Li Po, 2200 by Tu Fu, and 2800 by Po Chü-i. From Su Tung-p'o, the best-known poet of the Sung dynasty, we have 2400 different titles.

Since ability at versification as well as prose style were among the subjects tested on the civil service examinations, the majority of outstanding Chinese poets spent at least part of their lives in government service. The chief exception to this rule is Li Po (701-762)—probably the greatest lyricist of them all—whose carefree character and love of drink apparently precluded the serious study required for success on the examinations. But his more conscientious friend, Tu Fu (712-770), became a minor official who considered his failure to achieve official eminence a major personal tragedy. Po Chü-i (772-846)[1] rose to become the governor of a province; and Su Tung-p'o (1037-1101),[2] though his career was marked by sharp changes of

1. See his "Letter to Ch'en Ching," above, pp. 34-36.
2. See his "Letter to the Emperor Shen Tsung," above, pp. 49-51.

fortune, occupied several responsible posts. Indeed, two of the most eminent Sung poets—Ou-yang Hsiu[3] and Wang An-shih[4]—are nowadays probably better remembered for their politics than for their poetry.

The use of poetry as a vehicle for social commentary is of ancient date in China; and the practice continued under the T'ang and Sung dynasties. While those purely personal expressions of feeling which the Chinese term "flower, bird, wind, moon" never went out of fashion, many famous poets were also acutely aware of the problems of the larger society. A frequent poetic theme is the effect of political events or social custom upon the life of the individual. The traditional verse-form called *shih*,[5] having lines of five or seven syllables each, was most frequently employed for serious poetic expression; but a freer form known as the *tz'u*, with lines of irregular length which were sometimes set to popular tunes, came into common use by the ninth century. The typical Chinese poem continued to exhibit a highly literary vocabulary with numerous classical allusions, though Po Chü-i, for one, became enormously popular with his simple, almost vernacular style.

On the whole, however, the T'ang poets diverge sharply from those of the Sung in their typical attitudes toward society and the individual. All the great T'ang poets were deeply imbued both with philosophic Taoism and with Buddhism, which was then at the height of its influence in China. They thus tended to regard sorrow as the dominant quality of human existence. In their view, individual human beings are insignificant in the universal scheme of things, governed by forces beyond their control which inevitably lead to suffering. By contrast, the Sung poets were both more cheerful and more mundane. Many of them, notably Ou-yang Hsiu and Wang An-shih, were deeply involved in schemes for the betterment of society. Presumably this change in the character of poetry springs from that same changed attitude which led to the Confucian revival, with its emphasis upon social duty and the real possibility of improving earthly existence. In Sung poetry the day-to-day concerns of ordinary people constitute a frequent theme; and even those poems which are mainly sorrowful in tone manage to conclude on a note of hope.

3. See excerpts from his "New History of the T'ang Dynasty" and "Biographies of Eunuchs," above, pp. 14-17 and 47-49.

4. See "Discussion of the Agricultural Loans Measure" and "The Ten-Thousand-Word Memorial," above, pp. 23-29 and 36-45.

5. As in the Classic *Shih Ching* (*Book of Songs*).

POEMS OF LI PO

I Am a Peach Tree

[These two stanzas are taken from a poem written by Li Po on behalf of his wife, expressing her sentiment toward himself. (Tr.)]

I am a peach tree blossoming in a deep pit.
Who is there I may turn to and smile?
You are the moon up in the far sky;
Passing, you looked down on me an hour; then went on forever.

A sword with the keenest edge,
Could not cut the stream of water in twain
So that it would cease to flow.
My thought is like the stream; it flows and follows you on forever.

Chuang Chou and the Butterfly

[Chuang Chou (or Chuang Tzu), who lived in the late fourth century B.C., was the principal thinker of classical Taoism after Lao Tzu. His writings include a chapter describing how in a dream he became a butterfly.]

Chuang Chou in dream became a butterfly,
And the butterfly became Chuang Chou at waking.
Which was the real—the butterfly or the man?
Who can tell the end of the endless changes of things?
The water that flows into the depth of the distant sea
Returns anon to the shallows of a transparent stream.
The man, raising melons outside the green gate of the city,
Was once the Prince of the East Hill.[1]

From Shigeyoshi Obata, trans., *The Works of Li Po,* New York: Paragon Book Reprint Corp., 1965, nos. 69, 71, 97, 105, 118. Reprinted by permission of Paragon Book Reprint Corp.

1. I.e., the Marquis of Tung-ling, who was an important official under the Ch'in dynasty (221-206 B.C.). After the fall of that dynasty he was discovered growing melons on a patch of wasteland outside Ch'ang-an.

So must rank and riches vanish.
You know it, still you toil and toil,—what for?

The Nefarious War

[This poem was probably written not long after the two great Chinese military defeats of the year 751—one at the hands of the Nan-chao barbarians in Yünnan; the other by Arabs and Turks on the Talas River in northern Turkestan.]

Last year we fought by the head-stream of the Sang-kan,[2]
This year we are fighting on the Tsung-ho road.[3]
We have washed our armor in the waves of the Chiao-chi lake,[4]
We have pastured our horses on T'ien-shan's[5] snowy slopes.
The long, long war goes on ten thousand miles from home,
Our three armies are worn and grown old.

The barbarian does man-slaughter for[6] plowing;
On his yellow sand-plains nothing has been seen but
    blanched skulls and bones.
Where the Ch'in emperor built the walls against the Tartars,
There the defenders of Han[7] are burning beacon fires.
The beacon fires burn and never go out,
There is no end to war!—

In the battlefield men grapple each other and die;
The horses of the vanquished utter lamentable cries to heaven,
While ravens and kites peck at human entrails,
Carry them up in their flight, and hang them on the branches
    of dead trees.
So, men are scattered and smeared over the desert grass,
And the generals have accomplished nothing.

2. A river running through Shansi and Hopei provinces north of the Great Wall.
3. Running along the Kashgar-darya River in Turkestan.
4. In Parthia (southeast of the Caspian Sea).
5. High mountain range of northern Sinkiang.
6. I.e., instead of.
7. I.e., China. The Chinese were known as "men of Han."

Oh, nefarious war! I see why arms
Were so seldom used by the benign sovereigns.

A Letter from Chang-kan[8]

[A river-merchant's wife writes]

I would play, plucking flowers by the gate;
My hair scarcely covered my forehead, then.
You would come, riding on your bamboo horse,
And loiter about the bench with green plums for toys.
So we both dwelt in Chang-kan town,
We were two children, suspecting nothing.

At fourteen I became your wife,
And so bashful that I could never bare my face,
But hung my head, and turned to the dark wall;
You would call me a thousand times,
But I could not look back even once.

At fifteen I was able to compose my eyebrows,
And beg you to love me till we were dust and ashes.
You always kept the faith of Wei-sheng,[9]
Who waited under the bridge, unafraid of death,
I never knew I was to climb the Hill of Wang-fu[10]
And watch for you these many days.

I was sixteen when you went on a long journey,
Traveling beyond the Keu-Tang Gorge,
Where the giant rocks heap up the swift river,
And the rapids are not passable in May.
Did you hear the monkeys wailing
Up on the skyey height of the crags?

8. A suburb of Nanking.
9. Wei Sheng, who lived in the sixth century B.C., had promised to meet a girl under a bridge. When she did not appear and the water of the river began rising, he refused to leave the place and was drowned.
10. Wang-fu means "husband-watching." More than one hill has taken that name because of a similar tradition of a forlorn wife who climbed the height to watch for the return of her husband. (Tr.)

Do you know your foot-marks by our gate are old,
And each and every one is filled up with green moss?

The mosses are too deep for me to sweep away;
And already in the autumn wind the leaves are falling.
The yellow butterflies of October
Flutter in pairs over the grass of the west garden.
My heart aches at seeing them. . . .
I sit sorrowing alone, and alas!
The vermilion of my face is fading.

Some day when you return down the river,
If you will write me a letter beforehand,
I will come to meet you—the way is not long—
I will come as far as the Long Wind Beach[11] instantly.

To the Honorable Justice Hsin

Once we dwelt in the city of Ch'ang-an
In wild ecstasy of flowers and willow-green.
We drank our wine from the same bowls
With five princes and seven dukes.
Our hearts rose and grew blither,
Unflinching in the presence of a warrior lord;
Nor did we fall behind any one, when,
Delighting in wind and stream, we sought beauty.

You had red cheeks, then; and I was young, too.
We sped our horses to Chang-tai's pleasure mart,[12]
And lightly carried our crops of gold;
Offered our essays in the court examination;
And sat feasting at a tortoise table;
And there was endless singing and dancing; . . .
We thought it would last forever, you and I—
How were we to know that the grass would tremble
And the wind and dust come, roaring down?

11. Actually the Long Wind Beach is several hundred miles upriver from Nanking.
12. The prostitutes' quarter.

Down through the Han-ku Pass[13]
The Tartar horsemen came.
I am an exile now, traveling heavy-hearted,
Far away to the land of Yeh-lang.[14]
The peach and plum trees by the palace
Are opening their petals toward the light—
Ah, when will the Gold Cock[15] bring me pardon,
And I may return to you from banishment?

13. The pass through the mountains which controls the approaches to Ch'ang-an.
14. Yünnan.
15. Symbol which was hoisted when an amnesty was proclaimed.

POEMS OF TU FU

To the Official Wei, My Senior

[This poem was composed in A.D. 748, not long after Tu Fu had failed the national civil service examination for the second time. In fact the prime minister, Li Lin-fu, had arranged that no one should pass. Li was not well educated, and feared the competition of men more brilliant than himself.]

Youths clad in white silk breeches do not die of hunger;
A great detriment to my person is the scholar's cap.
Older friend, consider, listen quietly;
Lesser one, by your leave, will raise up and lay before you in sequence all details.
I, Fu, formerly, in youth's day,
Was soon satiated with seeing countries, visiting, paying respects.
I studied writings, thumbed and tattered ten thousand scrolls;
As if possessed by divine spirit, I brought down on the white silk my hair pencil.

From Florence Ayscough, *Tu Fu, The Autobiography of a Chinese Poet*, London: Jonathan Cape, 1929, pp. 92-94, 100-101, 176, 334-36.

In order to give the poems a more Chinese flavor, the translator has omitted some of the connectives usual in English and retained some of the original word order.

My prose pieces, I thought, competed with those of the writer Yang Hsiung;
My poems according to law I considered approached the work of Tzu Chien.
Li Yung, the high official, begged an introduction face to face;
Wang Han, the great scholar, was willing to live as my neighbour.
To myself I said, musing, this is an excess of swift advancement, of coming out from among my fellows;
I shall immediately rise to an important highway and reach the watercourse of recognition.
I shall transport my Lord, the Emperor, to the height of the ideal Rulers, Yao and Shun;
I will cause the wind of instruction to reform and again make pure and genuine the customs of the land.
Such my desire; contrary to this expectation I am lonely, poverty-stricken;
My running verses, songs, should not be for scholars out of office sitting by the waters of obscurity.
I ride my mule; thrice ten years have revolved;
I am eating the food of travellers at Flowery Capital[1] in Spring.
As the sun rises, I tap timidly at a rich fellow's door;
When the sun sets I follow, stumbling in the dust of sleek horses.
Dregs of wine cups and cold food;
Arriving at each place, I conceal my grief, my bitterness.

War Chariots

Lin! lin! chariots jangle; *hsiao! hsiao!* horses snort;
Men move forward; at his hip each wears arrows and a bow.
Fathers, mothers, wives, children, all come out to say farewell;
Dust in clouds: they cannot see the near-by Huo Yang Bridge.
They drag at the men's coats, fall beneath their feet, obstruct the road, weeping;
Sound of weeping rises straight; divides the soft white clouds.
On the road, passers-by question the marching men;
Marching men reply: 'Dots against our names; we are hurried away.'[2]

1. Ch'ang-an, where he had hoped to become an important official.
2. I.e., they were conscripted.

Followers who are ten years and five,[3] go North to guard the river;
When they reach four tens, go West to dig encampment fields.
On leaving, Village Senior wraps a cloth about their heads;
On returning, their hair is white: they have continuously kept watch at frontiers.
At frontier territories blood flows like waters of the sea;
To open those frontiers is the unceasing desire of the Military Emperor.[4]

Bewailing Autumn Rain

Who can reckon how many cotton-clad people in Ch'ang-an
Are locked behind their humble doors, patching the mud walls of their huts lest they melt?
The old man does not go out through the long grass and weeds,
But the little boys, without a care, paddle about in wind and rain.
Sound of rain *sou! sou!* mingles with northerly wind hastening early cold;
Wings of the wild goose are wet; high flight is difficult.
Since autumn came not once have we seen the white sun;
The mud is filthy! on what day will Empress Earth be dry?

The Newly Married Cut Apart

[According to old Chinese custom, the bride does not become a full member of her husband's family until the third day after the wedding, when she is formally presented to his parents.]

The trailing rabbit-silk[5] clings to wild chrysanthemums and hemp,
Therefore its outspread shoots do not reach high.
A maiden given in marriage to a fighting man,
Were better cast away beside the road.

3. Aged 15.
4. Emperor Hsüan Tsung, whose troops penetrated far into the northwest borderlands.
5. A parasitic plant with threadlike, clinging stem which lacks roots and leaves.

I knotted hair[6] and became my Lord's wife,
But sleeping-mat on my Lord's bed is not yet warmed.
Yesterday at yellow dusk you married wife; to-day at dawn say
must depart;
Is this not too hurried, too precipitate?
Albeit my Lord does not go far,
He hastens at Ho Yang to guard the lines.
Unworthy One's position is not yet clearly defined:
How can I lift two hands[7] in reverence before husband's mother,
husband's father?
At the time my father, mother, nourished me,
Day and night they treasured me in peaceful seclusion.
Every girl must have a place to return home to;
She should even follow a cock or a dog.[8]
My Lord now goes to death place;
Deep pain is driven to very centre of my bowels.
I long to go out, I swear it, to follow my Lord;
Shape and being are transformed; distraught, I tremble.
Do not because of your newly-married bride think anxious
thoughts;
Put forth the last effort of your strength: your business weapons,
warfare.
Were wife's person to be in midst of army corps,
Soldier's spirit would perhaps not rise in ardour.
Myself I sigh; woman of a stricken household!
I have always worn short coat and lower garments of openwork
silk gauze.
The silk gauze coat I will not use again;
Before my Lord I wash off red rouge and black eye-paint.
Throwing back my head, I look towards Heaven and see a hundred birds flying;
Large, small, destined to wheel in pairs.
In confusion, running contrariwise are all affairs of men;
I yearn to be united for ever with my Lord.

6. I.e., laid aside the headdress of a virgin.

7. At the ceremony of presentation.

8. Reference to a popular ditty which contains the lines: "Marry a cock, follow a cock/Marry a dog, follow a dog . . . /Be faithful to it and follow it on."

POEMS OF PO CHÜ-I

The Prisoner

[*Written in* A.D. *809*]

Tartars led in chains,
Tartars led in chains!
Their ears pierced, their faces bruised—they are driven into the land of Ch'in.
The Son of Heaven took pity on them and would not have them slain.
He sent them away to the south-east, to the lands of Wu and Yüeh.
A petty officer in a yellow coat took down their names and surnames.
They were led from the city of Ch'ang-an under escort of an armed guard.
Their bodies were covered with the wounds of arrows, their bones stood out from their cheeks.
They had grown so weak they could only march a single stage a day.
In the morning they must satisfy hunger and thirst with neither plate nor cup:
At night they must lie in their dirt and rags on beds that stank with filth.
Suddenly they came to the Yangtze River and remembered the waters of Chiao.[1]
With lowered hands and levelled voices they sobbed a muffled song.

1. In Turkestan. (Tr.)

Then one Tartar lifted up his voice and spoke to the other Tartars,
"*Your* sorrows are none at all compared with *my* sorrows."
Those that were with him in the same band asked to hear his tale:
As he tried to speak the words were choked by anger.
He told them "I was born and bred in the town of Liang-yüan.[2]
In the frontier wars of Ta-li[3] I fell into the Tartars' hands.
Since the days the Tartars took me alive forty years have passed:
They put me into a coat of skins tied with a belt of rope.
Only on the first of the first month might I wear my Chinese dress.
As I put on my coat and arranged my cap, how fast the tears flowed!
I made in my heart a secret vow I would find a way home:
I hid my plan from my Tartar wife and the children she had borne me in the land.
I thought to myself, "It is well for me that my limbs are still strong,"
And yet, being old, in my heart I feared I should never live to return.
The Tartar chieftains shoot so well that the birds are afraid to fly:
From the risk of their arrows I escaped alive and fled swiftly home.
Hiding all day and walking all night, I crossed the Great Desert:[4]
Where clouds are dark and the moon black and the sands eddy in the wind.
Frightened, I sheltered at the Green Grave,[5] where the frozen grasses are few:
Stealthily I crossed the Yellow River, at night, on the thin ice,
Suddenly I heard Han[6] drums and the sound of soldiers coming:

2. North of Ch'ang-an. (Tr.)
3. The period Ta-li, A.D. 766-780. (Tr.)
4. The Gobi Desert. (Tr.)
5. The grave of Chao-chün, a Chinese girl who in 33 B.C. was bestowed upon the Khan of the Hsiung-nu . . . Hers was the only grave in this desolate district on which grass would grow. (Tr.)
6. I.e., Chinese. (Tr.)

I went to meet them at the road-side, bowing to them as they
came.
But the moving horsemen did not hear that I spoke the Han
tongue:
Their Captain took me for a Tartar born and had me bound in
chains.
They are sending me away to the south-east, to a low and
swampy land:
No one now will take pity on me: resistance is all in vain.
Thinking of this, my voice chokes and I ask of Heaven above,
Was I spared from death only to spend the rest of my years in
sorrow?
My native village of Liang-yüan I shall not see again:
My wife and children in the Tartars' land I have fruitlessly
deserted.
When I fell among Tartars and was taken prisoner, I pined for
the land of Han:
Now that I am back in the land of Han, they have turned me
into a Tartar.
Had I but known what my fate would be, I would not have
started home!
For the two lands, so wide apart, are alike in the sorrow they
bring.
Tartar prisoners in chains!
Of all the sorrows of all the prisoners mine is the hardest to bear!
Never in the world has so great a wrong befallen the lot of
man,—
A Han heart and a Han tongue set in the body of a Turk."

Hermit and Politician

"I was going to the City to sell the herbs I had plucked;
On the way I rested by some trees at the Blue Gate.
Along the road there came a horseman riding,
Whose face was pale with a strange look of dread.
Friends and relations, waiting to say good-bye,
Pressed at his side, but he did not dare to pause.
I, in wonder, asked the people about me
Who he was and what had happened to him.
They told me this was a Privy Councillor

Whose grave duties were like the pivot of State.
His food allowance was ten thousand cash;
Three times a day the Emperor came to his house.
Yesterday his counsel was sought by the Throne;
To-day he is banished to the country of Yai-chou.[7]
So always, the Counsellors of Kings;
Favour and ruin changed between dawn and dusk!"

Green, green—the grass of the Eastern Suburb;
And amid the grass, a road that leads to the hills.
Resting in peace among the white clouds,
Can the hermit doubt that he chose the better part?

Remembering (His Daughter) Golden Bells

Ruined and ill—a man of two score;
Pretty and guileless—a girl of three.[8]
Not a boy—but still better than nothing:
To soothe one's feeling—from time to time a kiss!
There came a day—they suddenly took her from me;
Her soul's shadow wandered I know not where.
And when I remember how just at the time she died
She lisped strange sounds, beginning to learn to talk,
Then I know that the ties of flesh and blood
Only bind us to a load of grief and sorrow.
At last, by thinking of the time before she was born,
By thought and reason I drove the pain away.
Since my heart forgot her, many days have passed
And three times winter has changed to spring.
This morning, for a little, the old grief came back,
Because, in the road, I met her foster-nurse.

After Collecting the Autumn Taxes

From these high walls I look at the town below
Where the natives of Pa[9] cluster like a swarm of flies.

7. Remote island off Kwangtung in extreme southern China.
8. Probably about two years old by Western count. According to Chinese reckoning, a child is a year old at birth and becomes a year older each New Year's Day.
9. Semi-barbarous region in southwest China.

How can I govern these people and lead them aright?
I cannot even understand what they say.
But at least I am glad, now that the taxes are in,
To learn that in my province there is no discontent.
I fear its prosperity is not due to me
And was only caused by the year's abundant crops.
The papers I have to deal with are simple and few;
My arbour by the lake is leisurely and still.
In the autumn rain the berries fall from the eaves;
At the evening bell the birds return to the wood.
A broken sunlight quavers over the southern porch
Where I lie on my couch abandoned to idleness.

POEMS OF SU TUNG-P'O

Treading the Green[1]

East wind stirs fine dust on the roads:
First chance for strollers to enjoy the new spring.
Slack season—just right for roadside drinking,
Grain still too short to be crushed by carriage wheels.
City people sick of walls around them
Clatter out at dawn and leave the whole town empty.
Songs and drums jar the hills, grass and trees shake;
Picnic baskets strew the fields where crows pick them over.
Who draws a crowd there? A priest,[2] he says,
Blocking the way, selling charms and scowling:
"Good for silkworms—give you cocoons like water jugs!
Good for livestock—make your sheep big as deer!"

The first six poems are from Burton Watson, trans., *Su Tung-p'o. Selections from a Sung Dynasty Poet*, New York: Columbia University Press, 1965, nos. 3, 11, 16, 19, 20, 45. Reprinted by permission of Columbia University Press. "On the Birth of His Son" is from *Translations from the Chinese* by Arthur Waley. Copyright 1919, 1941 by Alfred A. Knopf, Inc., and renewed 1947 by Arthur Waley. Reprinted by permission of the publisher. In England the poem was published by Constable Publishers in *170 Chinese Poems* and is reprinted by permission.

1. "Treading the Green" refers to a festival held in early spring which was celebrated with picnics and outings.
2. *Tao-jen*, a term used for both Buddhist and Taoist priests (monks).

Passers-by aren't sure they believe his words—
Buy charms anyway to consecrate the spring.
The priest grabs their money, heads for a wine shop;
Dead drunk, he mutters: "My charms really work!"

New Year's Eve

New Year's Eve—you'd think I could go home early
But official business keeps me.[3]
I hold the brush and face them with tears:
Pitiful convicts in chains,
Little men who tried to fill their bellies,
Fell into the law's net, don't understand disgrace.
And I? In love with a meager stipend
I hold on to my job and miss the chance to retire.
Don't ask who is foolish or wise;
All of us alike scheme for a meal.
The ancients would have freed them a while at New Year's—
Would I dare do likewise? I am silent with shame.

Lament of the Farm Wife of Wu[4]

Rice this year ripens so late!
We watch, but when will frost winds come?
They come—with rain in bucketfuls;
The harrow sprouts mold, the sickle rusts.
My tears are all cried out, but rain never ends;
It hurts to see yellow stalks flattened in the mud.
We camped in a grass shelter a month by the fields;
Then it cleared and we reaped the grain, followed the wagon home,
Sweaty, shoulders sore, carting it to town—
The price it fetched, you'd think we came with chaff.
We sold the ox to pay taxes, broke up the roof for kindling;
We'll get by for a time, but what of next year's hunger?
Officials demand cash now—they won't take grain;

3. By custom, cases involving the death penalty had to be settled before the New Year. It was such cases that kept the poet at his office. (Tr.)

4. Wu is the old name for the region around the mouth of the Yangtze. (Tr.)

The long northwest border tempts invaders.
Wise men fill the court—why do things get worse?
I'd be better off bride to the River Lord!

Mountain Village

[The following verses are veiled attacks on Wang An-shih's administration, as the poet admitted later when he was called up for investigation. (Tr.)]

Old man of seventy, sickle at his waist:
Thank God for spring hills—their sprouts and ferns are sweet.
Is it Shao music's[5] made me forget how things should taste?
For three months now no salt for my food![6]

With goosefoot staff, boiled rice for the road, he hurries off;
Copper coins in no time will be lost to other hands.
What's left to show? My son speaks fancy language—
Over half the year we spend in town![7]

On First Arriving at Huang-chou

[In 1079 Su Tung-p'o was arrested and brought to trial for injudicious remarks he had made in a letter to the emperor. As punishment he was sent to a minor post at Huang-chou near Hankow, under orders that he was not to leave the district. Despite such setbacks, however, he seems never to have lost his good humor—or his habit of criticism.]

Funny—I never could keep my mouth shut;
It gets worse the older I grow.
The long river loops the town—fish must be tasty;
Good bamboo lines the hills—smell the fragrant shoots!

5. According to *Analects* VII, 13, Confucius was so moved by the music of Shao that for three months he forgot the taste of meat.

6. Reference to Wang An-shih's tightening of restrictions on the government salt monopoly, which made it difficult for the common people to obtain salt.

7. In order to receive and repay the agricultural loans sponsored by Wang An-shih, peasants were obliged to make frequent trips into town, where the government offices were situated.

An exile, why mind being a supernumerary?
Other poets have worked for the Water Bureau.
Too bad I was no help to the government
But still they pay me in old wine sacks.[8]

On the Birth of His Son

Families, when a child is born
Want it to be intelligent.
I, through intelligence,
Having wrecked my whole life,
Only hope the baby will prove
Ignorant and stupid.
Then he will crown a tranquil life
By becoming a Cabinet Minister.

8. Wine was a government monopoly under the Sung dynasty. Lesser officials were sometimes paid off in old sacks that had been used for squeezing wine, and which could be sold or bartered.

Social Commentary in Prose: Introduction

Confucianism in China has always been preoccupied with questions of propriety and decorum. Yet the purely descriptive sort of prose literature—dealing with the actual behavior of people, as opposed to how they ought to behave—has rarely been in favor among the intellectual elite. Century after century, Confucian scholars penned formal essays on the subject of proper social conduct; but these dealt usually with general principles and abstract considerations rather than concrete situations. Often as not, the moral examples they cite are drawn from legends concerning the ancient kings rather than from contemporary life.

Measured against the antiquity of other Chinese literary forms, the realistic novel and the drama are late developments in the history of China. The oldest extant Chinese novel (*The Romance of the Three Kingdoms*) dates only from the fourteenth century. Moreover, compared to the rigid structure of traditional essays, Chinese novels and plays lack form; and they are written in everyday language instead of in formal classical style. Though highly popular as entertainment, they were regarded as inferior or even frivolous forms of art, unworthy of the serious scholar's talents.

Nonetheless, to the Western mind this supposedly inferior literature generally speaks far more vividly and expressively than the traditional classical essay. Much of it, in fact, was produced by Confucian literati who wrote for their own amusement (and who themselves insisted on the insignificance of such creations). But aside from the question of literary merit, the popular genres provide a mine of information concerning Chinese notions of propriety and politeness, family relationships, and social distinctions. Far more than the didactic formal essays, the religious tales, humorous epigrams, and anecdotes as well as the more realistic novels and plays give important insights into the character of the Chinese people.

FROM THE MISCELLANEA OF I-SHAN

[I-shan, or Li Shang-yin (813-858), was a doctor of literature, a member of the Han-lin Academy (to which only the most eminent men of letters were admitted), and a distinguished poet and scholar. A number of works by him are extant in both poetry and prose, usually dealing with serious themes and having as their object the reform of contemporary social evils.

The *Miscellanea,* by contrast, is an informal composition, apparently considered so insignificant that it is not included in any of the major collections of I-shan's works. Consisting of over four hundred epigrams arranged under forty-one subject headings, it is terse and ironical in tone; its comparisons are particularly vivid and striking. As a reflection of the manners and morals of its period it is especially worthy of note, and indeed expresses many attitudes which were common in China well into the twentieth century.]

Incongruities

1. A poor Persian.
2. A sick physician.

From E. D. Edwards, trans., "The Miscellanea of I-shan," *Bulletin of the School of Oriental and African Studies,* V (1928-30). Reprinted by permission of Alan Barbary, executor for E. D. Edwards.

3. A (Buddhist) disciple addicted to drink.
4. Keepers of granaries coming to blows.[1]
5. A great fat bride.
6. An illiterate teacher.
7. A pork butcher reciting scriptures.[2]
8. A village elder riding in an open chair.[3]
9. A grandfather visiting courtesans.

Not To Be Despised

1. Coarse food when hungry.
2. A poor steed when travelling afoot.
3. Any seat after a long tramp.
4. Cold broth to drink when thirsty.
5. A small boat when travelling in haste.
6. A small house in a storm.

Resemblances

1. A metropolitan official, like a winter melon, grows in the dark.
2. A raven, like a hard-up scholar, croaks when hungry and cold.
3. A seal, like an infant, always hangs about one.
4. A magistrate, like a tiger, is vicious when disturbed.
5. Nuns, like rats, go into deep holes.
6. Swallows, like nuns, must go in pairs.
7. A slave, like a cat, finding any warm corner, stays.

Tantalizing

1. Happening upon a delicious odour when one's liver is out of order.
2. Making a night of it and the drinks giving out.
3. For one's back to itch when calling upon a superior.
4. For the lights to fail just when the luck begins to favour one at cards.
5. Inability to get rid of a worthless poor relation.

1. Too well-fed to fight. (Tr.)
2. Probably Buddhist sutras, since Buddhists were forbidden to eat meat.
3. Peculiar to military officials. (Tr.)

Exaggerations

1. To say that a courtesan feels affection.
2. To say that the pursuit of (Taoist) immortality brings wealth.
3. To say that an official's service-record is taken into consideration.
4. To say that the king understands.
5. To say what income one derives from one's land.[4]
6. To say that one's concubine is too young.
7. A needy magistrate prating about official probity.
8. To say of oneself that one studies hard.
9. To boast of the cost of one's plate.

Disheartening

1. Cutting with a blunt knife.
2. Catching the wind in a torn sail.
3. Trees shutting out the view.
4. A wall which hides the mountains.
5. No wine in flower time.
6. A feast spread away from the breeze in hot weather.

Waste

1. Being ill in flower time.
2. Being harassed in fine weather.
3. A eunuch with a handsome wife.
4. A festival day in a poor home.
5. A well-to-do family at loggerheads.
6. A poverty-stricken family with beautiful flowers.
7. Seeing a beautiful view and not making a poem.
8. A fine house and no entertaining.

Not Permissible

1. Priests joking with courtesans.
2. Servants imitating scholars.
3. Juniors behaving arrogantly to their betters.
4. Servants and concubines cutting into the conversation.
5. Soldiers and rustics trying to talk like scholars.

4. Where taxes were assessed on income.

Bad Form

1. To wrangle with one's fellow guests.
2. To fall from one's polo pony.
3. To eat or smoke in the presence of superiors.
4. Priests and nuns lately returned to ordinary life.
5. To vociferate orders at a banquet.
6. To cut into the conversation.
7. To go to another's bed in boots.
8. To preface remarks with a giggle.
9. To kick over tables when a guest.
10. To sing love-songs in the presence of one's wife's father or mother.
11. To reject distasteful food and put it back on the dish.
12. To lay chopsticks across a soup-bowl.

Mortifications

1. Failure of an honoured guest to accept one's invitation.
2. The arrival of a disliked person uninvited.
3. To be unable to rid oneself of a drunken man.
4. To be penniless when things are cheap.
5. To go for a stroll and run across a creditor.
6. To be seated next an enemy.
7. On a hot day to meet a person who does not drink.
8. A lovely concubine and a jealous wife.

II

India

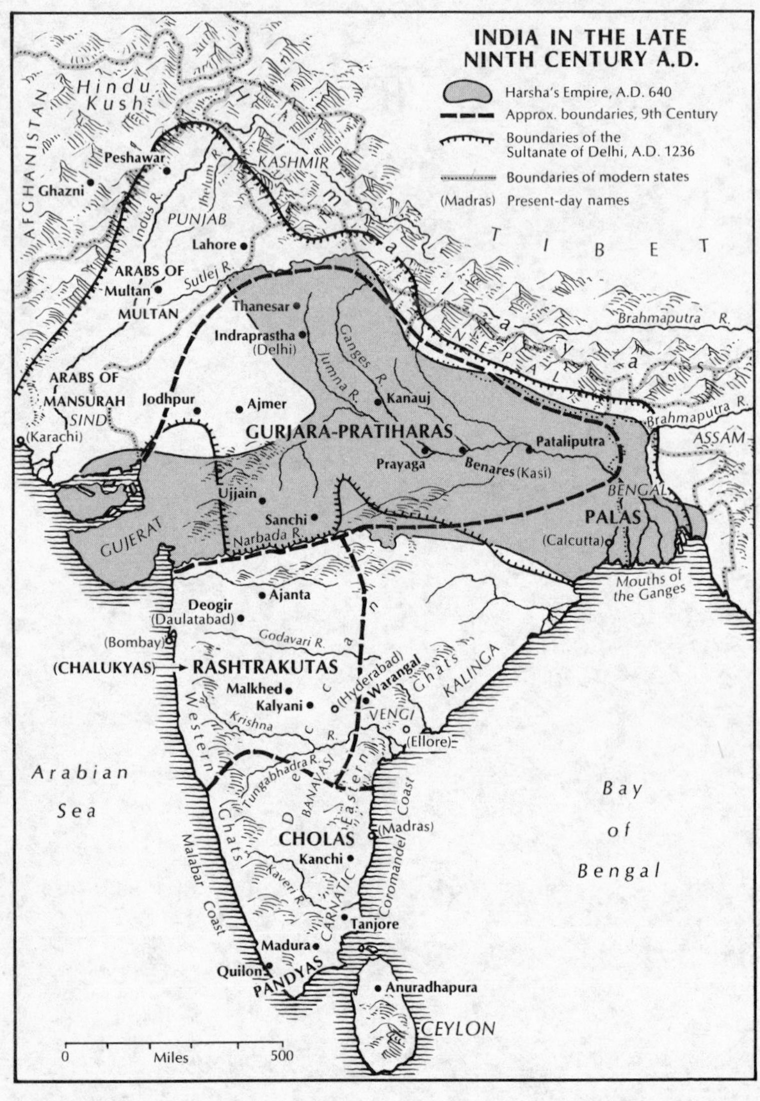

INDIA IN THE LATE NINTH CENTURY A.D.
Harsha's Empire, A.D. 640
Approx. boundaries, 9th Century
Boundaries of the Sultanate of Delhi, A.D. 1236
Boundaries of modern states
(Madras) Present-day names
AFGHANISTAN
Hindu Kush
Himalayas
KASHMIR
TIBET
NEPAL
Peshawar
Ghazni
Indus R.
Jhelum R.
PUNJAB
Lahore
Sutlej R.
ARABS OF Multan MULTAN
Thanesar
Indraprastha (Delhi)
Ganges R.
Jumna R.
Brahmaputra R.
ARABS OF MANSURAH
SIND
(Karachi)
Jodhpur
Ajmer
Kanauj
GURJARA-PRATIHARAS
Pataliputra
Prayaga
Benares (Kasi)
ASSAM
BENGAL
PALAS
(Calcutta)
Mouths of the Ganges
Ujjain
Sanchi
Narbada R.
GUJERAT
Ajanta
Deogir (Daulatabad)
(Bombay)
Godavari R.
Deccan
(CHALUKYAS)
RASHTRAKUTAS
Malkhed
Kalyani
(Hyderabad)
Warangal
Eastern Ghats
KALINGA
VENGI
Krishna R.
(Ellore)
Western Ghats
Arabian Sea
Tungabhadra R.
BANAVASI
Bay of Bengal
CHOLAS
(Madras)
Kanchi
Kaveri R.
CARNATIC
Coromandel Coast
Malabar Coast
Tanjore
Madura
Quilon
PANDYAS
Anuradhapura
CEYLON
0 Miles 500

Government

The Sources of Indian History: Introduction

With a few notable exceptions, the records of Indian history prior to the Muslim period are woefully inadequate and incomplete. In both Hindu and Buddhist India, historical knowledge was considered to be of small importance. To be sure, chronicles of current affairs were kept at various Indian courts; but these were not long preserved. Heat and moisture ensured the quick disappearance of any documents not engraved in stone or metal; and the preservation of written works depended upon constant re-copying.

An important source for Indian history are the inscriptions in stone or copper plate which abound in many parts of India. These record such matters as the genealogies of local kings, the granting of lands and description of their boundaries, an occasional military expedition, and those public works for which the ruler expected religious merit, that is, the building of temples or largesse to Brahmins. Sanskrit historical poems (*carita*) also provide some information, though with the exception of the Kashmiri chronicles they use history merely as a framework; their principal aim is to flatter their subjects and to demonstrate the poet's skill. Thus whereas we possess Indian religious texts of enormous antiquity (the Vedas and Upanishads; the Buddhist sutras), and secular literature from the time of the Gupta empire (A.D. 320-480), comprehensive or interpretive historical writing is almost totally absent. What is known of Indian history prior to the twelfth century A.D. must be laboriously reconstructed from stray references in religious and literary works, scattered inscriptions, coins, or the reports of foreign travelers—e.g. Muslim merchants and Buddhist pilgrims.

Beginning with the Muslim conquests, however, Indian historiography becomes far more detailed and complete than it had ever been in the days of Hindu supremacy. Unlike the Hindus, the Muslims were greatly interested in history. Their religion itself is historical, having a definite founder and holy scriptures of known date; and their tradition of history-writing dates back to the time of Muhammad.

The Muslim historians have as their chief object the propagation of the faith through example. Thus they take little note of ordinary people's affairs, but confine themselves largely to recounting the deeds of outstanding rulers, statesmen, and saints. Inevitably, they give a religious interpretation to events and tend to glorify whatever king had sponsored their work. But while writing of purely Indian affairs, the Muslim historians of India had a trans-national orientation. Their language was Persian, which was then the literary medium of the eastern Islamic world; and they participated in a culture which extended, with local variations, from Central Asia and the Middle East to Syria and Anatolia, North Africa and Spain.

Indian Government in the Middle Period: Introduction

From the time of the Hun invasions of the northwest (late fifth century A.D.) and the earliest of the major Muslim conquests (beginning 1175), India was divided into many kingdoms whose territories and ruling dynasties changed frequently according to the fortunes of war. With the brief exception of Harsha of Kanauj, whose empire extended from the Himalayas to the Narbada River, no single monarch in those centuries controlled more than a small fraction of the entire Indian sub-continent. Armed strife among the various kingdoms was almost uninterrupted. Warfare was the normal activity of a ruler, who was expected as a matter of course to attack his neighbors and attempt to increase his territories. Hindu religious texts treat war as a part of the warrior's *dharma* (i.e., duty), and therefore good in itself. Various rules of fair play were prescribed; and battle was begun only after suitable religious ceremonies had been conducted.

Military conquest, however, was not ordinarily accompanied by major changes in society as a whole. A change in the ruling dynasty of a kingdom did not usually disturb the basic forms of economic and social life, but merely substituted one set of military overlords and revenue-collectors for another. The hereditary chiefs of districts, called *rajas,* remained in control of local affairs, technically as vassals of the king; the village councils of elders continued to function no matter what dynasty prevailed. Even the rulers of larger states, when defeated in battle, could often retain their thrones by promising allegiance to the conqueror. Indian custom frowned upon the direct annexation of kingdoms; "lawful conquest," according to the ancient texts, meant merely the reduction of the conquered party to vassal status. The more important vassals sometimes even served as the conqueror's ministers of state. Often they retained their own armies and administrations, which made them a constant threat to the stability of the kingdom as a whole.

No Indian ruler of this period proved able to create a permanent official bureaucracy whose functions were divorced from landholding. Taxation in India was the province not of salaried officials, but of semi-independent vassal kings or rajas owing tribute and services to the overlord. Even royal appointees did not receive salaries, but rather the right to collect revenue from a specified portion of the crown lands. The result was to give local magnates an independent base of power and to encourage rebellion against the central government. Not until the time of Akbar, the great Mughal emperor (r. 1556-1605), was any consistent, large-scale effort made to establish a salaried bureaucracy responsible solely to the central government.

Introduction to Suleiman's Observations

Arab merchants were active in the trade with India at least from the time of the Roman empire; but undoubtedly their activities in that country became more extensive following the Arab conquest of Sind (the westernmost region of India) in the early eighth century. A number of such merchants have left us valuable travelogues which record their impressions of Hindu India, as seen through foreign and Muslim eyes.

The merchant Suleiman—author of the following passages—made several voyages to India and China in the middle of the ninth century. The kingdom of the "Balhara," described here, was then the leading power of the western Deccan, dominated by the Rashtrakuta family. In the Indian context, the kingdom of the Rashtrakutas was merely one of many medium-sized states which rose and fell in the course of Indian history. Nonetheless, its wealth and power were such as to make a profound impression upon foreigners accustomed to a simpler mode of life. Suleiman's account (dated A.D. 851) also makes clear that the Rashtrakuta sovereign exercised only a loose authority over his vassals and engaged in continual conflict with neighboring states.

FROM SULEIMAN: OBSERVATIONS ON THE COUNTRIES OF INDIA AND CHINA

The inhabitants of India and China agree that there are four great or principal kings in the world. They place the king of the Arabs (Caliph of Baghdad) at the head of these, for it is admitted without dispute that he is the greatest of kings. First in wealth, and in the splendour of his Court; but above all, as chief of that sublime religion which nothing excels. The king of China reckons himself next after the king of the Arabs. After him comes the king of the Greeks [Byzantium] and lastly the Balhara,[1] prince of the men who have their ears pierced.

The Balhara is the most eminent of the princes of India, and the Indians acknowledge his superiority. Every prince in India is master in his own state, but all pay homage to the supremacy of the Balhara. The representatives sent by the Balhara to other princes are received with most profound respect in order to show him honour. He gives regular pay to his troops, as the practice is among the Arabs. He has many horses and elephants, and immense wealth. The coins which pass in his country are the Tatariya dirhams,[2] each of which weighs a dirham and a half of the coinage of the king. They are dated from the year in which

From H. M. Elliot and John Dowson, eds., *The History of India as Told by Its Own Historians,* London: Trübner & Co., 1867, I, 3-7.

1. A corruption of "Vallabha Rai," the title borne by all members of the Rashtrakuta dynasty. Evidently it means something like "king of kings."

2. These may have been the coins (drachmas?) of the Tatirid dynasty which then ruled in Khurasan and Sistan (southwest Afghanistan).

the dynasty acquired the throne. They do not, like the Arabs, use the Hegira[3] of the prophet, but date their eras from the beginning of their kings' reigns; and their kings live long, frequently reigning for fifty years.[4] The inhabitants of the Balhara's country say that if their kings reign and live for a long time, it is solely in consequence of the favour shown to the Arabs. In fact, among all the kings there is no one to be found who is so partial to the Arabs as the Balhara; and his subjects follow his example.

Balhara is the title borne by all the kings of this dynasty. It is similar to the Khosrou (of the Persians), and is not a proper name. The kingdom of the Balhara commences on the sea side, at the country of Komkam [Konkan],[5] on the tongue of land which stretches to China. The Balhara has around him several kings with whom he is at war, but whom he greatly excels. Among them is the king of Jurz [Gujerat]. This king maintains numerous forces, and no other Indian prince has so fine a cavalry. He is unfriendly to the Arabs, still he acknowledges that the king of the Arabs is the greatest of kings. Among the princes of India there is no greater foe of the Muhammadan faith than he. His territories form a tongue of land. He has great riches, and his camels and horses are numerous. Exchanges are carried on in his states with silver (and gold) in dust, and there are said to be mines (of these metals) in the country. There is no country in India more safe from robbers.

By the side of this kingdom lies that of Tafak,[6] which is but a small state. The women are white, and the most beautiful in India. The king lives at peace with his neighbours, because his soldiers are so few. He esteems the Arabs as highly as the Balhara does.

3. The date of Muhammad's flight from Mecca to Medina (A.D. 622), the first year of the Muslim calendar.

4. The Rashtrakuta king Amoghavarsha in fact reigned for sixty-two years (815-877), though if the assumed date of Suleiman's book (A.D. 851) is correct, a large part of that king's reign still lay in the future.

5. Region south of modern Bombay. Suleiman's ignorance of the lands he had not himself visited evidently led him to suppose the region contiguous with China.

6. The location of Tafak is uncertain; evidently it lay to the north of Gujerat.

These three states border on a kingdom called Ruhmi,[7] which is at war with that of Jurz. The king is not held in very high estimation. He is at war with the Balhara as he is with the king of Jurz. His troops are more numerous than those of the Balhara, the king of Jurz, or the king of Tafak. It is said that when he goes out to battle he is followed by about 50,000 elephants. He takes the field only in winter, because elephants cannot endure thirst, and can only go out in the cold season. It is stated that there are from ten to fifteen thousand men in his army who are employed in fulling and washing cloths. There is a stuff made in his country which is not to be found elsewhere; so fine and delicate is this material that a dress made of it may be passed through a signet-ring. It is made of cotton, and we have seen a piece of it. Trade is carried on by means of kauris, which are the current money of the country. They have gold and silver in the country, aloes, and the stuff called *samara* [a kind of hair] of which [fly-whisks] are made. The striped [rhinoceros] is found in this country. It is an animal which has a single horn in the middle of its forehead, and in this horn there is a figure like unto that of a man. . . .

After this kingdom there is another situated in the interior of the country, away from the sea. It is called Kashbin.[8] The people are white, and pierce their ears. They are handsome, and dwell in the wilds and mountains.

Afterwards comes a sea, on the shores of which there is a kingdom called Kiranj.[9] Its king is poor and proud. He collects large quantities of amber, and is equally well provided with elephants' teeth. They eat pepper green in this country because it is scarce. . . .

When the king of Sarandib [Ceylon] dies, his corpse is carried on a low carriage very near the ground, with the head so attached to the back of the vehicle that the [back part of the

7. Ruhmi (or Rahma) was probably a region around the Bay of Bengal. Suleiman probably heard of it from Arab travelers who had visited its ports. His ignorance of the Indian interior led him to suppose that it bordered the Rashtrakuta domains.

8. Location unknown.

9. "Kiranj" may have been Kalinga; evidently it lay on the Coromandel coast.

skull] touches the ground, and the hair drags in the dust. A woman follows with a broom, who sweeps the dust on to the face of the corpse, and cries out, "O men, behold! This man yesterday was your king; he reigned over you and you obeyed his orders. See now to what he is brought; he has bid farewell to the world, and the angel of death has carried off his soul. Do not allow yourselves to be led astray by the pleasures of this life," and such like words. The ceremony lasts for three days, after which the body is burnt with sandal, camphor and saffron, and the ashes scattered to the winds. All the Indians burn their dead. Sarandib is the last of the islands dependent on India. Sometimes when the corpse of a king is burnt, his wives cast themselves upon the pile and burn with it; but it is for them to choose whether they will do so or not.

In India there are persons who, in accordance with their profession, wander in the woods and mountains, and rarely communicate with the rest of mankind. Sometimes they have nothing to eat but herbs and the fruits of the forest. . . . Some of them go about naked. Others stand naked with the face turned to the sun, having nothing on but a panther's skin. In my travels I saw a man in the position I have described; sixteen years afterwards I returned to that country and found him in the same posture. What astonished me was that he was not melted by the heat of the sun.

In all these kingdoms the nobility is considered to form but one family. Power resides in it alone. The princes name their own successors. It is the same with learned men and physicians. They form a distinct caste, and the profession never goes out of the caste.

The princes of India do not recognise the supremacy of any one sovereign. Each one is his own master. Still the Balhara has the title of "king of kings."

The Chinese are men of pleasure; but the Indians condemn pleasure, and abstain from it. They do not take wine, nor do they take vinegar which is made of wine. This does not arise from religious scruples, but from their disdain of it. They say "The prince who drinks wine is no true king." The Indians are surrounded by enemies, who war against them, and they say

"How can a man who inebriates himself conduct the business of a kingdom?"

The Indians sometimes go to war for conquest, but the occasions are rare. I have never seen the people of one country submit to the authority of another, except in the case of that country which comes next to the country of pepper [i.e., Malabar]. When a king subdues a neighbouring state, he places over it a man belonging to the family of the fallen prince, who carries on the government in the name of the conqueror. The inhabitants would not suffer it to be otherwise.

Introduction to the Deeds of Vikramanka

The Deeds of Vikramanka (*Vikramankadeva-carita*) is one of those rare Sanskrit poems which also has some claim to importance as a historical source. Written by the court-poet Bilhana in traditional panegyric style, its subject is a king of the south Indian Chalukya dynasty, Vikramaditya* VI (also known as Vikramanka or Vikrama), who reigned in the late eleventh and early twelfth centuries.

The Chalukyas were one of the most prominent (and longest-lasting) dynasties in the history of Hindu India. Coming to power in the mid-sixth century A.D., they subsequently dominated the western Deccan between the Narbada and the Tungabhadra Rivers for a total of over 400 years. Although supplanted in A.D. 757 by their vassals the Rashtrakutas,** the Chalukya family returned to power in 973 and ruled until *c.* 1190. Vikramaditya VI was the outstanding personality of this second Chalukya dynasty. In order to gain and then to keep the throne he defeated two brothers in battle; he fought many wars with neighboring states, particularly the powerful Chola kingdom to the south. His success was such that he maintained himself in power for the unusual period of fifty years (1076-1126), and proclaimed a new historical era bearing his name.

* This title was borne by many Indian kings, most notably Chandragupta II of the Gupta dynasty (r. A.D. 375-413).

** See Introduction to Suleiman's *Observations*, above p. 125.

The Deeds of Vikramanka is clearly intended as a demonstration of the poet's literary skill and as praise of his royal patron rather than as a true historical source. The object of the poem is to evoke aesthetic emotion, not to relate facts. Florid and prolix in style, it conforms to the rigid and complex canons of the traditional Sanskrit *kavya* (courtly poem).* Various literary embellishments, mythological references, pedantic moralizing, and descriptions of natural phenomena interrupt the main narrative. Much attention is devoted to the king's private life: his prowess in the hunt, his courtship and marriage, his private feelings and amorous pleasures. The figure of Vikramaditya himself is obviously idealized. Not only is he supreme in war and love; his conduct also conforms fully to the *dharma* of a warrior and king.

As history, *The Deeds of Vikramanka* is valuable chiefly as an account of eleventh-century court life as seen by a contemporary and eyewitness. The poet Bilhana has a purely religious concept of historical causation. Vikramaditya is a favorite of the god Shiva, who intervenes at crucial moments to dictate the course of events. The king's character is flawless; his opponents are wicked; and the god prefers virtue. Thus history represents the conflict of good and evil; and the result is preordained.

* For a discussion of the classical Sanskrit poetic style see "Introduction to Sanskrit Poetry," below, p. 184.

BILHANA: FROM THE DEEDS OF VIKRAMANKA

Canto XIV

1. As the rainy season attained maturity, with clouds rendered white as grey hairs, a reliable person approaching Vikramanka spoke in secret.
2. "Something cruel is being told by me, Oh lord of Kuntala![1] Forgive me on that account; because kings enjoy service only [from persons?] neglecting their own duty.
3. "Why do you, having resorted to affection [for Jayasimha,

S. C. Banerji and A. K. Gupta, trans., *Bilhana's Vikramankadeva Caritam*, Calcutta: Sambodhi Publications, 1965, pp. 223-26, 230-31, 233, 238, 241-45.

1. Kuntala was the realm ruled by Vikramaditya—the region now known as the Carnatic (modern Madras state).

your brother], transgress the path of political wisdom? Counsel which [in] the course of [events] becomes adverse is not distinguished from deadly poison.

4. "A great reversal of statesmanship exists in [the region of] Vanavasa,[2] on the part of your brother [Jayasimha, who was] sent [there] by you [as governor], aspiring after prosperity [after] having vanquished the king of Vengi[3] in battle.

5. "Having forsaken the path of righteousness, he has been amassing treasures, oppressing the subjects in general without any hesitation, and has thus rendered the land desolate.

11. "He, taking to unjust means, has brought under his sway the entire land of foresters.[4] It seems as though in the sinful darkness of night demons unite with sinners.

12. "Through ceaseless gifts he has been turning the king of Dravida[5] to his assistance. By what means does he not want to shatter this army of yours with disaffection?

13. "Or what is the use of much talk about strange things? Take it for certain, oh king, that within a few days he will confront you near the (River) Krishna."[6]

18. The king, an expert in polity, getting that [information] confirmed in many ways through eyes in the form of spies, and stricken with the anxiety as to what should be done, thought thus within himself.

19. "Oh dear [brother]! Why are you actuated by the goddess of royalty, with bad policy as her banner, to commit such misdeed? Do you not know that she avoids [even the sage] Narada[7] due to his delight in quarrels?

20. "True, some provinces were not given to you, (but) you

2. Vanavasa (or Banavasi) was the region just south of the Tungabhadra River where the king's brother had established himself.

3. Vengi was the eastern coastal region just south of the Godavari River. In an earlier war, Vikramaditya and his brother had joined forces to fight the king of Vengi.

4. I.e., the foothills of the western Ghats (low mountains of southwest India), which in ancient times were covered with trees.

5. Dravida was the Tamil-country (the extreme southeast of the Indian peninsula), then ruled by a king of the Chola family.

6. A major river of south India which ran through Vikramaditya's realm.

7. A legendary figure who was the patron of music.

possess a greater number of elephants emitting ichor[8] (than I do). In what are you deficient, excepting the designation of king, so that you take recourse to bad policy?

21. "Alas! wherefrom has this calamity befallen? What should I do? What counter-measures should be taken? Oh deities of the Chalukya race! May you yourselves dissuade my younger brother from improper activity!"

22. With this submission, the king sent hundreds of conciliatory proposals [to his brother], but could not restrain him from his misconduct. Whence does destiny run away?

48. The king of Kuntala, out of kindness, became eager to offer [to Jayasimha, his brother] the kingdom. What is the pain of the gracious-minded, aspiring after fame, in giving away wealth?

49. The king ceaselessly offered series of conciliatory proposals to him, but that thorn of the family, overpowered by the morbid affection of the windy humor of bad policy, did not accept any one of them.

50. While Vikrama was sitting down compassionately, thinking how this suffering could be removed, Jayasimha marched on to the banks of the River Krishna, due to the haughtiness of unexpected strength of arms.

51. Leaving Vikrama, many feudatory chiefs joined [Jayasimha's] army. Confusion of mind often arises in men when (their) defeat is going to take place.

52. Looking at the array of elephants with profuse ichor flowing down their temples, and at swift horses, [Jayasimha] realised his elder brother's vigorous method of fighting the battle.

54. He committed arson at one place, pillage at another and in some places captured people. [The] long series of his wicked deeds was like the sign of his downfall.

55. The king pardoned [his brother's] misconduct for [a long time]. Even oceans are not able to rival such a multitude of pure virtues [as those of Vikrama].

56. That despot [Jayasimha] incessantly sent abusive expressions to the king. What is there that is not done by dull-

8. Thin, watery fluid flowing from the ears of elephants in heat.

witted persons [who are] looked at with a crooked glance by evil fortune?

57. What more should I say? Rashness found in [Jayasimha] so much familiarity that he, being puffed up, advanced against the king in a hurry.

69. Agitated though the king was, out of anger, yet at heart he was eager for conciliation. Those who take recourse to misdeed for the sake of wealth are a different (kind of) kings, [who] defil[e] their race.

70. As the river-bank was drawing near, the hostile soldiers [who had] come at different places with equipments of war excited the wrath of the king of Kuntala.

71. Then the leader of the Chalukyas (i.e. Vikrama), mounting on an elephant, [and] desirous of bathing in the river of blood, invaded that land where he would make the River Krishna have its banks littered with the ribs of the heroes [who were] carried by water in the opposite direction.

72. The king, having encamped on that river-bank, resorted to expedients to win [his brother] over. But that crooked-natured fellow did not accept [Vikrama's] conciliatory terms. When there is misfortune, one's mind indeed becomes exceedingly unrestrained.

Canto XV

21. Then, due to the appearance of the heroic sentiment, [this] king of immense courage, which was strange in the world, smilingly set out in a flurry with a mind full of enthusiasm.

22. Having entered into the battlefield, being eager to embrace the goddess of victory, he appeared [in a mood] to have held a festival while entering the pleasure-house of his lady-love.

23. Then the king of severe valour, having advanced a little on the ground, saw the army of the enemy from which the sound of trumpets was emanating.

43. Then a terrible battle, like universal destruction, was commenced on two sides by good soldiers ready to churn the nectar of victory from the ocean of heroic sentiment.

44. When both the armies, having climbed up with the sticks of their arms, started shaking it, a number of fruits with a host of (dismembered) heads fell as it were from the battle-tree.

48. Gradually having reached the fathomless bloodstream that blocked the way, the good soldiers had not the joy of seeing one another for a moment.

52. Sparks of fire, dropped on the battlefield from the mutual striking of swords, became dear to the she-goblins in their cooking of flesh.

54. The waves of breeze, produced from the fans of the flapping ears (of elephants), became efficacious to those who, owing to swoon caused by arrows stuck to their hearts, were lying on the temples of elephants.

56. In the meantime the entire army of the king of Kuntala, agitated by the elephants of the adversary, became distracted and dispersed in (various) directions.

57. There was not a single mighty elephant or horse or an expert warrior who, struck by the wind of universal destruction in the form of enemies, did not move with his face turned against (the war).

58. Then the king of the Chalukyas, of boundless prowess, [with gooseflesh] on his cheeks, himself stood up with a tusker furiously in rut.

60. By means of the bud-like pearls dropping from the temples of wounded elephants he proclaimed that the tree of the fame of hostile heroes was shaken by his arms.

61. The fearless king, while striking at the frontal globes on the foreheads of elephants of the enemies, smiled remembering compact and plump breasts of ladies.

63. The king gladly looked at the series of arrows, shot by the soldiers of the opposite side, and clung to the rods of the banners borne by elephants like so many pillars of victory.

64. With swords and arrows accompanied by javelins, and with the sudden rushing of the elephants he, as if bearing a thousand arms, was engaged in the annihilation of the adversary.

70. Smashing the potsherds of the skulls of powerful rival[s]

with the feet of elephants, he, with fame capable of filling the receptacles of the three worlds, moved in the battle.

71. In the army of [Jayasimha] not a single expert soldier remained face to face with him by counter-discharge of arrows.

72. Swarms of bees, with flowers of gods, fell upon the Chalukya king [Vikrama], who, within a moment, annihilated the entire hostile army.

. . . .

Introduction to the River of Kings

The region of Kashmir has traditionally enjoyed a considerable degree of political isolation from the rest of India. Situated in the extreme north of the Indian sub-continent, it is surrounded by formidable mountain barriers. Great conquerors like Alexander, Mahmud of Ghazni (*c.* A.D. 1000), and Tamerlane (A.D. 1398) passed it by when they invaded India; some of the principal north Indian empires—that of the Guptas, Harsha of Kanauj, the sultans of Delhi—failed to include it among their territories. Nonetheless, for as long as history records, Kashmir has been bound to India by community of culture and religion. Until it became a Muslim state in 1339, Hindu monarchs ruled there, and Hindu social forms predominated; the kingdom was a center of Sanskrit learning. Buddhism flourished side by side with Hindu Shiva-worship; and Kashmir was an important way-station by which Buddhist religion and art passed into Khotan and Turkestan and thence into China.

The River of Kings (*Rajatarangini*) is the oldest and most complete extant record of Kashmiri history. Composed in 1148-49, it is a chronicle of the rulers of Kashmir from the legendary beginnings of time down to the date of writing. Consisting of 7,826 verses arranged into eight books, it is in form a Sanskrit poem in the classical *kavya** style. Kalhana, the author; was a poet well trained in the traditional canons of Sanskrit rhetoric, grammar, and poetic theory. In many respects his work is a conventional example of the

* The term *kavya* may denote either courtly poetry or poetic prose.

kavya, containing the abundant similes and metaphors, stock phrases, and elaborate descriptions of nature which were considered the true test of the poet's art. At the same time, *The River of Kings* differs strikingly from the typical Indian historical poem (*carita*). Its subject is not the life of a single king, but the entire history of a kingdom. By classical *kavya* standards, it contains relatively few rhetorical ornaments—a fact for which Kalhana apologized, explaining that the breadth of his theme made the work already long enough. In the part of the poem treating of recent events, his characters stand forth as real people, not idealized types. Kalhana was not a court poet; his creation is largely free of that exaggerated flattery typical of the *carita*. His opinions are outspoken and frequently critical, his tone sometimes sarcastic, his epithets uncomplimentary.

According to the rules of classical Sanskrit style, every poem should exhibit one characteristic sentiment. In *The River of Kings* the pervading sentiment is resignation. Kalhana's theme is the instability of fame and fortune, the capriciousness of events. He presents a somber picture of Kashmiri society as he knew it: greedy and oppressive feudal lords, corrupt officials, cowardly, boastful soldiers, arrogant and ignorant priests, a passive populace. Conceivably some of this pessimism arose out of the poet's personal circumstances. Kalhana was born a Brahmin of good family. His father had been an important minister in the reign of King Harsha (r. 1089-1101);* he himself may well have desired an official career. His lifetime, however, coincided with a period of internal disorganization and frequent armed upheavals in the state of Kashmir; and so far as is known, he never held any political office. Certainly the critical tone of his poem makes it unlikely that he ever expected royal employment.

As a historian, Kalhana shared many of the faults common to his age and milieu. He had slight knowledge of the outside world, and thus exaggerated the importance of Kashmir. He was uncritical in his acceptance of ancient legends. As a high-caste Hindu, he clearly sympathized with Brahmin pretensions to leadership in society. He took for granted the Hindu theory of world-cycles†—according to which the world progressively declines in virtue—and therefore idealized the remote past. The course of events he sometimes explained by reference to *karma*, the power of fate, or demon-posses-

* Not to be confused with Harsha of Kanauj, who ruled an empire in north India A.D. 606-647. On that Harsha see Vol. IV of this series, pp. 42-43.

† See Vol. IV, "World Cycles," pp. 268-74.

sion. Even so his merits as a historian are impressive, and by medieval Hindu standards exceptional. He utilized written sources where possible, for example, inscriptions and court records. In dealing with recent history, he took care to assign precise dates to events. His descriptions of individuals and social classes are frank and vivid, having the ring of authenticity. As a man in close contact with political life, he understood the realities of power, while retaining an independent viewpoint. Although in fact more than half his verses deal with events occurring within living memory,* he aimed at completeness, and began his poem with the earliest legends concerning his country's history.

Whether Kalhana was an innovator in the art of chronicle-writing is not known; his poem is the earliest surviving example of its type. Indeed, as a genre of historical writing, the Sanskrit poetic chronicle is apparently unique to Kashmir. While the *kavya* style existed throughout India wherever courtly literature was cultivated, only in Kashmir have true historical chronicles thus far come to light. Later Kashmiri poets continued Kalhana's work, with the result that the history of that kingdom is far better known than the history of any other region of India until the Muslim period. But in scope and concept, in historical accuracy and dispassionate judgment combined with a high degree of poetic art, *The River of Kings* stands alone among the extant works of ancient and medieval Hindu literature.

* I.e., from the year 1089.

KALHANA: FROM THE RIVER OF KINGS

Book VII

868. Many are the kings whom [my narrative has dealt with] some way or another and passed on. [But] now, O ill-luck, a path has been reached which is hard to traverse for the understanding.

869-873. How is it to be related, that story of King Harsha

From M. Aurel Stein, trans., *Kalhana's Rajatarangini. A Chronicle of the Kings of Kashmir*, London: Archibald Constable & Co., Ltd., 1900, Vol. I, pp. 335-36, 340-43, 351-53, 356, 400.

which has seen the rise of all enterprises and yet tells of all failures; which brings to light all [kinds of] settled plans and yet shows the absence of all policy; which displays an excessive [assertion of the] ruling power and yet has witnessed excessive disregard of orders; which [tells] of excessive abundance of liberality and of [equally] excessive persistence in confiscation; which gives delight by an abundant [display of] compassion and shocks by the superabundance of murders; which is rendered charming by the redundance of pious works and soiled by the superabundance of sins; which is attractive on all sides and yet repulsive, worthy of praise and deserving of blame; which sensible men must magnify and deride, regard with love and yet feel aggrieved at; which is to be blessed and to be condemned, worthy of memory and yet to be dismissed from the mind?

874. Surely he must have been born from atoms of light. How otherwise could he have been, even for the great, difficult to look at, just like the sun?

875. An appearance like his is not to be seen anywhere among mortals or gods. But if the wise were to look out for him [they would see him] among the chiefs of the demons.

876-878. He wore earrings which flashed like the reflected image of the sun; on his round, broad head-dress was fixed a high diadem; he used to look around like a pleased lion; his bushy beard was hanging down low; his shoulders were like those of a bull, his arms great, and his body of a dark-reddish complexion; he had a broad chest with a narrow waist, and his voice was deep like thunder. Thus even superhuman beings would have lost [before him] their presence of mind.

879. At the palace gate he hung up great bells in all four directions, to be informed by their sound of those who had come with the desire of making representations.

880. And when he had once heard their plaintive speech, he fulfilled their desire [as quickly] as the cloud in the rainy season [fulfils] that of the Cataka birds.

881. Nobody in his court was seen without brilliant dress, without gold ornaments, with a small following, or without a resolute bearing.

882. At that gate of the king's palace at which people from

various nations presented themselves, the riches of all countries seemed always to be piled up.

883. In the king's palace, councillors, chamberlains and other [attendants] moved about without number, adorned with golden chains and bracelets.

932. By addressing their prayers to him, beggars became able to support others, just as the clouds through the aid of the ocean [become] capable of refreshing all beings.

933. By the favours of this liberal king who showered gold about, all bands of singers came to vie with kings.

934. The king, who was the crest-jewel of the learned, adorned men of learning with jewels, and bestowed upon them the privileges of [using] litters, horses, parasols, etc.

941. Surely, not even (the sage) Brhaspati is able to name clearly all the sciences in which he was versed.

942. Even to this day, if one of the songs which he composed for the voice is heard, tears roll on the eye-lashes even of his enemies.

943. Ever fond of amusement, he slept for two watches of the day and kept awake at night, when he held his assemblies.

944. He passed his nights in the assembly-hall, which was illuminated by a thousand lamps, attending meetings of learned men, musical performances and dances.

945. When the conversation ceased, there was heard only the rustling sound from the chewing of betel, and that which was caused by the movement of the ladies' locks and the Shephali flowers [bound up with them].

946-949. What Brhaspati could fully describe the nightly court [held] by this king whose splendour surpassed that of (the god) Indra? The canopies were like clouds, the lights like a wall of fire; the golden sticks resembled the lightning and the multitudes of swords were like smoke; lovely ladies took the place of the Apsaras (nymphs) and ministers that of the stars; its scholars were like an assembly of Rishis (sages) and its singers like Gandharvas (heavenly musicians); it was the fixed meeting-place of (the gods) Kubera and Yama[1] and the one common pleasure-grove of liberality and terror.

1. Yama was the guardian deity of the southern quarter, Kubera of the northern quarter.

955. The king, who completely relieved the distress of his supplicants, profusely provided Brahmins with skins of black antelopes, cows with calves, and other presents.

956. Vasantalekha, the king's wife, who belonged to the Shahi family, founded Mathas[2] and Agraharas[3] in the City and at the holy Tripureshvara.[4]

957. Thus it seemed as if in some degree the flame of Shiva[5]-devotion was rising [at his court], yet one cannot call his reign one of noble transactions.

958. When the new ministers had gradually attained power, they caused delusions in the king's mind from spite against his former advisers.

959. The peacock, whose feet are attacked by leprosy, runs and catches the many-footed snake; the sun, which has a thousand feet (rays), is guided step by step by the Thighless (the Dawn). It is the amusement of fate that the strong are deceived by the weak, and that those who hold all affairs in their hands are confused by those without power.

960. [Thus it came to pass] that the lord of the people, who was eminent by the knowledge of all sciences, had his mind perverted, even by foolish ministers.

962. In his liberality he squandered right and left the riches which his greedy [father] had accumulated, and called him by the name of "Papasena" ("he whose army was one of villains").

963. Confused in his senses, verily the king placed three hundred and sixty women of doubtful character in his seraglio.

. . . .

1070. The kings whom fate ruins, clear their kingdom from rivals by killing their relatives who would preserve it, [with the result] that some one [else] enjoys it alone.

1071. The foolish Ashvattha tree, in order to make the well-grown comb of honey in the dense thicket of its numerous high branches easy to approach and seize by any lucky person, by

2. Residences for Hindu holy men.

3. Villages or land areas given to Brahmins.

4. Tripureshvara was a holy place where the god Shiva was said to have slain the demon Tripura.

5. Shiva is one of the two chief gods of popular Hinduism. He is the lord of death and time, an ascetic and patron of ascetics, and lord of the dance.

fate's instigation takes to shaking spontaneously, and puts the bees which guard that [honey] well out of the way by killing them with the blows of its [falling] leaves.

1072. The king, whose mind was perverted by the most sinful perfidies against his relatives, came then to be exploited by rogues [to such an extent] as would be incredible even of simpletons.

1089. As he was addicted to extravagant expenditure upon various corps of his army, his thoughts in consequence [of this addiction] became in time firmly fixed upon the spoliation of temples.

1090. Then the greedy-minded [king] plundered from all temples the wonderful treasures which former kings had bestowed there.

1091. In order to get hold of the statues of gods, too, when the treasures [of the temples] had been carried off, he appointed (an official named) Udayaraja "prefect for the overthrow of divine images."

1092. In order to defile the statues of gods he had excrements and urine poured over their faces by naked mendicants whose noses, feet and hands had rotted away.

1093. Divine images made of gold, silver, and other [materials] rolled about even on the roads, which were covered with night soil, as [if they were] logs of wood.

1094. Crippled naked mendicants and the like covered the images of the gods, which were dragged along by ropes round their ankles, with spittings instead of flowers.

1095. There was not one temple in a village, town or in the City which was not despoiled of its images by that Muslim,[6] King Harsha.

. . . .

1099. Those who are anxious to amass fortunes do not stop from evil actions, though in this world they may have reached riches which are a wonder for all. Thus the elephant, though he

6. The Islamic religion does not permit images to be made of sacred things. The use of the epithet in this context may also be meant to suggest that King Harsha, though a Shiva-worshipper, had secret Muslim sympathies.

is the pleasure-seat of the [lotus-born goddess] Lakshmi, yet somehow falls into the sin of destroying the lotus-tank [in his desire] to obtain the lotus-flowers.

1100-1101. O shame! Though he possessed his grandfather's and father's treasures and those which (his predecessor, King) Utkarsha at the commencement of his reign had brought from Lohara,[7] and though he had confiscated from the temples the riches [bestowed] by former kings, yet he endeavoured to secure [more] wealth by oppressing the householders.

1102. Merely upon his order the bad ministers then appointed numerous officers, who took their designation from frequent new imposts.

1133. When he desired to give magic perfection to his body, some (low-caste person) made him swallow a drink which, he pretended, was an elixir having that power.

1134. What object is there in relating the other foolish acts of this [king], who at the bidding of his parasites gave away portions of his life just as [if it were] a procurable property?

1135. What respectable man could relate the other even more shameful practices of his which he followed to obtain strength and beauty?

1136. Being of small intellect, he was thus for many a year thrown into absolute blindness by his own senselessness and the wickedness of evil advisers.

1137-1138. As there are at present persons of little faith whose minds are swayed by doubts in regard to the miraculous deeds of Meghavahana and other [ancient kings], so there will be surely in time people who will not believe these astonishing misdeeds which I relate.

1139. Afflicted with want of wisdom as he thus was, in a kingdom full of deceit, yet he was, while he lived, never at the mercy of enemies watching for weak points.

1140-1141. That he was never shot at with an arrow and killed, or wounded by one or the other enemy when at night he was standing upright in the illuminated hall, and teaching in person the dancing-girls how to act,—that must be due to [there

7. Lohara was a principality in the hills southwest of Kashmir, whose kings were close relatives of the Kashmiri kings.

having been] a balance of the life-period [allotted to him], or to the sinfulness of his subjects.

. . . .

1708. The fight at the king's last hour was not rendered glorious by lionlike roars [of brave men], nor by the sound of kettle-drums, nor the furious noise of [clashing] arms.

1709. On the contrary, the armed Damaras (noble landowners) got without noise into his hut, as cats [get round] a mouse which is inside a pot.

1710. Then another who had entered through the roof, attacked the king after striking (the king's servant) Prayagaka on the shoulder and head.

1711. This soldier, after parrying the king's weapon, struck him rapidly twice with a dagger in the breast.

1712. After uttering twice the word: "O Mahesvara,"[8] he fell dead to the ground, struck down like a tree which has been cut at the root.

1713. Sovereign as he was, he found a death which was fit for a thief who in his flight had entered a house.

1714. No other king has been seen in this epoch as powerful as he was, nor of any other [king] so shameful a funeral.

1715. It was his aversion to battle alone which destroyed the grandeur of this high-minded [king] with all its attending happiness.

1716. Or, his fault may have been only his want of independent judgment, and all errors which brought about his complete ruin [may have been] those of his ministers.

1717. His age was forty-two years and eight months, when he was slain on the fifth day of the bright half of Bhadrapada in the year [of the Laukika era four thousand one hundred] seventy-seven (A.D. 1101).

8. I.e., Shiva.

The Sultanate of Delhi: Introduction

Despite the chronic instability of the Hindu kingdoms, foreign conquest was a comparatively rare occurrence in India prior to the twelfth century A.D. The towering mountains and high seas surrounding the sub-continent served effectively to protect it from foreign incursions. From the time of the Hun inroads in the fifth and sixth centuries A.D. until the period of the Muslim conquests (beginning in 1175), India remained almost totally free of alien rule. Only Sind in the far west (captured by Arabs in the eighth century) and the Punjab in the northwest (annexed to the sultanate of Ghazni in the eleventh) came under foreign government in these centuries.

A new era of foreign conquest began in 1175 when Muhammad of Ghur, the ruler of a minor principality in Afghanistan, led his bands of Turkish tribesmen through the northwest mountain passes into India. Their first object was plunder and slave-raiding; but they stayed to govern. Uncouth and warlike mountaineers, Muhammad of Ghur's followers were also fanatic Muslims, convinced that the slaying of infidels was pleasing to God. In battle they relied upon the mobility of horse cavalry, upon the warriors' personal bravery, and upon their reputation for frightfulness. The enormous Hindu armies which sometimes opposed them—composed of individual contingents each obeying its own raja, and relying upon slow-moving elephants—were rarely able to withstand their quick attacks. At the time of his death in 1206, Muhammad of Ghur controlled the major part of both the Indus and the Ganges basins.

Thus was founded the so-called sultanate of Delhi—the first major Muslim state in India, in which an alien ruling class governed a vastly larger Hindu population. Its territories, though changing somewhat from time to time, were larger than those of any other Indian political unit since the short-lived empire of Harsha of Kanauj (r. A.D. 606-47). One of the sultans—Muhammad bin Tughluq—even managed briefly to subdue almost the entire Indian peninsula. The sultanate of Delhi lasted through three ruling dynasties and more than three centuries, until being displaced (in 1526) by another Muslim Turkish group from beyond the northwest frontier —the Mughals. While Muslims thus ruled the north, a succession of more or less ephemeral Hindu kingdoms shared the sovereignty of the Deccan. Only in the late sixteenth century, under the great Mughal emperor Akbar, did an empire come into being which united most of the Indian sub-continent.

On the whole, the sultans of Delhi did not fundamentally alter the traditional Indian relationship between rulers and subjects. Hindu cultivators were not ordinarily displaced from their traditionally held lands; they continued to practice their own religion; and Hindu officials remained in subordinate government positions, though Muslims held the chief posts. Inevitably, a degree of amalgamation occurred between Hindu and Muslim culture. A new language came into being as a lingua franca for much of north India—Urdu, containing mostly Arabic and Persian words superimposed upon Hindi grammar. A distinct style of Indo-Muslim architecture developed. Men like Kabir and Nanak* founded new religions which incorporated both Hindu and Muslim notions of God. But whereas previous invaders of India had quickly become absorbed into the Hindu caste system, the Muslims neither sought nor achieved assimilation. Though always a minority group, they considered themselves an elite and took care to cultivate their separate religion, law, and customs. Indeed, the Mongol eruptions into the Near East in the thirteenth and fourteenth centuries caused many leading intellects of the Muslim world to seek refuge in India, which then became in its own right a center of Muslim culture.

* For "Poems of Kabir" and "Hymns of Nanak" see below, pp. 177-83.

Introduction to Zia-ud-din Barni: Firuz Shah's History

Zia-ud-din Barni (*c.* 1285-1357) was a political theorist as well as a major historian of Muslim India. Belonging to a family of high officials, he was for many years a close associate of the conqueror-sultan Muhammad bin Tughluq (r. 1325-51). When that ruler died Barni fell from grace, retired to private life, and devoted himself to writing, evidently in hopes of returning to favor under the new sultan, Firuz Shah. Of his two chief works, one—the *Rulings on Temporal Government*—sets forth his conception of the Muslim ruler's duties toward religion. The other, entitled *Firuz Shah's History* (*Tarikh-i Firuz Shahi*) in honor of the reigning monarch, records the important acts of eight sultans of Delhi between 1266 and 1357, the year of writing.

The following excerpts are taken from Barni's account of the reign of Ala-ud-din Khilji, sultan of Delhi 1296-1316. Ala-ud-din won the throne through an act of treachery against his uncle, the previous sultan. Fierce and cruel, he killed off rivals and enemies, sought to increase his territories through aggressive war, and accumulated vast quantities of plunder. But in the typical fashion of the Delhi sultans, he was also a devout Muslim who patronized men of learning and constructed magnificent mosques and religious colleges. The administrative measures which Barni describes in the following passages were designed to strengthen Ala-ud-din's still precarious throne.

ZIA-UD-DIN BARNI: FROM FIRUZ SHAH'S HISTORY

The Sultan [Ala-ud-din] next directed his attention to the means of preventing rebellion, and first he took steps for seizing upon property. He ordered that, wherever there was a village held by proprietary right, in free gift, or as a religious endowment, it should by one stroke of the pen be brought back under the exchequer. The people were pressed and amerced, money was exacted from them on every kind of pretence. Many were left without any money, till at length it came to pass that, excepting army officers, officials, and bankers, no one possessed even a trifle in cash. So rigorous was the confiscation that, beyond a few thousand *tankas*,[1] all the pensions, grants of land, and endowments in the country were appropriated. The people were all so absorbed in obtaining the means of living, that the name of rebellion was never mentioned.

From H. M. Elliot and John Dowson, eds., *The History of India as Told by Its Own Historians*, London: Trübner & Co., 1871, III, 179-83, 191-95.

1. A silver or gold coin, worth approximately 67 grains.

Secondly, he provided so carefully for the acquisition of intelligence, that no action of good or bad men was concealed from him. No one could stir without his knowledge, and whatever happened in the houses of nobles, great men, and officials, was communicated to the Sultan by his reporters. Nor were the reports neglected, for explanations of them were demanded. The system of reporting went to such a length, that nobles dared not speak aloud even in the largest palaces, and if they had anything to say they communicated by signs. In their own houses, night and day, dread of the reports of the spies made them tremble. No word or action which could provoke censure or punishment was allowed to transpire. The transactions in the bazaars, the buying and selling, and the bargains made, were all reported to the Sultan by his spies, and were kept under control.

Thirdly, he prohibited wine-drinking and wine-selling, as also the use of beer and intoxicating drugs. Dicing also was forbidden. Many prohibitions of wine and beer were issued. Vintners and gamblers and beer-sellers were turned out of the city, and the heavy taxes which had been levied from them were abolished. . . . The sellers, the importers, and drinkers of wine were subjected to corporal punishment, and were kept in prison for some days. But their numbers increased so much that holes for the incarceration of offenders were dug outside the Badaun gate, which is a great thoroughfare. Wine-bibbers and wine-sellers were placed in these holes, and the severity of the confinement was such that many of them died. . . .

Fourthly, the Sultan gave commands that noblemen and great men should not visit each other's houses, or give feasts, or hold meetings. They were forbidden to form alliances without consent from the throne, and they were also prohibited from allowing people to resort to their houses. To such a length was this last prohibition carried that no stranger was admitted into a nobleman's house. Feasting and hospitality fell quite into disuse. Through fear of the spies, the nobles kept themselves quiet; they gave no parties and had little communication with each other. No man of a seditious, rebellious, or evil reputation was allowed to come near them. If they went to the *sarais*,[2] they could not lay

2. Inns.

their heads together, or sit down cosily and tell their troubles. Their communications were brought down to a mere exchange of signs. This interdict prevented any information of conspiracy and rebellion coming to the Sultan, and no disturbance arose.

After the promulgation of these interdicts, the Sultan requested the wise men to supply some rules and regulations for grinding down the Hindus, and for depriving them of that wealth and property which fosters disaffection and rebellion. There was to be one rule for the payment of tribute applicable to all, and the heaviest tribute was not to fall upon the poorest. The Hindu was to be so reduced as to be left unable to keep a horse to ride on, to carry arms, to wear fine clothes, or to enjoy any of the luxuries of life. To effect these important objects of government two regulations were made. The first was that all cultivation, whether on a small or large scale, was to be carried on by measurement at a certain rate for every *biswa*.[3] Half (of the produce) was to be paid without any diminution, and this rule was to apply to [everyone] without the slightest distinction. The second [regulation] related to buffaloes, goats, and other animals from which milk is obtained. A tax for pasturage, at a fixed rate, was to be levied, and was to be demanded for every inhabited house, so that no animal, however wretched, could escape the tax. Heavier burdens were not to be placed upon the poor, but the rules as to the payment of the tribute were to apply equally to rich and poor. Collectors, clerks, and other officers employed in revenue matters, who took bribes and acted dishonestly, were all dismissed. . . . The same rules for the collection of the tribute applied to all alike, and the people were brought to such a state of obedience that one revenue officer would string twenty [people] together by the neck, and enforce payment by blows. No Hindu could hold up his head, and in their houses no sign of gold or silver or of any superfluity was to be seen. These things, which nourish insubordination and rebellion, were no longer to be found. . . . Blows, confinement in the stocks, imprisonment and chains, were all employed to enforce payment [of the tribute]. There was no chance of a single *tanka* being taken dishonestly, or as bribery, from any Hindu or Musulman.

3. Unit of land.

The revenue collectors and officers were so coerced and checked that for five hundred or a thousand *tankas* they were imprisoned and kept in chains for years. Men looked upon revenue officers as something worse than fever. Clerkship was a great crime, and no man would give his daughter to a clerk. Death was deemed preferable to revenue employment. Ofttimes fiscal officers fell into prison, and had to endure blows and stripes. . . .

The Sultan next turned his attention to the increase of his forces, and consulted and debated with wise men by night and day as to the best means of opposing and overcoming the Mongols.[4] After much deliberation between the Sultan and his councillors, it was decided that a large army was necessary, and not only large, but choice, well armed, well mounted, with archers, and all ready for immediate service. This plan, and this only, seemed to recommend itself as feasible for opposing the Mongols. The Sultan then consulted his advisers as to the means of raising such a force, for it could not be maintained without heavy expenditure, and what was arranged for one year might not be continuous. On this point he said, "If I settle a large amount of pay on the army, and desire to maintain the pay at the same rate every year, then, although the treasury is now full, five or six years will clear it out, and nothing will be left. Without money government is impossible. I am very desirous of having a large army, well horsed, well accoutred, picked men and archers, ready for service year after year. I would pay them 234 *tankas* regularly, and I would allow seventy-eight *tankas* to those who keep two horses, requiring in return the two horses, with all necessary appointments. So also as regards the men of one horse, I would require the horse and his accoutrements. Inform me, then, how this large army can be regularly maintained on the footing I desire." His sagacious advisers thought carefully over the matter, and after great deliberation made a unanimous report to the Sultan. "The ideas which have passed through your Majesty's mind as to maintaining a large and permanent army upon a low scale of pay are quite impracticable.

4. The Mongols made a number of inroads into India in this period. In 1299, shortly before the events described here, they nearly captured Delhi itself.

Horses, arms, and accoutrements, and the support of the soldier and his wife and family, cannot be provided for a trifle. If the necessaries of life could be bought at a low rate, then the idea which your Majesty has entertained of maintaining a large army at a small expense might be carried out, and all apprehension of the great forces of the Mongols would be removed." The Sultan then consulted with his most experienced ministers as to the means of reducing the prices of provisions without resorting to severe and tyrannical punishments. His councillors replied that the necessaries of life would never become cheap until the price of grain was fixed by regulations and tariffs. Cheapness of grain is a universal benefit. So some regulations were issued, which kept down the price for some years. This scale of prices was maintained as long as Ala-ud-din lived, and grain never rose one *dang*, whether the rains were abundant or scanty. This unvarying price of grain in the markets was looked upon as one of the wonders of the time.

To secure the cheapness of grain, Malik Kabul Ulugh Khan, a wise and practical man, was appointed controller of the markets. He received a large territory and used to go round (the markets) in great state with many horse and foot. He had clever deputies, friends of his own, who were appointed by the crown. Intelligent spies also were sent into the markets.

The Sultan gave orders that all the *Khalsa*[5] villages of the Doab[6] should pay the tribute in kind. The corn was brought into the granaries of the city (of Delhi). In the country dependent on the [Delhi government], half the Sultan's portion (of the produce) was ordered to be taken in grain. In Jhain[7] also, and in the villages of Jhain, stores were to be formed. These stores of grain were to be sent into the city in caravans. By these means so much royal grain came to Delhi that there never was a time when there were not two or three royal granaries full of grain in the city. When there was a deficiency of rain, or when for any reason the caravans did not arrive, and grain became scarce

5. Lands administered directly by the crown.
6. Region between the Ganges and the lower Jumna River. The word means "space between rivers."
7. District southwest of Delhi.

in the markets, then the royal stores were opened and the corn was sold at the tariff price, according to the wants of the people. Grain was also consigned to the caravans from [Delhi]. Through these two rules, grain never was deficient in the markets, and never rose one *dang* above the fixed price.

The Sultan placed all the [corn dealers and] carriers of his kingdom under the controller of the markets. Orders were given for arresting the head carriers and for bringing them in chains before the controller of the markets, who was directed to detain them until they agreed upon one common mode of action and gave bail for each other. Nor were they to be released until they brought their wives and children, beasts of burden and cattle, and all their property, and fixed their abodes in the villages along the banks of the Jumna. An overseer was to be placed over the carriers and their families, on behalf of the controller of the markets, to whom the carriers were to submit. Until all this was done the chiefs were to be kept in chains. Under the operation of this rule, so much grain found its way into the markets that it was unnecessary to open the royal stores, and grain did not rise a *dang* above the standard.

The fifth provision for securing the cheapness of grain was against regrating. This was so rigidly enforced that no merchant, farmer, corn-chandler, or any one else, could hold back secretly [the slightest quantity] of grain and sell it at his shop for a *dang* above the regulated price. If regrated grain were discovered, it was forfeited to the Sultan, and the regrater was fined. Engagements were taken from the governors and other revenue officers in the Doab that no one under their authority should be allowed to regrate, and if any man was discovered to have regrated, the deputy and his officers were fined, and had to make their defence to the throne.

Engagements were taken from the provincial revenue officers and their assistants, that they would provide that the corn-carriers should be supplied with corn by the [cultivators] on the field at a fixed price. The Sultan also gave orders that the overseers and other revenue officers in the countries of the Doab, near the capital, should so vigorously collect the tribute that the cultivators should be unable to carry away any corn from the fields into their houses and to regrate. They were to be compelled to sell their corn in the fields to the corn-carriers at a low price, so that the dealers should have no excuse for neglecting to bring the corn into the markets. A constant supply was thus secured. To give the villagers a chance of profit, they were permitted to carry their corn into the market and sell it at the regulation price.

Reports used to be made daily to the Sultan of the market rate and of the market transactions from three distinct sources. 1st. The superintendent made a report of the market rate and of the market transactions. 2nd. The reporters made a statement. 3rd. The spies made a report. If there was any variance in these reports, the superintendent received punishment. The various officials of the market were well aware that all the ins and outs of the market were reported to the Sultan through three different channels, and so there was no opportunity of their deviating from the market rules in the smallest particular.

All the wise men of the age were astonished at the evenness of the price in the markets. If the rains had fallen (regularly), and the seasons had been (always) favourable, there would have been nothing so wonderful in grain remaining at one price; but the extraordinary part of the matter was that during the reign of Ala-ud-din there were years in which the rains were deficient, but instead of the usual scarcity ensuing, there was no want of corn in Delhi, and there was no rise in the price either in the grain brought out of the royal granaries, or in that imported by the dealers. This was indeed the wonder of the age, and no other monarch was able to effect it. . . .

Introduction to the Autobiography of Firuz Shah

Firuz Shah Tughluq (r. 1351-89) was the most humane of all the sultans of Delhi. Ascending the throne at the death of Muhammad bin Tughluq, the cruel conqueror who for a brief period had ruled most of India, he sought to abolish many of his predecessor's oppressive practices. Himself an undistinguished general, Firuz Shah led several expensive campaigns with negligible result, but made no attempt to reconquer the Deccan, which had risen in rebellion. Like most of the Delhi sultans, he was diligent in building: cities and towns, mosques and colleges, forts and canals were among the works he sponsored. But with all his merits, Firuz Shah shared the religious prejudices of his age, and was ruthless in defense of the faith. Toleration of idolatry (i.e., Hinduism) or of Muslim sectarianism he considered heinous, and the purchase of conversions (by exempting Muslims from the poll-tax) pleasing to God.

Firuz Shah's remarkable autobiography, from which the following excerpts are taken, bears witness to his deep religious feeling and sincere desire to rule justly according to his lights.

FROM THE AUTOBIOGRAPHY OF FIRUZ SHAH

Praises without end, and infinite thanks to that merciful Creator who gave to me his poor abject creature Firuz, son of Rajab, the slave of Muhammad Shah son of Tughluq Shah,[1] His impulse for the maintenance of the laws of His religion, for the repression of heresy, the prevention of crime, and the prohibition of things forbidden; who gave me also a disposition for discharging my lawful duties and my moral obligations. . . . My desire is that, to the best of my human power, I should recount and pay my thanks for the many blessings He has bestowed upon me, so that I may be found among the number of His grateful servants. First I would praise Him because when irreligion and sins opposed to the Law prevailed in Hindustan,[2] and mens' habits and dispositions were inclined towards them, and were averse to the restraints of religion, He inspired me, His humble servant, with an earnest desire to repress irreligion and wickedness, so that I

From H. M. Elliot and John Dowson, eds., *The History of India as Told by Its Own Historians*, London: Trübner & Co., 1871, III, 374-88.

1. I.e., Muhammad bin Tughluq, the previous sultan.
2. The portion of India north of the Deccan.

was able to labour diligently until with His blessing the vanities of the world, and things repugnant to religion, were set aside, and the true was distinguished from the false.

In the reigns of former kings the blood of many Musulmans had been shed, and many varieties of torture employed. Amputation of hands and feet, ears and noses; tearing out the eyes, pouring molten lead into the throat, crushing the bones of the hands and feet with mallets, burning the body with fire, driving iron nails into the hands, feet, and bosom, cutting the sinews, sawing men asunder; these and many similar tortures were practised. The great and merciful God made me, His servant, hope and seek for His mercy by devoting myself to prevent the unlawful killing of Musulmans, and the infliction of any kind of torture upon them or upon any men. . . . Through the mercy which God has shown to me these severities and terrors have been exchanged for tenderness, kindness, and mercy. Fear and respect have thus taken firmer hold of the hearts of men, and there has been no need of executions, scourgings, tortures, or terrors. But this blessed result is altogether due to the mercy and favour of the Creator. . . . By God's help I determined that the lives of Musulmans and true believers should be in perfect immunity, and whoever transgressed the Law should receive the punishment prescribed by the Book[3] and the decrees of judges. . . .[4]

In former reigns they used to collect frivolous, unlawful, and unjust cesses at the public treasury. . . . I had all these abolished and removed from the accounts, and any revenue collector who exacted these cesses from the people was to be brought to punishment for his offence. The money received in the public treasury should be derived from sources recognized by the Sacred Law, and approved by books of authority. First the tenth from cultivated lands, then the alms, then the *jizya* or poll tax on Hindus and other separatists,[5] then the fifth of the spoil and

3. I.e., the Koran.
4. The Sacred Law of Islam.
5. Whether the *jizya* was actually enforced upon Hindus is historically in doubt. But because the levying of this tax upon non-Muslims was considered a sacred duty, orthodox Muslim writers felt impelled to state that it was in fact collected.

of (the produce of) mines. No tax unauthorized by the declarations of the Book should be received in the public treasury.

The sect of *Shi'as*,[6] also called *Rawafiz*, had endeavoured to make proselytes. They wrote treatises and books, and gave instruction and lectures upon the tenets of their sect, and traduced and reviled the first chiefs of our religion (on whom be the peace of God!). I seized them all and I convicted them of their errors and perversions. On the most zealous I inflicted punishment, and the rest I visited with censure and threats of public punishment. Their books I burnt in public, and so by the grace of God the influence of this sect was entirely suppressed. . . .

There was in Delhi a man named Rukn-ud-din, who was called Mahdi,[7] because he affirmed himself to be the Imam[8] Mahdi who is to appear in the latter days, and to be possessed of knowledge by inspiration. He said that he had not read or studied under anyone, and that he knew the names of all things, a knowledge which no prophet had acquired since Adam. He pretended that the mysteries of the science of letters had been revealed to him in a way never made known to any other man, and that he had written books upon the subject. He led people astray into mystic practices, and perverted ideas by maintaining that he was Rukn-ud din, the prophet of God. The elders brought the facts of this case to my attention, and gave evidence of what they had heard him say. When he was brought before me I investigated the charges of error and perversion brought against him, and he was convicted of heresy and error. The doctors of the Law said he was an infidel, and worthy of death, for having spread such vile and pernicious ideas among the people of Islam. If any delay were made in putting them down they would spread like a pestilence, and many Musulmans would stray from the true faith. A revolt (against religion) would follow; and many men would fall into perdition. I ordered that this vile fellow's rebellion and wickedness should be communicated

6. The Shi'a (which in turn includes many subdivisions) are one of the two principal branches of the Islamic faith. Firuz Shah belonged to the other, or Sunni persuasion.

7. Muslims believe that a Prophet called the Mahdi will appear on earth shortly before the end of the world.

8. The title of "Imam" is applied to various Muslim religious leaders.

to all societies of learned men, and be made public to all men, high and low: and that in accordance with the decision of the doctors learned in the holy Law, the guilty should be brought to punishment. They killed him with some of his supporters and disciples, and the people rushing in tore him to pieces and broke his bones into fragments. Thus was his iniquity prevented. God in His mercy and favour, made me, His humble creature, the instrument of putting down such wickedness, and abolishing such heresy; and guided me to effect a restoration of true religion. Thanks for this are due to the great and glorious God. Upon hearing or reading the facts here recorded, every well-wisher of His religion will admit that this sect was deservedly punished, and for this good action I hope to receive future reward. . . .

The Hindus and idol-worshipers had agreed to pay the money for toleration, and had consented to the poll tax (*jizya*), in return for which they and their families enjoyed security. These people now erected new idol temples in the city and the environs in opposition to the Law of the Prophet which declares that such temples are not to be tolerated. Under Divine guidance I destroyed these edifices, and I killed those leaders of infidelity who seduced others into error, and the lower orders I subjected to stripes and chastisement, until this abuse was entirely abolished. . . .

Some Hindus had erected a new idol-temple in the village of Kohana, and the idolaters used to assemble there and perform their idolatrous rites. These people were seized and brought before me. I ordered that the perverse conduct of the leaders of this wickedness should be publicly proclaimed, and that they should be put to death before the gate of the palace. I also ordered that the infidel books, the idols, and the vessels used in their worship, which had been taken with them, should all be publicly burnt. The others were restrained by threats and punishments, as a warning to all men, that no *zimmi*[9] could follow such wicked practices in a Musulman country. . . .

9. The word *zimmi* means "protected unbeliever." Strictly speaking, only "people of the Book" (meaning "revealed Book"), i.e., Jews, Christians, and Zoroastrians, may enjoy this status.

Among the gifts which God bestowed upon me, His humble servant, was a desire to erect public buildings. So I built many mosques and colleges and monasteries, that the learned and the elders, the devout and the holy, might worship God in these edifices, and aid the kind builder with their prayers. The digging of canals, the planting of trees, and the endowing with lands are in accordance with the directions of the Law. The learned doctors of the Law of Islam have many troubles; of this there is no doubt. I settled allowances upon them in proportion to their necessary expenses, so that they might regularly receive the income. . . .

Again, by the guidance of God, I was led to repair and rebuild the edifices and structures of former kings and ancient nobles, which had fallen into decay from lapse of time; giving the restoration of these buildings the priority over my own building works.[10] . . . The expense of repairing and renewing these tombs and colleges was provided from their ancient endowments. In those cases where no income had been settled on these foundations in former times for (procuring) carpets, lights, and furniture for the use of travelers and pilgrims in the least of these places, I had villages assigned to them, the revenues of which would suffice for their expenditure in perpetuity. . . .

All the fortifications which had been built by former sovereigns at Delhi I repaired.

For the benefit of travelers and pilgrims resorting to the tombs of illustrious kings and celebrated saints, and for providing the things necessary in these holy places, I confirmed and gave effect to the grants of villages, lands, and other endowments which had been conferred upon them in olden times. In those cases where no endowment or provision had been settled, I made an endowment, so that these establishments might for ever be secure of an income, to afford comfort to travelers and wayfarers, to holy men and learned men. May they remember those (ancient benefactors) and me in their prayers.

I was enabled by God's help to build a hospital for the benefit of every one of high or low degree, who was suddenly attacked

10. This attention to the buildings of his predecessors was unusual; more commonly such edifices were allowed to decay.

by illness and overcome by suffering. Physicians attend there to ascertain the disease, to look after the cure, to regulate the diet, and to administer medicine. The cost of the medicines and the food is defrayed from my endowments. All sick persons, residents and travelers, gentle and simple, bond and free, resort thither; their maladies are treated, and, under God's blessing, they are cured.

Under the guidance of the Almighty I arranged that the heirs of those persons who had been executed in the reign of my late lord and patron Sultan Muhammad [bin Tughluq] and those who had been deprived of a limb, nose, eye, hand, or foot, should be reconciled to the late Sultan and be appeased with gifts, so that they executed deeds declaring their satisfaction, duly attested by witnesses. These deeds were put into a chest, which was placed at the head of the tomb of the late Sultan, in the hope that God, in his great clemency, would show mercy to my late friend and patron, and make those persons feel reconciled to him.

Another instance of Divine guidance was this. Villages, lands, and ancient patrimonies of every kind had been wrested from the hands of their owners in former reigns, and had been brought under the Exchequer. I directed that every one who had a claim to property should bring it forward in the law-court, and, upon establishing his title, the village, the land, or whatever other property it was should be restored to him. By God's grace I was impelled to this good action, and men obtained their just rights.

I encouraged my infidel subjects to embrace the religion of the prophet, and I proclaimed that every one who repeated the creed and became a Musulman should be exempt from the *jizya*, or poll-tax. Information of this came to the ears of the people at large, and great numbers of Hindus presented themselves, and were admitted to the honour of Islam. Thus they came forward day by day from every quarter, and, adopting the faith, were exonerated from the *jizya*, and were favoured with presents and honours.

Through God's mercy the lands and property of his servants have been safe and secure, protected and guarded during my reign; and I have not allowed the smallest particle of any man's property to be wrested from him. Men often spoke to me officiously, saying that such and such a merchant had made so many *lacs*,[11] and that such and such a revenue collector had so many *lacs*. By reproofs and punishments I made these informers hold their tongues, so that the people might be safe from their malignity, and through this kindness men became my friends and supporters.

Under God's favour my heart was occupied with an earnest desire to succour the poor and needy and to comfort their hearts. Wherever I heard of a *fakir*[12] or religious recluse, I went to visit him and ministered to his necessities, so that I might attain the blessing promised to those who befriend the poor.

. . . When any government servant filling an important and responsible position was carried off under the decrees of God to the happy future life, I gave his place and employment to his son, so that he might occupy the same position and rank as his father and suffer no injury. . . .

The greatest and best of honours that I obtained through God's mercy was, that by my obedience and piety, and friendliness and submission to the Caliph,[13] the representative of the holy Prophet, my authority was confirmed; for it is by his sanction that the power of kings is assured, and no king is secure until he has submitted himself to the Caliph, and has received a confirmation from the sacred throne. A diploma was sent to me fully confirming my authority as deputy of the Caliphate, and the leader of the faithful was graciously pleased to honour me. He also bestowed upon me robes, a banner, a sword, a ring, and a foot-print as badges of honour and distinction.

My object in writing this book has been to express my gratitude to the All-bountiful God for the many and various blessings He has bestowed upon me. Secondly, that men who desire to be good and prosperous may read this and learn what is the proper course. There is this concise maxim, by observing which, a man may obtain God's guidance: Men will be judged according to their works, and rewarded for the good that they have done.

11. The sum of 100,000 (in modern India: 100,000 rupees).
12. An itinerant Muslim holy man who lives by begging.
13. The highest religious authority of the Muslim world, then residing in Egypt.

Religion

Introduction to Hinduism in the Middle Period

Hinduism can probably best be defined as the totality of rites, customs and legends recorded in the Vedas,* the epics,† and the ancient law-books** of India. Of all these books the most sacred are the four Vedas; and acceptance of the Vedas as divine revelation (*shruti*) is one criterion of Hindu orthodoxy. But in Hinduism there is no central institution empowered to define truth and reject error, nor can Hindu religious practices and beliefs be traced back to any known historical founder and his teaching. Within Hinduism the most diverse ideas are tolerated or even welcomed; and even apparently contradictory beliefs are regarded as aspects of a single truth. Custom and ritual are more important in Hinduism than doctrine. Groups like the Buddhists or Jains were regarded by Hindus as heterodox not on grounds of dogma, but because they refused to accept the sacredness of the Vedas and the validity of the caste system.

In pre-Muslim India, as nowadays, the unity of Hinduism rested rather upon the universal acceptance of its social system than upon any definition of orthodox belief. From ancient times Hindu society has been divided into four principal social classes (*varnas*), each with its specific rights and duties. In the course of time these *varnas* became divided into a variety of castes (*jats*) and sub-castes; new castes were added as alien groups (e.g., foreign invaders or uncivilized tribes) were absorbed within the Hindu framework. Members of a caste were permitted to intermarry and share meals together, while their social relations with members of other castes were subject to precise regulation. The Hindu who transgressed a law of his

* Including the Brahmanas, Aranyakas, and Upanishads.
† The *Mahabharata* (which includes the *Bhagavad Gita*) and the *Ramayana*.
** The Dharma Sutras and Dharma Shastras for example, the *Laws of Manu*).

caste became "polluted" thereby, and was required to undergo ritual purification; serious failure to conform resulted in loss of caste and expulsion from all normal social relations. Though prior to the sixth or seventh century (the period of Hun invasions) the boundaries between castes were still somewhat fluid, in the following centuries these distinctions became more and more rigid, especially after the twelfth century in response to the Muslim conquests.

In its religious as well as its social aspect, Hinduism in the middle period was largely the outgrowth of myths and traditions recorded in the Vedas. But some of its gods and rites apparently originated with the non-Aryan inhabitants of India,* and entered Hinduism only in the post-Vedic period (i.e., after *c.* 500 B.C.). Though the precise stages of this assimilative process are impossible to describe, owing to the dearth of source material, a great deal of amalgamation between Aryan and non-Aryan religious ideas unquestionably occurred. New gods came to prominence while others were forgotten; all, however, were regarded as *avatars* (incarnations) of the older Vedic deities.

But whereas the Vedas include prayers, hymns, and invocations addressed to many gods, popular Hinduism in the middle period was directed chiefly to the worship of one of two principal deities—Vishnu and Shiva. Despite theoretical reverence for the Vedas and the widespread cult of images—later stigmatized by Muslims as idol-worship—the Vishnuites described Vishnu, and the Shivaites Shiva, as a single, universal Supreme Being. While neither Vishnuites nor Shivaites expressly rejected the other Hindu deities, they generally addressed their prayers only to their special god. Especially in south India, with its primarily Dravidian (i.e., non-Aryan) population, the seventh to the twelfth centuries saw the proliferation of sects stressing complete devotion (*bhakti*) to one's chosen God, surrender to his will, and salvation through faith and divine grace. At the highest intellectual level, philosophers too took note of the new religious spirit. The great Shankara (*c.* A.D. 800) recognized the belief in a personal God as a lower stage of truth, supposedly leading toward the higher (and more difficult) Upanishadic concept of Brahman; while Ramanuja (twelfth century A.D.) re-interpreted the Brahman-doctrine to make it harmonize with the newer Vishnu-worship.

* For as long as history records, the principal non-Aryan population of India has been Dravidian. The home of the Dravidians nowadays is the far south of the Indian peninsula; their chief languages (all linguistically related) are Tamil, Telugu, Kanarese, and Malayalam.

But despite the monotheistic tendencies of the *bhakti* sects, most Hindus continued to accept the basic assumptions of the older faith as expressed in the Vedas, the epics, and the law-books. They believed in a cyclic world-process without beginning or end; in world-ages of unfathomable length; in a plurality of worlds; in *karma*—the notion of reward or punishment in another world or another earthly life for one's acts in this life; and in the transmigration of souls, not only from one human body to another, but also into animals and plants. Buddhism—the great rival of Hinduism—was already in decline by the seventh century, and had virtually disappeared from India by the twelfth; while the challenge of Islam, despite the influence of a few sects which sought to synthesize Hindu with Muslim beliefs, led rather to a stiffening of Hindu custom than to its modification.

Introduction to the Puranas

The Puranas are a group of popular religious books—generally reckoned as eighteen in number—which relate a variety of myths and legends about the Hindu gods. In many instances they merely repeat, with variations, stories which already appear in the Vedas, the *Mahabharata,* or the *Ramayana.* But in contrast to these older texts, the Puranas concentrate upon a few selected divinities—especially Vishnu and Shiva—and add new tales to illustrate the power and mercy of those gods. Many Puranas also include extensive descriptions of the leading rites and observances directed to the god in question and prescribe ceremonies, prayers, and invocations for his worship. Ancient Indian sources list the subject matter of the Puranas as follows: (1) original creation; (2) secondary creation, meaning the rise and destruction of worlds; (3) genealogies of the gods; (4) reigns of the Manus—the law-givers who inaugurate each new era on earth; and (5) histories of the solar and lunar deities and their human descendants. Not every Purana includes all of these themes, though each contains some of them.

The evident purpose of the Puranas is religious instruction. But whereas only selected persons were allowed to study the Vedas, the Puranas could be read or heard by anyone, including women and members of the lowest social classes. Their dates of composition are difficult to determine precisely (the word "Purana" means old). Certainly much of their content is very ancient, though no Purana in its present form antedates the Gupta dynasty (A.D. 320-480). Their style is generally straightforward and easy; the form is dialogue. The Puranas are popular rather than esoteric religious treatises; and many of the legends they record were also transmitted by word of mouth among the illiterate Indian masses.

FROM THE VISHNU PURANA

Krishna and the Milkmaids

[Unquestionably the most popular avatar of Vishnu is the god Krishna, who is the subject of a vast religious literature in India. In the most ancient versions of the legend Krishna is a hero-god—the destroyer of wicked kings and demons; the adviser to the Pandavas in the great war recounted in the *Mahabharata;* Arjuna's divine charioteer in the *Bhagavad Gita.* In another of his aspects he is depicted as a lovable child-god; in still another he is a divine youth, brought up among herdsmen, who performs many miracles and pranks.

In this latter, pastoral form Krishna is pictured as sporting with the wives and daughters of the cowherds, calling them with his flute to dance with him in the moonlight. His love for these milkmaids and their utter devotion to him—though to all outward appearances purely erotic in nature—is invariably interpreted in India as symbolic of God's love for the human soul and the soul's devotion to its God.*]

CHAPTER XIII

The cowherds said to Krishna, whom they had seen holding up [the mountain] Govardhana: "We have been preserved, together with our cattle, from a great peril, by your supporting the mountain (above us). But this is very astonishing child's play, unsuitable to the condition of a herdsman; and all thy

From H. H. Wilson, trans., *The Vishnu Purana,* London: Trübner & Co., 1868, Vol. IV, pp. 322-31, and Vol. III, pp. 217-21.

* Jews and Christians interpret the love-poetry of the *Song of Solomon* (*Song of Songs*) in the Old Testament in the same way.

actions are those of a god. Tell us what is the meaning of all this . . . our minds are filled with amazement. Assuredly, we repose at the feet of Hari [Krishna], O thou of unbounded might. For, having witnessed thy power, we cannot believe thee to be a man. . . . The deeds that thou has wrought, which all the gods would have attempted in vain; thy boyhood, and thy prowess; thy lowly birth amongst us,—are contradictions that fill us with doubt, whenever we think of them. Yet, reverence be to thee, whether thou be a god or a demon, or an earth-spirit [Yaksha] or a celestial musician [Gandharva], or whatever we may deem thee; for thou art our friend." When they had ended, Krishna remained silent for some time, as if hurt and offended, and then replied to them: "Herdsmen, if you are not ashamed of my relationship; if I have merited your praise; what occasion is there for you to engage in any discussion (concerning me)? If you have (any) regard for me; if I have deserved your praise; then be satisfied to know that I am your kinsman. I am neither god nor earth-spirit nor celestial musician nor enemy of the gods [Danava]. I have been born your relative; and you must not think differently of me." Upon receiving this answer, the cowherds held their peace, and went into the woods, leaving Krishna apparently displeased.

But Krishna, observing the clear sky, bright with the autumnal moon, and the air perfumed with the fragrance of the wild water-lily, in whose buds the clustering bees were murmuring their songs, felt inclined to join with the milkmaids [Gopis] in sport. Accordingly, he and [his brother] Rama commenced singing sweet low strains in various measures, such as the women loved; and they, as soon as they heard the melody, quitted their homes, and hastened to meet [Krishna], the foe of [the demon] Madhu. One damsel gently sang an accompaniment to his song; another attentively listened to his melody. One, calling out upon his name, then shrunk abashed; whilst another, more bold, and instigated by affection, pressed close to his side. One, as she came forward, beheld some of the seniors (of the family), and dared not venture forth, contenting herself with meditating on Krishna with closed eyes and entire devotion, by which, immediately, all acts of merit were effaced by rapture, and all sin was expiated by regret at not beholding him; and others again, reflecting upon the cause of the world in the form of the supreme Brahma, obtained final emancipation by their sighing. Thus surrounded by the milkmaids, Krishna thought the lovely moonlight night of autumn propitious to the Rasa-dance.[1]

Many of the milkmaids imitated the different actions of Krishna, . . . and beguiled their sorrow[2] by mimicking his sports. Looking down upon the ground, one damsel calls to her friend, as the light downy hair upon her body stands erect (with joy), and the lotuses of her eyes expand: "See, here are the marks of Krishna's feet, as he has gone along sportively, and left the impressions of the banner, the thunderbolt, and the goad. What lovely maiden has been his companion, inebriate with passion, as her irregular footmarks testify? Here Krishna has gathered flowers from on high; for we see alone the impressions of the tips of his feet. Here a nymph has sat down with him, ornamented with flowers, fortunate in having propitiated Vishnu in a prior existence. Having left her in an arrogant mood, because he had offered her flowers, [Krishna] the son of Nanda has gone by this road. See, unable to follow him with equal steps, his associate has here tripped along upon her toes, and holding his hand, the damsel has passed, as is evident from the uneven and intermingled footsteps. But the rogue has merely taken her hand, and left her neglected; for here the paces indicate the path of a person in despair. Undoubtedly, he promised that he would quickly come again; for here are his own footsteps returning with speed. Here he has entered the thick forest, impervious to the rays of the moon; and his steps can be traced no further." Hopeless, then, of beholding Krishna, the milkmaids returned and repaired to the banks of the Yamuna [River], where they sang his songs; and presently they beheld the preserver of the three worlds, with a smiling aspect, hastening towards them. On which one exclaimed "Krishna! Krishna!" unable to articulate anything else; another affected to contract her

1. This is danced by men and women holding hands, going around in a circle, and singing.

2. I.e., jealousy at not being singled out by Krishna for special attention.

forehead with frowns, as drinking, with the bees of her eyes, the lotus of the face of Hari [Krishna]; another, closing her eyelids, contemplated his form internally, as if engaged in an act of devotion.

Then Madhava [Krishna], coming amongst them, conciliated some with soft speeches, some with gentle looks; and some he took by the hand: and the illustrious deity sported with them in the stations of the dance. As each of the milkmaids, however, attempted to keep in one place, close to the side of Krishna, the circle of the dance could not be constructed; and he, therefore, took each by the hand, and when their eyelids were shut by the effects of such touch, the circle was formed. Then proceeded the dance, to the music of their clashing bracelets, and songs that celebrated, in suitable strain, the charms of the autumnal season. Krishna sang of the moon of autumn,—a mine of gentle radiance; but the nymphs repeated the praises of Krishna alone. At times, one of them, wearied by the revolving dance, threw her arms, ornamented with tinkling bracelets, round the neck of the destroyer of Madhu [Krishna]; another, skilled in the art of singing his praises, embraced him. The drops of perspiration from the arms of Hari [Krishna] were like fertilizing rain, which produced a crop of down upon the temples of the milkmaids. Krishna sang the strain that was appropriate to the dance. The milkmaids repeatedly exclaimed "Bravo, Krishna!" to his song. When leading, they followed him; when returning they encountered him; and, whether he went forwards or backwards, they ever attended on his steps. Whilst frolicking thus, they considered every instant without him a myriad of years; and prohibited (in vain) by husbands, fathers, brothers, they went forth at night to sport with Krishna, the object of their affection.

Thus, the illimitable being, the benevolent remover of all imperfections, assumed the character of a youth amongst the females of the herdsmen of [the district of] Vraja; pervading their natures and that of their lords by his own essence, all-diffusive like the wind. For even as the elements of ether, fire, earth, water, and air are comprehended in all creatures, so also is he everywhere present, and in all.

The Reincarnation of Shatadhanu

CHAPTER XVIII

[The following tale, while evidently intended as propaganda against Buddhists or Jains, serves incidentally to illustrate Hindu notions of reincarnation and wifely faithfulness.]

It is related that there was formerly a king named Shatadhanu, whose wife Shaibya was (a woman) of great virtue. She was devoted to her husband, benevolent, sincere, pure, adorned with every female excellence, with humility and discretion. The Raja and his wife daily worshipped the god of gods, Janardana [Vishnu], with pious meditations, oblations to fire, prayers, gifts, fasting, and every other mark of entire faith and exclusive devotion. On one occasion, when they had fasted during the full moon of [the month of] Karttika, and had bathed in the Ganges River, they beheld a heretic[3] approach them as they came up from the water. This heretic was the friend of the Raja's military preceptor. The Raja, out of respect to the latter, entered into conversation with the heretic; but not so did the princess. Reflecting that she was observing a fast, she turned from him and cast her eyes up to the sun. On their arrival at home, the husband and wife, as usual, performed the worship of Vishnu in accordance with the [prescribed] ritual. After a time the Raja died, triumphant over his enemies; and the princess ascended the funeral-pile of her husband.[4]

In consequence of the fault committed by Shatadhanu, by speaking to an infidel when he was engaged in a solemn fast, he was born again as a dog. His wife was born as the daughter of the Raja of Kashi, with a knowledge of the events of her preexistence, accomplished in every science (*vijnana*), and endowed with every virtue. Her father was anxious to give her in marriage to some suitable husband: but she constantly opposed his design, and prevented the king from accomplishing

3. I.e., a Buddhist or Jain.

4. The devoted Hindu wife was supposed to commit suicide in this fashion (called *sati* or *suttee*) after her husband's death.

her nuptials. With the eye of divine intelligence, she knew that her own husband had been reborn as a dog. Going once to the city of Vaidisha, she saw the dog and recognized her former lord in him. Knowing that the animal was her husband, she placed upon his neck the bridal garland, accompanying it with the marriage-rites and prayers: but he, eating the delicate food presented to him, expressed his delight after the fashion of his species. At this she was much ashamed, and bowing reverently to him, thus spake to her degraded spouse: "Recall to memory, illustrious prince, the ill-timed politeness on account of which you have been born as a dog, and are now fawning upon me. In consequence of speaking to a heretic, after bathing in a sacred river, you have been condemned to this abject birth. Do you not remember it?" Thus reminded, the Raja recollected his former condition, and was lost in thought, and felt deep humiliation. With a broken spirit, he went forth from the city, and, falling dead in the desert, was born anew as a jackal. In the course of the following year the princess knew what had happened, and went to the mountain Kolahala to seek for her husband. Finding him there, the lovely daughter of the king of the earth said to her lord, thus disguised as a jackal: "Dost thou not remember, O king, the circumstance of conversing with a heretic, which I called to thy recollection, when thou wast a dog?" The Raja, thus addressed, knew that what the princess had spoken was true, and thereupon desisted from food, and died. He then became a wolf; but his blameless wife knew it, and came to him in the lonely forest, and awakened his remembrance of his original state. . . . The king next became a peacock, which the princess took to herself, and petted and fed constantly, with such food as is agreeable to birds of its class.

The king of Kashi at that time instituted the solemn sacrifice of a horse. In the ablutions with which it terminated, the princess caused her peacock to be bathed; also bathing herself: and she then reminded Shatadhanu how he had been successively born as various animals. On recollecting this he resigned his life. He was then born as the son of a person of distinction. As the princess now assented to the wishes of her father to see her wedded, the king of Kashi caused it to be made known that she would elect a bridegroom from those who should present themselves as suitors for her hand. When the election took place the princess made choice of her former lord, who appeared amongst the candidates, and again invested him with the character of her husband. They lived happily together; and, upon her father's decease Shatadhanu ruled over the country of Videha.

FROM THE AGNI PURANA

Places of Pilgrimage

CHAPTER CIX

[In medieval India, just as in medieval Europe, pilgrimages to sacred places were a popular means of gaining religious merit.]

[Agni] the fire god said:—Now I shall describe the greatness of all the sacred pools and places which people resort to in India. A man who has perfect control over the doings of his hands and feet, and who has got ample education, practised penances, secured a good name in the world, and has mastered his own mind, is fit to start on a pilgrimage to the sanctuaries mentioned above. A pilgrim who has refrained from taking alms, lives on a spare diet, who has put his passions and propensities under a healthy curb, and becomes absolved of all sins, attains the merit of performing all sacrifice by resorting to a sacred place or attains the same merit without pilgrimage if he observes a fast for three consecutive days.

A person who does not make a gift of gold, cows, etc., at a sacred place takes birth as an indigent pauper in his next existence. A man attains the same merit by visiting a sacred place as by performing a sacrifice.

O Brahmin, [the lake] Pushkara[1] is the greatest of all sacred places in respect of sanctity and merit. A man should dwell at

From Manmatha Nath Dutt, trans., *Agni Puranam,* Calcutta: H. C. Das, Elysium Press, 1903, Vol. I, pp. 437-38, 440, 443.

1. Near the modern city of Ajmer in north central India.

least three nights within its holy precincts. O thou, twice-born one,[2] ten millions of sacred places are in Pushkara. The god Brahma accompanied by all the gods lives in that great sanctum. The sages (*munis*) resort to the place with the most willing heart, and the *devas* (gods) attained the ends of their beings on the banks of that sacred pool. A bather in the waters of Pushkara attains the merit of a hundred horse-sacrifices, by worshipping the demigods (*pitris*) and the gods on its banks. A man who doles out rice on its banks on the moon-light night of the month of Karttika becomes absolved of all sins and goes to the region of Brahma. O Brahmin, Pushkara is difficult to get at and very austere is the penance which is practised in Pushkara. Hard it is to dole out alms and charities in Pushkara, and the articles are exceptionally hard to procure. A man who lives for a year in Pushkara and repeats his prayer and performs the Shraddha ceremony[3] of his fathers [thereby] assists the souls of his hundred departed spirits from the nether regions. . . .

CHAPTER CX

Thus said [Agni] the god of fire:—Now I shall describe the sanctity of the river Ganges, which imparts to men enjoyment of earthly cheers in this life and salvation in the next. The countries which the Ganges meanders through should be deemed as hallowed grounds. The river Ganges is the earthly door to salvation for men who long for emancipation from this prison house of life. The river Ganges duly worshipped aids, from the nether regions, the two branches of the family of a bather therein. The man who drinks the water of the holy Ganges attains the merit of a thousand sin-expiating rites; and a person enjoys the benefit of performing all the sacrifices by worshipping (bathing in) the river Ganges continuously for a month. The goddess Ganges destroys all sins and gives to her devotees access to all the celestial regions. Continuance amidst the waters of the river Ganges is identical with one's stay in heaven. The blind and the dupes of nature become the rivals of the gods

2. The twice-born were men of the three highest *varnas* who had undergone the ancient rite marking their initiation as full members of their class.
3. A Hindu sacrificial rite.

by bathing in the river Ganges. A man who carries clay dug out of the bed of that hallowed stream becomes free of all sin, and shines as resplendent as the sun god with the native effulgence of his unclouded soul. Hundreds, nay thousands, of impious persons become sinless and pure by seeing, touching, or drinking of the river Ganges or by calling out to the goddess, as "Oh mother Ganges!"

CHAPTER CXII

Said [Agni] the god of fire:—[The holy city of] Benares excels all other sacred pools and places in respect of sanctity, and imparts to its inmates who recite the name of the god Hari [Vishnu] both enjoyment of the sweets of this life and salvation in the next.

[The storm-god] Rudra said:—Benares, which is the sacred abode of the goddess Gouri, is never forsaken by me and by the latter goddess and by those who are bent on working out their own salvation. Any prayer repeated, any penance practised, any offering cast into the sacrificial fire in Benares bears immortal fruit. A man should take up his lodging for good in Benares, after having rubbed off the dust from his feet with a stone slab.

O god, the city of Benares is the most mysterious of all sacred places under my protection. The city extends over a space of two yojanas in the east, and half a yojana (four miles) in the opposite direction. The holy city is washed on its two sides by the rivers Asi and Varuna, and the [making of an] offering, resignation from life, worshipping a god, performing a Shraddha ceremony, and making gifts at this place, lead to salvation and earthly prosperity.

Introduction to Shankara's Hymn to Shiva

Shankara (*c.* A.D. 788-820) is by common consent the greatest of all Indian philosophers. Born a Brahmin of south India, he was raised as a Shivaite, became an ascetic, and wandered widely throughout India preaching his interpretation of the holy scriptures and debating with opponents. His philosophy is founded upon those verses of the Upanishads which speak of Brahman as the undifferentiated world-essence; and he supported his convictions with a wealth of logical subtlety and a complex theory of knowledge. While teaching a strict monism or non-duality (Advaita), he regarded belief in a personal God as a lower form of truth, permissible for those who cannot comprehend the pure Brahman-doctrine.

Because of Shankara's great fame, many compositions have traditionally been attributed to him which may well have emanated from his followers. One such is the ecstatic *Hymn to Shiva*, which is difficult to reconcile in any logical fashion with the philosopher's notion of higher and lower truth. But whoever its author was, the work is a particularly striking example of that *bhakti*-religion prevalent in Shankara's lifetime and afterward. The worshipper of the *Hymn* expresses utter devotion to Shiva, total reliance upon his protection, and fervent hope of a life in paradise hereafter.

SHANKARA: FROM THE HYMN TO SHIVA

1 May this my obeisance be to the two Auspicious Ones (Shiva and his consort Parvati), who constitute the essence of all learning, who wear on the head the crescent-moon as embellishment, who are, each to the other, the fruit of their own respective penances, who confer benefits on the devotees, who make all the three worlds blessed, who appear repeatedly in the heart, and who engender the experience of manifest happiness!

2 O Shambhu[1] (Shiva)! Victory be to the Flood of Shiva-Bliss, which flows from the river of Thy story, removes the dust of sin, courses through the channels of the intellect, yields the destruction of sorrow caused by wandering in *samsara*,[2] and remains in the lake-land of my mind!

3 In my heart do I worship Shiva who is knowable through

From T. M. P. Mahadevan, trans., *Sankara's Hymn to Siva* (*Sivanandalahari*), Madras: Ganesh & Co., 1963, pp. 1-14, 19-21, 35, 37, 41.

1. This title means "source of good fortune."

2. *Samsara* (or *sansara*) denotes the flux of earthly existence, the transient world of phenomena as opposed to eternal Being.

the three Vedas, who is delightful to the heart, who destroyed the three Cities,[3] who is primeval and has three eyes, who looks majestic with a profusion of matted locks,[4] who wears the wriggling snakes as ornaments and bears an antelope, who is the great God, the Divinity, who is gracious to me, who is the lord of souls, and the basic consciousness, who is in the company of His Spouse, and who enacts the ways of the world.

4 Thousands of gods there are in the world who grant puerile benefits; even in my dreams I do not think of following them or of the benefits granted by them. O Shambhu! O Shiva! What I have been for a long time asking for is the worship of Thy lotus-feet, which does not come easily even to those that are near Thee, such as (the gods) Vishnu and Brahma.

5 I am not learned in the Traditional Codes, or in the philosophical texts,[5] in the art of medicine, or in the articulation of the science of portents, poesy or music, or in the ancient lore, or in the technique of mystic formulas, or in the arts of praising, dancing and humouring. How, then, will the kings be pleased with me? O Lord of souls, the omniscient and renowned One! O the all-pervading Lord! Save me, who am a soul, through Thy Grace!

6 Whether it be a pot or lump of clay, or atom, whether it be smoke, fire, or mountain, whether it be cloth or thread—will any of these serve as a remedy for horrible death! You are only straining your throat unnecessarily by logic-chopping! O wise one, hasten to worship the lotus-feet of Shambhu, and attain the supreme happiness.

7 O the supreme Shiva! Let my mind stay at Thy lotus feet; let my speech be engaged in uttering Thy praise; my hands in Thy worship; my sense of hearing in listening to Thy story; my intellect in meditation on Thee; and my eyes in looking at Thy splendid form! This being so, through which other sense-organs will I learn other texts?

3. This refers to a tale in the *Mahabharata*, in which Shiva destroys three castles occupied by demons.

4. The matted locks (uncombed hair) are characteristic of ascetics; Shiva was their patron deity.

5. If Shankara, the great philosopher, is the true author of this *Hymn* he is being modest.

8 O Great God! O Lord of souls! Just as one perceives mother-of-pearl as silver, glass-bead as gem, water mixed with flour as milk, and mirage as water, so also the fool worships what is other than Thee under the delusion that it is deity, not contemplating Thee, the Lord, with the mind.

13 O Lord of souls! It is but proper that Thou shouldst protect me through Thy great compassion—me who am blind, and who revolve foolishly in the essenceless *samsara* that is far away from one's real goal. To Thee, who can be poorer in spirit than I? And, to me, who can be a better expert than Thou, in protecting the poor and in offering refuge in all the three worlds?

14 O Lord of souls! Art not Thou, who art the Lord, the greatest friend of the poor. And, of them, I am the foremost. Is not this, then, the relationship between us? O Shiva! All my transgressions should be forgiven by Thee alone. Even through effort, protection should be given to me. This, indeed, is the way pursued by relations.

24 When shall I live in Kailasa (the abode of Shiva), in the Hall of gold and emeralds, in the company of the divine attendants, in the presence of Shambhu, and with folded hands gleaming on my head, addressing thus "O the all-pervading One! O, the One with the Devi (goddess); O Master! O the supreme Shiva! Protect me!" and spend in happiness aeons of Brahma (-day)s[6] as if they were seconds?

26 O Mountain-Dweller![7] Beholding Thee, and holding with my hands Thy gracious Feet, pressing them against my head, eyes, and chest, embracing them, and smelling the sweet scents of the full-blown lotuses, when am I to enjoy the happiness that does not come even to (the god) Brahma and others?

29 O all-pervading One! I worship Thy lotus-feet; I meditate daily on Thee that art supreme; I seek refuge in Thee that art the Lord; through words I beg of Thee alone; cast on me the look of Thy eyes that are full of grace, the look for which the gods have been praying for long. O Shambhu! O World-Teacher! Give to my mind the instruction about happiness!

6. A day of Brahma (or *kalpa*) is reckoned as 4,320 million earthly years.
7. Kailasa, the home of Shiva, was a high mountain.

Introduction to Hindu-Muslim Syncretism

The Muslim conquests beginning in the late twelfth century introduced a new and unassimilable element into the religious life of India. Unlike previous invaders of that country, who became absorbed into the Hindu caste system and adopted the worship of Hindu gods, the Muslims maintained their separate religious identity. Indeed, the rigid monotheism of Islam forms the sharpest possible contrast to the religious diversity of Hinduism, which includes a primitive polytheism and adoration of images side by side with devotional monotheism and the esoteric philosophy of mystic union with Brahman, the world-essence. While Hindus regarded Muslims as unclean barbarians who polluted the soil of India, Muslims thought of Hindus as idolators; and the divergent religious practices of the two faiths gave rise to mutual hostility.

But despite religious antagonisms, a degree of mutual accommodation between Hindus and Muslims in India could scarcely be avoided. Muslims in the villages began to adopt certain Hindu social customs, and in turn were treated by Hindus as merely another caste. In some areas of India local sects arose which combined Hindu and Muslim rituals in rather indiscriminate fashion. From about the mid-fifteenth century, a few religious thinkers began to encourage the idea that the fundamental beliefs of both Hinduism and Islam are identical. This notion was made plausible by the undoubted monotheistic tendencies of Hindu *bhakti*-religion after the sixth or seventh century. In practice, the syncretists generally borrowed the Hindu elements in their thought from Vishnu-worship. They taught the existence of a single God whom they called by both Muslim and Vishnuite names; they denied the efficacy of ritual, rejected the Hindu cult of images, and refused to respect the distinctions of caste. Though none of the syncretistic sects ever attracted more than a tiny minority of the Indian population, they exercised an influence far beyond the circle of their own immediate adherents.

The most successful creators of syncretistic religions were Kabir (1440-1518), a simple Muslim weaver of Benares, and Nanak (1469-

1539), the Hindu founder of the community of Sikhs (i.e., "disciples"). In the best tradition of Indian holy men, both were ascetic wanderers who attracted many followers through their personal sanctity and magnetism. Kabir, though a Muslim by upbringing, became a pupil of the Hindu reformer and saint Ramananda, who was an advocate of *bhakti*-worship. Kabir's own religion combined various Hindu devotional practices with the Muslim's total submission to a single God. He recorded his teachings in a number of works in the vernacular tongue—mostly rhymed verses in which he spoke to himself. The sect he founded, though small, continues to exist even nowadays in India; and his verses are beloved by many who fail to share his religious views.

Among Kabir's spiritual successors was Nanak, the first Guru (i.e., Teacher) of the Sikhs. His aim was to found a faith that both Hindus and Muslims could accept; and like Kabir, he insisted on the unity of God, the abolition of caste, and the uselessness of religious ceremonies. Nanak wandered through all of India preaching his doctrine and even made the pilgrimage to Mecca, disguised as a Muslim. Famous in his own lifetime as a learned and holy man, he founded a sect which became of considerable importance in the modern religious and political history of India. Though Sikhism was in origin a peaceful religious movement, under Nanak's successors it evolved into a military brotherhood which made war on the Mughal government, and in the early nineteenth century established an independent state in the Punjab. Even today in India the Sikhs remain a separate group, marked off from other Indians by their long hair and distinctive garb, though many of them now describe themselves as Hindus and neglect to observe the Sikh sacraments.

FROM THE POEMS OF KABIR

I

O servant, where dost thou seek Me?
Lo! I am beside thee.

From Rabindranath Tagore, *One Hundred Poems of Tabir,* Evelyn Underhill, trans. London: The India Society, 1914, nos. I, II, III, IX, XLII, XLV.

I am neither in temple nor in mosque: I am neither in Kaaba[1] nor in Kailash:[2]
Neither am I in rites and ceremonies, nor in Yoga and renunciation.
If thou art a true seeker, thou shalt at once see Me: thou shalt meet Me in a moment of time.
Kabir says, "O Sadhu! God is the breath of all breath."

II

It is needless to ask of a saint the caste to which he belongs;
For the priest, the warrior, the tradesman, and all the thirty-six castes, alike are seeking for God.
It is but folly to ask what the caste of a saint may be;
The barber has sought God, the washerwoman, and the carpenter—
Even Raidas was a seeker after God.
The Rishi Swapacha was a tanner[3] by caste.
Hindus and Moslems alike have achieved that End, where remains no mark of distinction.

III

O friend! hope for Him whilst you live, know whilst you live, understand whilst you live: for in life deliverance abides.
If your bonds be not broken whilst living, what hope of deliverance in death?
It is but an empty dream, that the soul shall have union with Him because it has passed from the body:
If He is found now, He is found then,
If not, we do but go to dwell in the City of Death.
If you have union now, you shall have it hereafter.
Bathe in the truth, know the true Guru, have faith in the true Name!

1. The small stone building at Mecca which contains the Black Stone sacred to all Muslims.

2. A famous Hindu temple cut out of rock, located at Ellore in Hyderabad state and dedicated to the god Shiva.

3. Since Hinduism forbade the killing of animals, the profession of tanner was one of the lowest conceivable.

Kabir says: "It is the Spirit of the quest which helps; I am the slave of this Spirit of the quest."

IX

O how may I ever express that secret word?
O how can I say He is not like this, and He is like that?
If I say that He is within me, the universe is ashamed:
If I say that He is without me, it is falsehood.
He makes the inner and the outer worlds to be indivisibly one;
The conscious and the unconscious, both are His footstools.
He is neither manifest nor hidden, he is neither revealed nor unrevealed:
There are no words to tell that which He is.

XLII

There is nothing but water at the holy bathing places; and I know that they are useless, for I have bathed in them.
The images are all lifeless, they cannot speak; I know, for I have cried aloud to them.
The Purana and the Koran are mere words; lifting up the curtain, I have seen.
Kabir gives utterance to the words of experience; and he knows very well that all other things are untrue.

LXV

O brother! when I was forgetful, my true Guru showed me the Way.
Then I left off all rites and ceremonies, I bathed no more in the holy water:
Then I learned that it was I alone who was mad, and the whole world beside me was sane; and I had disturbed these wise people.
From that time forth I knew no more how to roll in the dust in obeisance:
I do not ring the temple bell:
I do not set the idol on its throne:

I do not worship the image with flowers.
It is not the austerities that mortify the flesh which are pleasing to the Lord,
When you leave off your clothes and kill your senses, you do not please the Lord:
The man who is kind and who practises righteousness, who remains passive amidst the affairs of the world, who considers all creatures on earth as his own self,
He attains the Immortal Being, the true God is ever with him.
Kabir says: "He attains the true Name whose words are pure, and who is free from pride and conceit."

FROM THE HYMNS OF NANAK

1

Pilgrimages, penances, compassion and almsgiving
Bring a little merit, the size of sesame seed.
But he who hears and believes and loves the Name[1]
Shall bathe and be made clean
In a place of pilgrimage within him.

All goodness is Thine, O Lord, I have none;
Though without performing good deeds
None can aspire to adore Thee.
Blessed Thou the Creator and the Manifestation,
Thou art the word, Thou art the primal Truth and Beauty,
And Thou the heart's joy and desire.

When in time, in what age, in what day of the month or week
In what season and in what month did'st Thou create the world?
The Pundits[2] do not know or they would have written it in the Puranas;

From Trilochan Singh *et al.*, trans., *Selections from the Sacred Writings of the Sikhs,* London: George Allen & Unwin, Ltd., 1960, pp. 40, 43-44, 45-46, 76, 77. Reprinted by permission of George Allen & Unwin, Ltd. Numbers of the poems have been supplied by the present editors.

1. I.e., the name of God.
2. Brahmins learned in Hindu religion and law.

The Qazis[3] do not know, or they would have recorded it in the Koran;
Nor do the Yogis know the moment of the day,
Nor the day of the month or the week, nor the month nor the season.
Only God Who made the world knows when He made it.

Then how shall I approach Thee, Lord?
In what words shall I praise Thee?
In what words shall I speak of Thee?
How shall I know Thee?
O Nanak, all men speak of Him, and each would be wiser than the next man;
Great is the Lord, great is His Name,
What He ordaineth, that cometh to pass,
Nanak, the man puffed up with his own wisdom
Will get no honour from God in the life to come.

2

The Vedas proclaim Him,
So do the readers of the Puranas;
The learned speak of Him in many discourses;
Brahma and Indra speak of Him,
Shivas speak of Him, Siddhas speak of Him,[4]
The Buddhas He has created, proclaim Him.

The demons and the gods speak of Him,
Demigods, men, sages and devotees
All try to describe Him;
Many have tried and still try to describe Him;
Many have spoken of Him and departed.

If as many people as lived in all the past
Were now to describe Him each in His own way,
Even then He would not be adequately described.

3. (Also called Cadis or Qadis); experts in the Islamic Sacred Law; judges.
4. Brahma, Indra, and Shiva are all important Hindu deities; the Siddhas are a class of demigods.

The Lord becometh as great as He wishes to be.
If anyone dares to claim that he can describe Him,
Write him down as the greatest fool on earth.

3

Going forth a begging,
Let contentment be thine earnings,
Modesty thy begging bowl,
Smear thy body with ashes of meditation,
Let contemplation of death be thy beggar's rags;

Let thy body be chaste, virginal, clean,
Let faith in God be the staff on which thou leanest;
Let brotherhood with every man on earth
Be the highest aspiration of your Yogic Order.
Know that to subdue the mind
Is to subdue the world.

Hail, all hail unto Him,
Let your greetings be to the Primal God;
Pure and without beginning, changeless,
The same from age to age.

4

Perversity of the soul is like a woman of low caste,
Lack of compassion like a butcher woman;[5]
The desire to find fault with others
Is like a scavenger woman,[5]
The sin of wrath is like an utter outcast;
What use is it to draw a line around your kitchen[6]
If four such vices keep you company.

Make your discipline the practice of truth,

5. Only persons of the most debased castes engaged in such activities as butchering or scavengering.

6. Orthodox Hindus thus enclose their kitchens; if anyone not of the proper caste crosses the line, the food is considered polluted.

Make the square you draw round your kitchen
The practice of virtue;
Make the ceremonial cleansing of your body
The meditation of Holy Name.
Saith Nanak: Those alone shall be deemed good and pure
That walk not in the way of sin.

5

Let compassion be thy mosque,
Let faith be thy prayer mat,
Let honest living be thy Koran,
Let modesty be the rules of observance,
Let piety be the fasts thou keepest;
In such wise strive to become a Moslem:
Right conduct the Kaaba; Truth the Prophet,
Good deeds thy prayer;
Submission to the Lord's Will thy rosary;
Nanak, if this thou do, the Lord will be thy Protector.

Society

Introduction to Sanskrit Poetry

The Sanskrit language bears much the same relation to India as Latin does to medieval Europe. In its oldest known form it was the speech of the Aryan tribes who filtered into north India between *c.* 1500 and 1000 B.C. This "pre-classical" tongue, the language of the *Rig Veda* (earliest of the Vedas), is an elder relative of nearly all the modern languages of Europe.* But as Sanskrit continued to develop through the addition of new words and the loss of certain inflections, doubts arose as to the correct meaning and pronunciation of the older Vedic texts. From the fifth century B.C. onward, a series of grammarians—most notably Panini (late fourth century B.C.)—conducted exhaustive investigations into the ancient sacred writings with the object of preserving their original purity.† Precise and complex rules for correct usage were laid down; and thenceforth the language came to be called "Sanskrit," meaning "perfected" or "refined" in contrast to the "unrefined" spoken dialects (called Prakrits) which developed naturally.

The work of Panini and other linguists resulted in the standardization of Sanskrit grammar, which thenceforth remained unchanged, though additions to the vocabulary of the language continued to be made. The Gupta dynasty (A.D. 320-480) witnessed an enormous efflorescence of Sanskrit literature; and for a thousand years afterward, Sanskrit remained the principal written language of north India for compositions of all sorts. Already in Panini's time Sanskrit had been the lingua franca of Brahmin priests throughout India; from the Gupta period it was that of the governing classes also, until its replacement by Persian in the Muslim states which

* The exceptions are Finnish, Estonian, Hungarian, Turkish, and Basque.

† The Aryans believed that unless the Vedic texts were recited with total accuracy they would have no magical effect, and might even cause harm.

arose after the twelfth century. But Sanskrit was artificial in the sense of being no one's native tongue. It was cultivated only by educated people, who had first learned some vernacular form of speech at home.

The great period of Sanskrit poetry may be calculated as *c.* A.D. 300 to 1200, though the earliest known example of the classical style dates from the first century A.D., and poems of this genre have continued to be written down to the present day. Classical Sanskrit poetry was a highly intellectualized form of art, which developed almost entirely within the entourages of kings and rajas. The poems were designed for recitation or performance either at courts or in small groups of literati. At an early date this poetry became circumscribed by a number of rigid conventions. Various theoretical works were composed on the art of poetry-writing; and most extant Sanskrit authors conform closely to their rules.

The purpose of poetry, according to the theorists, is not to tell a story but to evoke an emotion. Not only each complete poem, but each single verse within it, should exhibit one of about eight accepted moods or "flavors" (*rasa*). These were not the more violent emotions of terror or hate, but quieter sensations like love, anger, mirth, surprise. In sharp contrast to Western poetry, a tragic ending was forbidden. In form, each verse was supposed to contain only four lines of no more than twenty-three syllables and conform to one of about fifty specified metrical patterns.

That poetry could flourish at all under such restrictions is a tribute to the flexibility of the Sanskrit language. Highly inflected, it permits almost any word order, and contains an extraordinary number of synonyms and homonyms. Partly for this reason, one of the principal techniques of Sanskrit verse is suggestion or punning—the careful selection of words not only for their primary meaning, but also for secondary and tertiary connotations. Other types of ornamentation were employed also: simile and metaphor, alliteration and generalization. A striking characteristic of Sanskrit poetry is the fact that persons are seen only as types, not as individuals with unique features; often they are given no names. Perhaps for this reason, true tragedy is unknown in classical Sanskrit literature: the characters lack the capacity for making genuine choices.

Introduction to Vidyakara's Treasury

Vidyakara's *Treasury of Well-Turned Verse* (*Subhashita-ratnakosha*) is an anthology of 1739 Sanskrit verses drawn from a variety of sources: epic and lyric poems, dramas, inscriptions, and religious hymns. Most were composed between A.D. 700 and 1050; all are neatly classified under fifty distinct headings. Vidyakara, the compiler, was a Buddhist monk and scholar of the latter half of the eleventh century. Apparently he lived and worked at the monastery of Jagaddala in Bengal—then an important center of learning—and used the library there in making his choices. Despite this background, his taste is eclectic and predominantly secular: among the subjects of the verses he selected are natural phenomena and the seasons, personality types, earthly fame and praise, and a large variety of amorous situations. Perhaps limited by the contents of the monastery library, he chose primarily from among the poets of eastern India, especially his native Bengal. His *Treasury* includes excerpts from about 250 identifiable authors as well as many who remain anonymous—an indication of the widespread cultivation of Sanskrit poetry in India long after the age of the great Gupta empire.

VIDYAKARA: FROM THE TREASURY OF WELL-TURNED VERSE

SHIVA[1]

Rising up as in the monsoon rains,
pouring with Ganges water[2] from a thousand streams,

From Daniel H. H. Ingalls, trans., *An Anthology of Sanskrit Court Poetry: Vidyakara's "Subhasitaratnakosa"* (Harvard Oriental Series, Vol. 44), Cambridge, Mass.: Harvard University Press, 1968, nos. 63, 346, 440, 687, 784, 830, 1019, 1053, 1081, 1170, 1213, 1270, 1312, 1320, 1321. Reprinted by permission of Harvard University Press.

Titles at left are the headings under which the poems that follow are classified.

1. One of the two chief gods of popular Hinduism.
2. "Bearer of the Ganges" was one of Shiva's titles.

terrible from the unseasonable heat
of his swiftly shaken forehead-eye,[3]
noisy with the slapping of the wind
emitted from the hollows of its skulls,[4]
may this cloud, the head of kindly Shiva,
bring you kindliness.

ADOLESCENCE

She longs to hear of gambling games of lovers;
in learning double meanings takes delight.
She holds a mirror ever in her hand,
and acts the teacher to her crowd of friends.
Anxious to copy grown-up women's conduct,
she's yet too shy with youth.
There is a charming progress of coquetry
as womanhood begins.

YOUNG WOMAN

Had the Creator once seen her he would never have let her go,
this gazelle-eyed beauty
with face as golden as saffron-paste.
Again, had he closed his eyes he could never have made such features.
From which we see
that the Buddhist doctrine is best:
that all is uncreated.

THE WOMAN OFFENDED

You've paid no heed to anything your friends have said,
and as for me who lie before your feet
you have not touched me even with your toe.
Hard-hearted lady, this vicious vow of silence
is not the way to keep one's proud position
but the way to lose a servant.

3. Shiva had three eyes; from his forehead eye the heat of creation was emitted.

4. Shiva is often depicted wearing a necklace of skulls; he is the god of death.

THE LOVER SEPARATED FROM HIS MISTRESS

If my absent bride were but a pond,
her eyes the waterlilies and her face the lotus,
her brows the rippling waves, her arms the lotus stems;
then might I dive into the water of her loveliness
and cool of limb escape the mortal pain
exacted by the flaming fire of love.

THE WANTON

My husband is no easy fool,
the moon is bright, the way is mire
and people love a scandal;
yet it is hard to break a lover's promise.
Driven by such thoughts, a certain beauty
in going to a meeting set for love
starts from her house door many times
only to turn back.

ALLEGORICAL EPIGRAMS

Go forth, oh perfect pearl, and make a house resplendent.
Bring to full fruit
your virtues and the necklace of a king.
Why pass your life unnoticed in an oyster-shell?
The sea is wide and deep;
who is there here will know your worth?

You were born on the heights of Malabar,[5]
yet woodsmen found you and brought you to a distant land
where men have ground you into scented ointment.
Grieve not, sandalwood, my friend;
it is your virtues have undone you.

We only asked a little water from you, ocean,
for we were weary and your wealth is great.
Why then toss high your waves in anger?
Have mercy! We take our leave. On every side
we can find peaceful lotus ponds aplenty.

5. The southwest coastal region of India.

CHARACTERIZATION

The religious student carries a small and torn umbrella;
his various possessions are tied about his waist;
he has tucked *bilva* leaves in his topknot;
his neck is drawn, his belly frightening from its sunkenness.
Weary with much walking, he somehow stills
the pain of aching feet and goes at evening
to the brahmin's house to chop his wood.

THE GOOD MAN

To ask no favors from the wicked;
to beg not from a friend whose means are small;
to be in manner kindly and correct,
in conduct spotless even at the hour of death;
to keep one's stature in misfortune
and follow in the footsteps of the great:
in these rules, though hard to travel as a sword blade,
good men require no instruction.

THE VILLAIN

It is beyond the reach of charms,
beyond the skill of born physicians,
beyond ambrosia's cure,
so strange and secret are its workings.
Clearly it took no less an intellect than God's
to make for the confusion of the world
a plague so contrary to nature
as is a villain.

POVERTY AND MISERS

When the rain pours down on the decrepit house
she dries the flooded barley grits
and quiets the yelling children;
she bails out water with a potsherd
and saves the bedding straw.
With a broken winnowing basket on her head
the poor man's wife is busy everywhere.

Often the pauper's children go to others' houses.
With their little hands leaning against the doorways,
hungry, but with voices hushed by shame,
they cast half glances at those who eat within.

You gave me feet to tire of travel,
a wife to leave me, a voice for begging
and a body for decrepitude.
If you never are ashamed, oh God,
do you not at last grow weary of your gifts?

Social Commentary in Prose: Introduction

While Sanskrit classical poetry and drama are highly refined forms of literary expression, capable of appealing only to educated persons, an extensive folk literature also existed in traditional India. Handed on by word of mouth from generation to generation, many popular tales and anecdotes eventually were written down in classical Sanskrit prose, whereby they have come down to us.

All such stories contain a strong element of moralizing, in which religion and custom are virtually inseparable. Especially prominent is the notion—already enunciated in the *Bhagavad Gita*—that each person's supreme obligation is to perform the duties pertaining to his social class, sex, and stage of life. Class status, in turn, was religiously justified as being the consequence of the person's deeds in previous existences, as determined by the law of *karma*. Even the precise details of one's duty in daily life were regarded as divinely ordained if based on prescriptions found in the ancient and holy Vedas.

Indian popular literature also includes a strong supernatural component. Gods and goddesses intermingle freely with men and women, and take a direct interest in the latters' affairs. The course of events is frequently ascribed to magic or to divine intervention. Moreover, even the human characters in these stories are not drawn from life: on the whole, they are types rather than real people. The realistic, descriptive novel or play, as found in China or the West, is lacking in traditional Indian culture.

Nonetheless, from the vast quantity of extant popular literature, a fairly coherent picture of Indian society emerges. The stories unquestionably illustrate the social ideas of their authors, e.g. the importance of male progeny; the loyalty and submissiveness expected of wives; the importance of religious ceremonies; the respect owed to Brahmins. While admittedly didactic in purpose, these tales still express ideals which innumerable Hindus must have cherished in their real lives. Finally, amid the moralizing and the fantastic occurrences, Indian popular literature often makes reference to actual customs and conditions, thereby providing valuable information concerning Indian society in the middle period.

Introduction to the Adventures of Vikrama

The *Adventures of Vikrama* (*Vikrama-carita*) is a popular collection of moral tales revolving about an ancient king named Vikrama. Scholarly opinion is divided as to his identity. He may have been the monarch who founded the Vikrama era of time-reckoning, which began in 58 B.C., but more likely he was Chandragupta II (r. *c.* A.D. 375-413), the powerful ruler of the Gupta dynasty, who bore the title of Vikramaditya ("sun of prowess"). In any event, the Vikrama of our storybook is a figure of pure legend. He is represented as an exemplary ruler, whose generosity and unselfishness set a high standard of conduct for later kings to follow.

In form the *Adventures* consists of a long frame-story followed by thirty-two separate story sequences, each composed of a series of related incidents leading one into the other. They embody a kind of popular wisdom, in which the narrative serves merely as a framework for drawing moral lessons. Frequently the tales are rambling and disconnected: their plots are either weak or non-existent. Though recorded in classical Sanskrit, the stories themselves represent popular notions of morality, and undoubtedly originated within the centuries-old store of folk-wisdom transmitted orally among the common people.

According to the frame-story, King Vikrama possessed a magic throne which was discovered many years afterward by King Bhoja, a ruler whose virtues are described as equal to those of Vikrama himself. Each of the story-sequences was told to Bhoja by one of the thirty-two statuettes supporting Vikrama's throne. This King Bhoja is a definite historical figure (r. A.D. 840-890), a member of the powerful Gurjara dynasty which controlled large areas of northwest

India in the ninth and tenth centuries A.D. In view of its praise of Bhoja, the *Adventures* may conceivably have been written by one of the king's own panegyrists. But a more likely date is the twelfth or thirteenth century, when Bhoja, like Vikrama himself, had been transformed by the popular memory into an ideal monarch-type: glorious, just, and enlightened.

FROM THE ADVENTURES OF KING VIKRAMA

The Fruit That Gave Immortality

In this city there was a certain brahman, who knew all the books of science, and had an exceptional acquaintance with charm-textbooks; yet he was a pauper. By the performance of incantations he propitiated the Queen of the Earth [Parvati]. She, being propitiated, said to the brahman: "Brahman, choose a wish." The brahman said: "O goddess, if you are pleased with me, then make me immune to old age and death." Then the goddess gave him a divine fruit, and said: "My son, eat this fruit, and you shall be immune to old age and death."

Then the brahman took that fruit, and went back to his own house; and when he had bathed and performed divine service, before he ate the fruit this thought occurred to his mind: "How now! After all I am a pauper; if I become immortal who will be helped by me? No, even if I live a very long time I am bound to do nothing but go a-begging. Now even a short life, if a man be a benefactor of others, amounts to something. Moreover, he who lives but a very short time, blest with intelligence and high position and such advantages, his life it is that bears fruit. And thus it is said:

1. Fruitful shall be the life of a man who lives only for a short time, but endowed with renowned wisdom, manliness, high rank, and such qualities, say the righteous. As for

From Franklin Edgerton, trans., *Vikrama's Adventures* (Harvard Oriental Series, Vol. 26), Cambridge, Mass.: Harvard University Press, 1926, pp. 6-7, 67-68, 228-30. Reprinted by permission of Harvard University Press.

Titles of these anecdotes have been supplied by the present editors.

(merely) living a long time, even a crow does that, devouring scraps of food that are thrown to him. And so:

2. Real life is that which is lived by glorious and righteous men. A crow may live for a long time, by gulping morsels of rotten food. Moreover:

3. He truly lives through whose life many (others) live; does not even a crane fill his *own* belly with his beak? Moreover:

4. A thousand times insignificant are those who merely fill their bellies in the business of their own support; he whose own interest is the interest of others, that man alone is a leader of the just. Thus the underworld-fire drinks up the ocean to fill its own insatiable belly; but the cloud (does so) to relieve the heat of the earth accumulated by the summer.

5. A man who effects no useful end either by his caste, his deeds, or his virtues, his birth serves only for a name, like an accidentally-formed word.

If with this idea in mind this fruit should be given to the king, he, being immune to old age and death, would be a righteous benefactor to all the four castes." Accordingly he took the fruit and came into the king's presence, and first recited this blessing:

6. "May he [Shiva] who wears a garland of snakes, and also he [Vishnu] who assumes a yellow-clad form—I say, may Hara and Hari [Shiva and Vishnu] bless you, O king!"

And giving the fruit into the king's hands he said: "O king, eat this matchless fruit, which was obtained by the favor of a goddess's boon, and you shall be immune to old age and death."

So the king took that fruit, and gave him many grants of land, and dismissed him.

A Brahman Desires a Son

While Vikramaditya was king there dwelt in that city a certain brahman, who was learned in all branches of knowledge and adorned with all virtues, but had no offspring. One time his wife said to him: "My dear lord, the learned in tradition say that a householder cannot get along [or, "cannot go to heaven"] without a son. And so:

1. There is no help [or, "no going to heaven"] for a man who has no son; paradise is never, never for him. Therefore only after seeing his son's face should a man become an ascetic.

2. The moon is the light of night; the sun is the light by day; religion is the light of the three worlds; a good son is the light of the family. And so:

3. The glory of an elephant is his passion; of water, lotuses; of night, the full moon; of a woman, her good character; of a horse, his swiftness; of a house, constant festivals; of speech, good grammar; of rivers, pairs of mating swans; of a council chamber, wise men; of a family, a good son; of the earth, a king; of the three worlds, the sun."

The brahman replied: "My dear, you have spoken truly; but though wealth may be obtained by great effort, and knowledge also by obeying a teacher, glory and offspring cannot be obtained without propitiating the Supreme Lord [Shiva]. And it is said:

4. If a longing for endless happiness makes itself felt in the heart, let one only make a firm resolve and worship constantly the Lord of Bhavani [Shiva]."

His wife answered: "My lord, there is no one more learned than you; you know all things. So undertake some service or the like to win the favor of the Supreme Lord." He replied: "My dear, what you say is quite reasonable, and I assent to your suggestion. Since:

5. Wise counsel should be heeded even if it comes from a child, while a man of judgment should never accept bad advice, even though it comes from an old man."

So speaking the brahman undertook the Rudra-rite, in order to win the favor of the Supreme Lord. One night after that the Supreme Lord appeared to the brahman in a dream, wearing his (characteristic) hair-braid and crest, in his bull-drawn chariot, with his consort sitting on his left thigh, and said: "Brahman, perform a *pradoshavrata* ["evening rite," a Shivaite ceremony]; by performing this rite you shall obtain a son." In the morning the brahman told of his dream before the elders. They said: "Brahman, this dream will come true. And it is said in the Book of Dreams:

6. A man shall make his decision in accordance with whatever is said in dreams by a god, a brahman, a guru, cows, ancestors, or bearers of lingas [signs of Shiva].

Upon performing this rite you shall beget a son." When the brahman heard their words he instituted a *pradoshavrata,* on the thirteenth day of the bright half of the month Margashirsa, on a Saturday, observing the rules prescribed in the ritual books. The Supreme Lord became propitiated thru the performance of that rite, and gave him a son.

The Clever Magician

Once King Vikrama, attended by all his vassal princes, had ascended his throne. At this time a certain magician came in, and blessing him with the words "Live forever!" said: "Sire, you are skilled in all the arts; many magicians have come into your presence and exhibited their tricks. So today be so good as to behold an exhibition of my dexterity." The king said: "I have not time now; it is the time to bathe and eat. Tomorrow I will behold it." So on the morrow the juggler came into the king's assembly as a stately man, with a mighty beard and glorious countenance, holding a sword in his hand, and accompanied by a lovely woman; and he bowed to the king. Then the ministers who were present, seeing the stately man, were astonished, and asked: "O hero, who are you, and whence do you come?" He said: "I am a servant of Great Indra; I was cursed once by my lord, and was cast down to earth; and now I dwell here. And this is my wife. Today a great battle has begun between the gods and the Daityas [demons], so I am going thither. This King Vikramaditya treats other men's wives as his sisters, so before going to the battle I wish to leave my wife with him." Hearing this the king also was greatly amazed. And the man left his wife with the king and delivered her over to him, and sword in hand flew up into heaven. Then a great and terrible shouting was heard in the sky: "Ho there, kill them, kill them, smite them, smite them!" were the words they heard. And all the people who sat in the court, with upturned faces, gazed in amazement. After this, when a moment had past by, one of the man's arms, holding his sword and stained with blood, fell from the sky into the king's assembly. Then all the people, seeing it, said: "Ah, this great hero has been killed in battle by his opponents; his sword and one arm have fallen." While the people who sat in the court were even saying this, again his head fell also; and then his trunk fell too. And seeing this his wife said: "Sire, my husband, fighting on the field of battle, has been slain by the enemy. His head, his arm, his sword, and his trunk have fallen down here. So, that this my beloved may not be wooed by the heavenly nymphs, I will go to where he is. Let fire be provided for me." Hearing her words the king said: "My daughter, why will you enter the fire? I will guard you even as my own daughter; preserve your body." She said: "Sire, what is this you say? My lord, for whom this body of mine exists, has been slain on the battlefield by his foes. Now for whose sake shall I preserve this body? Moreover, you should not say this, since even fools know that wives should follow their husbands. For thus it is said:

1. Moonlight goes with the moon, the lightning clings to the cloud, and women follow their husbands; even fools know this.

And so, as the learned tradition has it:

2. The wife who enters into the fire when her husband dies, imitating Arundhati [a star, regarded as the wife of one of the "Seven Rishis" (the Dipper), and as a typical faithful spouse] in her behavior, enjoys bliss in heaven.
3. Until a wife burns herself in the fire after the death of her husband, so long that woman can in no way be (permanently) freed from the body.
4. A woman who follows after her husband shall surely purify three families: her mother's, her father's, and that into which she was given (in marriage). And so:
5. Three and a half crores [a crore is 10,000,000] is the number of the hairs on the human body; so many years shall a wife who follows her husband dwell in heaven.
6. As a snake-charmer powerfully draws a snake out of a hole, so a wife draws her husband upward (by burning herself) and enjoys bliss with him.
7. A wife who abides by the law of righteousness (in burn-

ing herself) saves her husband, whether he be good or wicked; yes, even if he be guilty of all crimes.

Furthermore, O king, a woman who is bereft of her husband has no use for her life. And it is said:

8. What profit is there in the life of a wretched woman who has lost her husband? Her body is as useless as a banyan tree in a cemetery.

9. Surely father, brother, and son measure their gifts; what woman would not honor her husband, who gives without measure?

Moreover:

10. Though a woman be surrounded by kinsfolk, though she have many sons, and be endowed with excellent qualities, she is miserable, poor wretched creature, when deprived of her husband. And so:

11. What shall a widow do with perfumes, garlands, and incense, or with manifold ornaments, or garments and couches of ease?

12. A lute does not sound without strings, a wagon does not go without wheels, and a wife does not obtain happiness without her husband, not even with a hundred kinsfolk.

13. Woman's highest refuge is her husband, even if he be poor, vicious, old, infirm, crippled, outcast, and stingy.

14. There is no kinsman, no friend, no protector, no refuge for a woman like her husband.

15. There is no other misery for women like widowhood. Happy is she among women who dies before her husband."

Thus speaking she fell at the king's feet, begging that a fire be provided for her. And when the king heard her words, his heart being tender with genuine compassion, he caused a pyre to be erected of sandalwood and the like, and gave her leave. So she took leave of the king, and in his presence entered the fire together with her husband's body.

(U.S.S.R.)
HOKKAIDO
(MANCHURIA)
Yalu R.
KOGURYO
Sea
of
Japan
Po Hai
(Gulf of Chihli)
KOREA
(SHANTUNG)
Yellow
Sea
SILLA
PAEKCHE
CHINA
(KIANGSU)
AINU
(Sendai)
J A P A N
H O N S H U
Kamakura
Heian
ISE
SHIKOKU
KYUSHU
Pacific
Ocean
Korean states prior to
unification of Korea in A.D. 668
0
Miles
500
KOREA
(Matsue)
HOKI
INABA
IZUMO
MIMASAKA
H
IWAMI
BITCHU
TSUSHIMA
BINGO
AKI
(Hiroshima)
Korea Strait
NAGATO
Dan-no-Ura
SUO
Inland
Yashima
SANUKI
AWA
CHIKUZEN
SHIKOKU
BUZEN
IYO
TOSA
HIZEN
BUNGO
KYUSHU
(Nagasaki)
HIGO
P a
HYUGA
SATSUMA

Sea of Japan
SADO
(Niigata)
DEWA
AINU TRIBES
(Sendai)
MATSU
ECHIGO
NOTO
(Takaoka)
ETCHU
SHIMOTSUKE
KOZUKE
KAGA
HIDA
HITACHI
SHINANO
ECHIZEN
MUSASHI
SHIMOSA
(Tokyo)
MINO
KAI
SAGAMI
Lake Biwa
HIEI
Kamakura
(Yokohama)
MT. FUJI
OWARI
(Nagoya)
OMI
YAMASHIRO
MIKAWA
TOTOMI
SURUGA
IZU
Nara
(Osaka)
ISE
SHIMA
YAMATO
Ocean
EARLY JAPAN AND KOREA
Province boundaries
Circuit boundaries
(Tokyo) Present-day names
0
Miles
150
V. Gray

III

Japan

Government

Chinese Influence in Early Japan: Introduction

The early history of Japanese civilization is inseparable from the story of Chinese influence in Japan, and indeed may best be understood as an interaction between native Japanese ways of thought and the more advanced Chinese models. In the early seventh century A.D., when China under the Sui and T'ang dynasties was a far-flung empire governed by a complex, centralized bureaucracy, the islands of Japan were divided among numerous clan units (called *uji*), each held together by its (real or presumed) descent from a common ancestor and ruled by a chieftain whose power was hereditary. While China possessed an imposing classical literature and a philosophical tradition dating back more than a thousand years, Japan had no written literature at all, or even a system of writing; her intellectual heritage was a composite of myth, legend, and custom. While Buddhism and Taoism in China had developed elaborate doctrines of man's relationship to the supernatural and an advanced notion of ethics, the native religion of Japan (Shinto) was a form of nature worship, its ethics consisting only of custom, ritual, and taboo. While China possessed great cities with hundreds of thousands of inhabitants, Japan had no cities at all or even any permanent architecture. It was scarcely surprising, then, that for many centuries Chinese high culture overshadowed the native achievements in Japan, or that the Japanese sought to imitate Chinese examples.

While a conscious and sustained attempt to acquire Chinese culture began only with the seventh century A.D. in Japan, archaeological evidence indicates that contacts between the two countries occurred even in prehistoric times. Some of the earliest known inhabitants of Japan were immigrants from northeast Asia who brought with them at least a superficial acquaintance with Chinese civilization. The principal route of communication passed through Korea, which is separated from mainland Japan by only 115 miles of open sea. In Han times a Chinese colony was established in north Korea, and the entire peninsula was strongly subject to Chinese influence. From the third century A.D. onward, the Japanese themselves were frequently active in Korea, attempting to exert political and military influence there by supporting one of the main Korean states against the others. In Han times and afterward, a number of Japanese kingdoms occasionally dispatched embassies or messengers to the Chinese court. By the early fifth century we hear of Japanese rulers employing scribes to keep records and conduct correspondence in the Chinese language. Without question, therefore, many aspects of Chinese culture had filtered into Japan long before the seventh century A.D.

Beginning in the seventh century, however, the flow of Chinese ideas into Japan accelerated sharply. One reason for the change, no doubt, was the political reunification of China following nearly four centuries of disunion. To Japanese eyes the power and splendor of the Chinese empire must now have appeared overwhelming; and Chinese forms of government, literature, religion, and art acquired a new prestige. By this time also, the indigenous Japanese culture had evidently reached a point where its adherents were able to appreciate and at least partially to assimilate many of China's achievements. Moreover, the adoption of Chinese ways served the purposes of powerful elements within Japanese society. Whereas the islands had previously been divided among numerous small kingdoms, there now existed a much larger state, centered in the Yamato area of southern Honshu but exercising a degree of control over central and western Japan as well. The Yamato government was based upon the old clan system; its ruler was merely the most powerful of the clan chieftains. He governed through the lesser chiefs, who derived their influence not from him, but from their own hereditary status as the heads of extended families. By contrast, the Chinese system was highly centralized: all lower officials received their power from an emperor who was in theory supreme. Obviously, then, the adoption of Chinese governmental forms aided the Yamato rulers in maintaining their primacy within the state. Buddhism, too, as a means of influencing the supernatural, was regarded as an instrument of power. By encouraging its spread, the Yamato government clearly expected to curry favor with the Buddhas and Bodhisattvas and thereby obtain concrete material benefits.

The Sinification of Japan thus began as a conscious, voluntary effort by leading members of Yamato society to revamp their own culture and institutions in accordance with Chinese prototypes. In the seventh century the Yamato government introduced the Chinese system of landholding and taxation and divided the country into districts and provinces on the Chinese model; supported the spread of Buddhism through the patronage of Buddhist learning and the building of temples and monasteries; and introduced Chinese-style law codes where previously the ritual precepts of the native religion had sufficed. Monks, civil servants, scholars, artists and artisans were sent to China in officially-sponsored embassies with the express purpose of acquiring knowledge of Chinese government, technology, religion, and literature. On their return to Japan, such men became the leading propagators of Chinese methods and ideas in their respective fields. Still other Japanese travelled unofficially to China in private merchant ships, often bringing back valuable books and art objects; while immigrant Koreans played an important role both in the dissemination of Buddhism and in teaching the Chinese language.

The height of Chinese influence in Japan was reached during the Nara period (A.D. 710-784), so named for Japan's first capital city, which was laid out in imitation of Ch'ang-an. The government at Nara made a serious effort to make the borrowed Chinese institutions function; and its successes were impressive. But although Chinese administrative structures and titles could be copied, the spirit behind them could not. For example, Japanese leaders never accepted the important Chinese notion that government officials should be selected on the basis of merit. No Board of Censors—an essential element in Chinese government—was ever established in Japan. The administrators of the new Japanese districts and provinces were the old clan leaders, whose power was based upon family solidarity and transmitted by heredity. The doctrines of Buddhist religion were understood only imperfectly: the Japanese borrowed the ceremonies and art forms of Buddhism rather than its asceticism and its complex philosophy. Indeed, Buddhism was regarded as a novel form of magic, which soon became assimilated to the native religion by the simple process of regarding Japanese deities as local incarnations of the Buddha or the Bodhisattvas.

By the ninth century, Japanese borrowings from China had decreased considerably, while native customs and traditions gradually returned to favor. The imported Chinese administrative system now broke down almost completely; the decrees of the central government carried little weight outside of the capital. But the cultural and economic achievements of the period of Sinification were more permanent. The Chinese tax system, which was based upon individual rather than clan responsibility, had led to the growth of private agricultural estates not owned by kinship groups; and enormous amounts of new land had been brought into cultivation. Buddhism continued to flourish; and in the tenth century the Japanese began to develop their own schools of Buddhism, clearly distinct from those of the mainland. Though the Chinese language was still used in official documents and in all "serious" writing, Chinese characters were increasingly adapted to the Japanese tongue, and a native Japanese literature developed. The most striking benefit from Chinese contacts came in the realm of art and architecture, where the language barrier scarcely existed: Japanese artists soon produced paintings and temples equal in quality to those of China itself. By the tenth and eleventh centuries, Japanese government, religion, art, and literature had largely freed themselves from direct Chinese inspiration. Having gone to school in China, literally or figuratively, for a period of about two hundred years, the Japanese now created a culture which—despite the profound debt it owed to China—nonetheless bore a character distinctly its own.

The Sources of Early Japanese History: Introduction

One important by-product of Chinese influence in Japan was the fact that the Japanese produced extensive historical records at an extremely early period of their cultural development. Together with Chinese political institutions, religion, and literature, they adopted the notion that record-keeping is an important function of government. Moreover, until Japanese men-of-letters learned to adapt Chinese characters to their own very different language—a process which required centuries for completion—all such histories were written in Chinese.

The earliest extant accounts of Japanese history are the *Kojiki* ("Record of Ancient Matters") and the *Nihongi* ("Chronicles of Japan"). The *Kojiki* is written partly in Chinese, partly in Chinese characters used to represent Japanese words or ideas; the *Nihongi* is in pure Chinese. Both works begin by recording ancient native myths of the gods and the genealogies of legendary rulers on earth, and pass on to more factual events of relatively recent date. Compiled respectively in A.D. 712 and 720, they obviously attempt to present Japanese traditions in a way which will enhance the prestige of the reigning family of Yamato. Both accounts, therefore, give a false picture of centralized rule in Japan dating back for many centuries, and trace the descent of the Yamato rulers back to the Sun Goddess. But while the *Kojiki* is almost entirely mythological in content, the *Nihongi* provides fairly reliable information for at least the sixth and seventh centuries A.D.

The *Nihongi* was succeeded by five more official histories, also written in Chinese. Known collectively as the "Six National Histories" (*Rikkokushi*), they provide a reasonably complete and accurate outline of Japanese political affairs down to the year 887. Their scope, however, is limited: they focus almost exclusively upon matters of direct interest to the imperial court. Moreover—like the Chinese court records on which they were modelled—they are chronicles rather than true histories. Dry and matter-of-fact in style, they merely state a series of bare facts, making no attempt to evaluate the respective importance of events or to place them in a broader historical framework.

Introduction to the Constitution of Prince Shotoku

Prince Shotoku Taishi (A.D. 573-621) was the dominant political figure in Japan during the reign of his aunt, the Empress Suiko (r. 592-628), and the principal Japanese advocate of Sinification in his time. He was without question a man of unusual ability and strength of character. Shotoku encouraged the study of things Chinese through his own personal example: he was a sincere Buddhist and a dedicated Chinese scholar. Among his practical contributions to Sinification were his sponsorship of embassies to the Chinese mainland; the institution (in A.D. 603) of a Chinese-style system of ranks for court officials; and his generous financial support of Buddhist institutions.

Shotoku's seventeen-article Constitution, issued in A.D. 604, is in no way a binding legal code, but merely a collection of moral precepts addressed to the hereditary clan leaders. Its generalized language reflects the Confucian belief that broad ethical principles rather than specific and detailed laws should set the standard for official conduct. Sixteen of its seventeen articles enunciate typically Confucian notions: for example, the need for harmony between superiors and inferiors, the importance of personal uprightness in government, and the requirement that officials take responsibility for the popular welfare. It sets forth the Chinese theory of centralized government, according to which the emperor is the fount of all political power and the local authorities merely his delegates.

The actual situation in Japan in Shotoku's time was almost exactly the opposite of that described in his Constitution. Political office was hereditary, while the various clans (*uji*) engaged in periodic strife; the Japanese emperor was not the supreme authority in the state, but merely the first among equals. Japan had no indigenous moral code beyond custom and the ceremonial injunctions of the national religion (Shinto), and no political theory or set of precepts for officials. Thus Shotoku's Constitution expresses a concept of government which by Japanese standards was revolutionary. It had no immediate practical effect, but served rather to prepare the ground for the events of the following century, when the Japanese attempted a thorough overhaul of their institutions to accord with the Chinese example.

FROM THE CONSTITUTION OF PRINCE SHOTOKU

[A.D. 604]. Summer, 4th month, 3rd day. The Prince Imperial in person prepared laws for the first time. There were seventeen clauses, as follows:—

I. Harmony is to be valued,[1] and an avoidance of wanton opposition to be honoured. All men are influenced by class-feelings, and there are few who are intelligent. Hence there are some who disobey their lords and fathers, or who maintain feuds with the neighbouring villages. But when those above are harmonious

From W. G. Aston, trans., *Nihongi. Chronicles of Japan from the Earliest Times to A.D. 697*, London: George Allen & Unwin Ltd., 1896, 1956, Vol. II, pp. 128-33. Reprinted by permission of George Allen & Unwin, Ltd.

1. Quotation from *Analects* I, 12.

and those below are friendly, and there is concord in the discussion of business, right views of things spontaneously gain acceptance. Then what is there which cannot be accomplished!

II. Sincerely reverence the three treasures. The three treasures, viz. Buddha, the Law and the Priesthood, are the final refuge of the four generated beings,[2] and are the supreme objects of faith in all countries. What man in what age can fail to reverence this law? Few men are utterly bad.[3] They may be taught to follow it. But if they do not betake them to the three treasures, wherewithal shall their crookedness be made straight?

III. When you receive the Imperial commands, fail not scrupulously to obey them. The lord is Heaven, the vassal is Earth.[4] Heaven overspreads, and Earth upbears. When this is so, the four seasons follow their due course, and the powers of Nature obtain their efficacy.[5] If the Earth attempted to overspread, Heaven would simply fall in ruin. Therefore is it that when the lord speaks, the vassal listens; when the superior acts, the inferior yields compliance. Consequently when you receive the Imperial commands, fail not to carry them out scrupulously. Let there be a want of care in this matter, and ruin is the natural consequence.

IV. The Ministers and functionaries should make decorous behaviour their leading principle, for the leading principle of the government of the people consists in decorous behaviour.[6] If the superiors do not behave with decorum, the inferiors are disorderly: if inferiors are wanting in proper behaviour, there must necessarily be offences. Therefore it is that when lord and vassal behave with propriety, the distinctions of rank are not confused:[7] when the people behave with propriety, the Government of the Commonwealth proceeds of itself.

2. Living beings were supposedly generated in four ways: from eggs, from wombs, through moisture, or by metamorphosis.

3. Orthodox Confucian doctrine held that human nature is inherently good.

4. Similarly—according to Chinese theory—the emperor is the Son of Heaven, his subjects the children of the Earth.

5. This is the Chinese principle that an all-embracing harmony exists between Heaven and Earth, whereby events in nature are the consequences of human acts.

6. In Chinese: *li* (i.e. "rites" or "ceremonies").

7. Chinese political theory laid great stress upon government by example.

V. Ceasing from gluttony and abandoning covetous desires, deal impartially with the suits which are submitted to you. Of complaints brought by the people there are a thousand in one day. If in one day there are so many, how many will there be in a series of years? If the man who is to decide suits at law makes gain his ordinary motive, and hears causes with a view to receiving bribes, then will the suits of the rich man be like a stone flung into water,[8] while the plaints of the poor will resemble water cast upon a stone. Under these circumstances the poor man will not know whither to betake himself. Here too there is a deficiency in the duty of the Minister.

VI. Chastise that which is evil and encourage that which is good. This was the excellent rule of antiquity. Conceal not, therefore, the good qualities of others, and fail not to correct that which is wrong when you see it. Flatterers and deceivers are a sharp weapon for the overthrow of the State, and a pointed sword for the destruction of the people. Sycophants are also fond, when they meet, of dilating to their superiors on the errors of their inferiors; to their inferiors, they censure the faults of their superiors. Men of this kind are all wanting in fidelity to their lord, and in benevolence towards the people. From such an origin great civil disturbances arise.

VII. Let every man have his own charge, and let not the spheres of duty be confused. When wise men are entrusted with office, the sound of praise arises. If unprincipled men hold office, disasters and tumults are multiplied. In this world, few are born with knowledge: wisdom is the product of earnest meditation. In all things, whether great or small, find the right man, and they will surely be well managed: on all occasions, be they urgent or the reverse, meet but with a wise man, and they will of themselves be amenable. In this way will the State be lasting and the Temples of the Earth and of Grain will be free from danger. Therefore did the wise sovereigns of antiquity seek the man to fill the office, and not the office for the sake of the man.

VIII. Let the Ministers and functionaries attend the Court early in the morning, and retire late. The business of the State does not admit of remissness, and the whole day is hardly

8. I.e., they meet with no resistance. (Tr.)

enough for its accomplishment. If, therefore, the attendance at Court is late, emergencies cannot be met: if officials retire soon, the work cannot be completed.

IX. Good faith is the foundation of right. In everything let there be good faith, for in it there surely consists the good and the bad, success and failure. If the lord and the vassal observe good faith one with another, what is there which cannot be accomplished? If the lord and the vassal do not observe good faith towards one another, everything without exception ends in failure.

X. Let us cease from wrath, and refrain from angry looks. Nor let us be resentful when others differ from us. For all men have hearts, and each heart has its own leanings. Their right is our wrong, and our right is their wrong. We are not unquestionably sages, nor are they unquestionably fools. Both of us are simply ordinary men. How can any one lay down a rule by which to distinguish right from wrong? For we are all, one with another, wise and foolish, like a ring which has no end. Therefore, although others give way to anger, let us on the contrary dread our own faults, and though we alone may be in the right, let us follow the multitude and act like them.

XI. Give clear appreciation to merit and demerit, and deal out to each its sure reward or punishment. In these days, reward does not attend upon merit, nor punishment upon crime. Ye high functionaries who have charge of public affairs, let it be your task to make clear rewards and punishments.

XII. Let not the provincial authorities[9] or the [local clan leaders] levy exactions on the people. In a country there are not two lords; the people have not two masters. The sovereign is the master of the people of the whole country. The officials to whom he gives charge are all his vassals. How can they, as well as the Government, presume to levy taxes on the people?

XIII. Let all persons entrusted with office attend equally to their functions. Owing to their illness or to their being sent on missions, their work may sometimes be neglected. But whenever they become able to attend to business, let them be as accommodating as if they had had cognizance of it from before, and not

9. I.e., the official representatives of the central government.

hinder public affairs on the score of their not having had to do with them.

XIV. Ye ministers and functionaries! Be not envious. For if we envy others, they in turn will envy us. The evils of envy know no limit. If others excel us in intelligence, it gives us no pleasure; if they surpass us in ability, we are envious. Therefore it is not until after a lapse of five hundred years that we at last meet with a wise man, and even in a thousand years we hardly obtain one sage. But if we do not find wise men and sages, wherewithal shall the country be governed?

XV. To turn away from that which is private, and to set our faces towards that which is public—this is the path of a Minister. Now if a man is influenced by private motives, he will assuredly feel resentments, and if he is influenced by resentful feelings, he will assuredly fail to act harmoniously with others. If he fails to act harmoniously with others, he will assuredly sacrifice the public interests to his private feelings. When resentment arises, it interferes with order, and is subversive of law. Therefore in the first clause it was said, that superiors and inferiors should agree together. The purport is the same as this.

XVI. Let the people be employed (in forced labour) at seasonable times. This is an ancient and excellent rule. Let them be employed, therefore, in the winter months, when they are at leisure. But from Spring to Autumn, when they are engaged in agriculture or with the mulberry trees, the people should not be so employed. For if they do not attend to agriculture, what will they have to eat? if they do not attend to the mulberry trees, what will they do for clothing?

XVII. Decisions on important matters should not be made by one person alone. They should be discussed with many. But small matters are of less consequence. It is unnecessary to consult a number of people. It is only in the case of the discussion of weighty affairs, when there is a suspicion that they may miscarry, that one should arrange matters in concert with others, so as to arrive at the right conclusion.

Introduction to the Taika Reforms

The efforts of Prince Shotoku in the early seventh century to introduce Chinese political institutions into Japan remained without immediate effect. But by the middle of the same century, knowledge of Chinese ways had increased in Japan to a point where reforms based upon Chinese models were feasible. This time the leader of the reformers was Kamatari, chief of the powerful Nakatomi clan which then dominated the imperial court. The immediate object of Kamatari's policy was to make the authority of the central government supreme in the provinces. As a preliminary measure in A.D. 645, his government appointed imperial governors to the outlying (i.e., Eastern) provinces of Japan, where the clans were least powerful. Some months later, it issued an edict in four articles which—in intention if not always in practice—inaugurated radical changes in the prevailing forms of land tenure, taxation, and local government in Japan. Consequently the years 645-650, in which the new system went into effect, are known in Japanese history as Taika, or "Great Reform."

Though Kamatari's government clearly desired to maximize its own power vis-a-vis that of the hereditary clan leaders, it obviously could not deprive so many influential persons of their authority and possessions all at once. For this reason, the reformers on the whole altered merely the *de jure* distribution of power in the provinces, while confirming it *de facto*. The existing great estates were left untouched, except that their owners now held the land theoretically as vassals of the crown. The more important clan chiefs were appointed as provincial governors supposedly representing the imperial government; the clan leaders were compensated for lost authority by increases in their official court rank.

The immediate effect of the Taika appears to have been economic rather than political. The new tax system was designed to ensure that the imperial government received its share of the provincial revenue. For this reason, detailed and up-to-date land registers were essential, showing the location and amount of land allotted to each individual and the tax liability upon it. Corresponding population registers recorded the age and status of each person within the district to determine which of them were taxable (various high officials were exempt). Politically, the clan leaders retained most of their earlier authority. But the land and population registers were carefully kept; and the tax receipts which accrued to the central government did much to support the subsequent cultural flowering of the Nara period (A.D. 710-84).

The Taika system ultimately broke down for some of the same reasons which led to the replacement of its Chinese prototype in the late eighth century. The per capita assessment of taxes placed the heaviest burden upon the poor. As a result, tax evasion was widespread, registrars were given false information, and farmers absconded in large numbers to outlying districts. The clan leaders were able to evade the regulations in order to build up large tax-free estates; and as the tax base decreased, the claims upon remaining taxpayers grew. By the end of the Nara period the attempt to apply Chinese models of government to Japan was abandoned as an obvious failure. The power of the central government, while not disappearing entirely, became more theoretical than real. Actual power in the provinces rested with the clan leaders, who often were also the owners of great estates, while the society of the court and capital maintained its own separate existence.

FROM THE TAIKA REFORM EDICTS

1st year of Taika [A.D. 645], 8th month, 5th day. Governors of the Eastern provinces were appointed. Then the Governors were addressed as follows:—"In accordance with the charge entrusted to Us by the Gods of Heaven, We propose at this present (moment) for the first time to regulate the myriad provinces.

"When you proceed to your posts, prepare registers of all the free subjects of the State and of the people under the control of others,[1] whether great or small. Take account also of the acreage

From W. G. Aston, trans., *Nihongi. Chronicles of Japan from the Earliest Times to A.D. 697*, London: George Allen & Unwin, Ltd., 1896, 1956, Vol. II, pp. 200-201, 204-208.

Words in square brackets have been supplied by the present editors to replace Japanese terms confusing to the general reader.

1. I.e., tenant-farmers (here called serfs).

of cultivated land. As to the profits arising from the gardens and ponds, the water and land, deal with them in common with the people.[2] Moreover it is not competent for the provincial Governors, while in their provinces, to decide criminal cases, nor are they permitted by accepting bribes to bring the people to poverty and misery. When they come up to the capital they must not bring large numbers of the people in their train. They are only allowed to bring with them the [local clan chiefs] and the district officials. But when they travel on public business they may ride the horses of their department, and eat the food of their department. From the rank of [Assistant Governor] upwards those who obey this law will surely be rewarded, while those who disobey it shall be liable to be reduced in cap-rank. On all, from the rank of [Assistant District Chief] downwards, who accept bribes a fine shall be imposed of double the amount, and they shall eventually be punished criminally according to the greater or less heinousness of the case. Nine men are allowed as attendants on a Chief Governor, seven on an assistant, and five on a secretary. If this limit is exceeded, and they are accompanied by a greater number, both chief and followers shall be punished criminally.

"If there be any persons who lay claim to a title, but who, not being [chiefs of local or Imperial clans or district custodians of (tax) grain] by descent, unscrupulously draw up lying memorials, saying:—'From the time of our forefathers we have had charge of this [granary] or have ruled this district'—in such cases, ye, the Governors, must not readily make application to the Court in acquiescence in such fictions, but must ascertain particularly the true facts before making your report.

"Moreover on waste pieces of ground let arsenals be erected, and let the swords and armour, with the bows and arrows of the provinces and districts, be deposited together in them. In the case of the frontier provinces which border close on the [Ainu],[3] let all the weapons be mustered together, and let them remain in the hands of their original owners. In regard to the six districts of

2. I.e., take them into your counsel. (Tr.)

3. Tribesmen of the far north of Japan, having lighter skins than the typical Japanese and speaking a different language.

the province of Yamato, let the officials who are sent there prepare registers of the population, and also take an account of the acreage of cultivated land.

"This means to examine the acreage of the cultivated ground, and the numbers, houses, and ages of the people.

"Ye Governors of provinces, take careful note of this and withdraw." Accordingly presents were made them of silk and cloth, which varied in the case of each person.

. . . .

9th month, 19th day. Commissioners were sent to all the provinces to take a record of the total numbers of the people. The Emperor on this occasion made an edict, as follows:—

"In the times of all the Emperors, from antiquity downwards, subjects have been set apart for the purpose of making notable their reigns and handing down their names to posterity. Now the [chiefs of clans] have each one set apart their own vassals, whom they compel to labour at their arbitrary pleasure. Moreover they cut off the hills and seas, the woods and plains, the ponds and rice-fields belonging to the provinces and districts, and appropriate them to themselves. Their contests are never-ceasing. Some engross to themselves many tens of thousands of [acres] of rice-land, while others possess in all patches of ground too small to stick a needle into. When the time comes for the payment of taxes, the [clan chiefs] first collect them for themselves and then hand over a share. In the case of repairs to palaces or the construction of [Imperial tombs], they each bring their own vassals, and do the work according to circumstances. The *Book of Changes*[4] says: 'Diminish that which is above: increase that which is below: if measures are framed according to the regulations, the resources (of the State) suffer no injury, and the people receive no hurt.'

"At the present time, the people are still few. And yet the powerful cut off portions of land and water, and converting them into private ground, sell it to the people, demanding the price yearly. From this time forward the sale[5] of land is not allowed.

4. Or *I Ching:* one of the Five Classics of the Chinese.
5. By sale is evidently meant letting. (Tr.)

Let no man without due authority make himself a landlord, engrossing to himself that which belongs to the helpless."

The people were greatly rejoiced.

. . . .

2nd year [A.D. 646], Spring, 1st month, 1st day. As soon as the ceremonies of the new year's congratulations were over, the Emperor promulgated an edict of reforms, as follows:—

"I. Let the people established by the ancient Emperors, etc., as representatives of children[6] be abolished, also the [granaries][7] of various places and the people owned as serfs by [chiefs of clans and villages]. Let the farmsteads [of serfs] in various places be abolished." Consequently fiefs were granted for their sustenance[8] to those of the rank of Daibu[9] and upwards on a descending scale. Presents of cloth and silk stuffs were given to the officials and people, varying in value.

"Further We say. It is the business of the Daibu[9] to govern the people. If they discharge this duty thoroughly, the people have trust in them, and an increase of their revenue is therefore for the good of the people.

II. The capital is for the first time to be regulated, and Governors appointed for the Home provinces and districts. Let barriers, outposts, guards, and post-horses, both special and ordinary, be provided, bell-tokens[10] made, and mountains and rivers regulated.[11]

For each ward in the capital let there be appointed one alderman, and for four wards one chief alderman, who shall be charged with the superintendence of the population, and the examination of criminal matters. For appointment as chief aldermen of wards let men be taken belonging to the wards, of

6. These were the "namesake" groups established by the crown upon hitherto uncultivated land. They paid taxes directly to the imperial government and were frequently named after imperial offspring.

7. These were the granaries where tax-grain was collected and stored. Thus the custodians of granaries were in fact the local tax authorities.

8. I.e., in place of the serfs taken from them.

9. *Daibu*, meaning "great man," is a general term for high officials.

10. Small round bells indicating the number of horses to which the bearer was entitled—a Chinese device.

11. I.e., guards to be provided at ferries and mountain passes.

unblemished character, firm and upright, so that they may fitly sustain the duties of the time. For appointments as aldermen, whether of rural townships or of city wards, let ordinary subjects be taken belonging to the township or ward, of good character and solid capacity. If such men are not to be found in the township or ward in question, it is permitted to select and employ men of the adjoining township or ward.

. . . Districts of forty townships[12] are constituted Greater Districts, of from thirty to four townships are constituted Middle Districts, and of three or fewer townships are constituted Lesser Districts. For the district authorities, of whatever class, let there be taken [local clan chiefs] of unblemished character, such as may fitly sustain the duties of the time, and made [Greater and Lesser Governors]. Let men of solid capacity and intelligence who are skilled in writing and arithmetic be appointed assistants and clerks.

The number of special or ordinary post-horses given shall in all cases follow the number of marks on the posting bell-tokens. When bell-tokens are given to (officials of) the provinces and barriers, let them be held in both cases by the chief official, or in his absence by the assistant official.

III. Let there now be provided for the first time registers of population, books of account and a system of the receipt and regranting of distribution-land.

Let every fifty houses be reckoned a township, and in every township let there be one alderman who shall be charged with the superintendence of the population,[13] the direction of the sowing of crops and the cultivation of mulberry trees, the prevention and examination of offences, and the enforcement of the payment of taxes and of forced labour.

[The edict concludes by specifying the amount of tax—payable in rice, silk floss, or cloth—which was due upon each unit of land. Groups of fifty or one hundred households were assigned to furnish a horse for the public service, weapons, servants for high officials, and waiting-women for the Palace.]

12. A township consisted of fifty houses. See below, Article III.
13. I.e., of the population registers. (Tr.)

The Fujiwara Dominance: Introduction

The transfer of the capital of Japan to Heian (modern Kyoto) in the year 794 is generally taken to mark the onset of a new period in Japanese history. The centralized administrative system copied from China now scarcely functioned: real power in the provinces rested with the local clan leaders, the holders of large landed estates. Provicial officials now generally remained at the capital, where a refined and elegant society flourished, largely divorced from the life of the countryside. The organs of centralized government were retained in theory, but scarcely in fact; the emperor was the titular head of government, but his power was now regularly exercised by the chiefs of leading clans. Thus was firmly established that system of dual government by which Japan was ruled until the latter part of the nineteenth century: the emperor was the head of state, treated with elaborate ceremonial reverence; but real power rested with someone else.

In the three centuries from 857 until 1160, the Fujiwara clan dominated the court and government so thoroughly that this entire period is generally called by their name. The heads of the family often, though not invariably, bore the title of Regent (*Kampaku*). But the power of successive Fujiwara chiefs was such that they could dictate which of the imperial princes would succeed to the throne, and when the reigning emperor must retire—often after a rather brief reign. Fujiwara men held most of the top government posts, while their daughters became the consorts or concubines of princes and emperors. But while the sovereign himself was restricted to purely ceremonial functions, his religious prestige—derived from his alleged direct descent from the Sun Goddess—served to legitimate the government. The Fujiwara regents always maintained the fiction that they served only as the emperor's delegate; and while dictating his policy, they never attempted to usurp his title.

The power of the Fujiwara house rested first and foremost upon their great wealth in land. In the general scramble for tax-free estates which led to the breakdown of centralized government in the late eighth century, they had been among the principal offenders.

Now they were the richest family in Japan, holding estates throughout the country, and bound together by that strong sense of family solidarity characteristic of Japanese society. Moreover, they were the maternal relatives of the emperor, with all that this meant in terms of Confucian filial piety; and they controlled the coveted titles and honors which only an emperor could bestow. Finally, the family produced a number of able leaders. By skillfully utilizing the ambitions and dissensions within other great houses, the Fujiwara regents ensured that no rival family, however supreme in its own domains, could challenge their authority on a national scale. In sharp contrast to the military regime which followed upon their downfall, the Fujiwara dominance was exercised through cleverness and political dexterity; only rarely did they use, or threaten to use, force.

The height of Fujiwara magnificence was attained under Michinaga, who controlled the imperial court and government from 995 until his death in 1027. Michinaga's position, his good fortune, and his personal qualities all combined to make him the outstanding man of his time. His rise to power, though aided by the accidental death or disgrace of leading rivals, was nonetheless meteoric. He was extraordinarily handsome physically, as well as a fine poet—qualities much prized by the elegant high society of Heian. His dominance over the court was such that four of his daughters married emperors; two emperors were his nephews and three his grandsons. It was no wonder that he was afterward remembered with nostalgia. Shortly after his death the Fujiwara power began its slow decline, culminating in its overthrow in 1160 and the establishment of military rule over Japan in 1185.

Introduction to the Great Mirror

The *Great Mirror* (*Okagami*), in which the following account of Michinaga's career appears, is an example of that Japanese literary genre known as the historical tale (*rekishi monogatari*). Resembling the "Six National Histories"* in its respect for facts, the historical tale at the same time attempts to provide literary interest. The *Great*

* See "The Sources of Early Japanese History," above, pp. 206-7.

Mirror, which covers the period 850-1025, is one of eight extant examples of this genre, and an important historical source.

The tone of the *Great Mirror* is informal and conversational: it tells its story in the words of two fictitious old men, 140 and 150 years old respectively, who personally recall nearly all the events of which they speak. In structure it resembles the *Historical Records* (*Shih Chi*) of Ssu-ma Ch'ien,* with which the author evidently was acquainted. Like the latter, it is divided into five parts; emperors and ministers receive separate treatment; and the handling of events is anecdotal. The identity of the author of the *Great Mirror* is unknown. He claims to have composed the work in 1025, at the height of Michinaga's career; but internal evidence suggests that a more likely date is 1115.

* On Ssu-ma Ch'ien see Vo.l V of this series, pp. 132-52.

FROM THE GREAT MIRROR (OKAGAMI)

Prime Minister Michinaga

Concerning this Grand Minister Michinaga: he is His Excellency, the present[1] Lay Priest.[2] He is the father-in-law of the Retired Emperors Ichijo and Sanjo, and the grandfather of the present Emperor (Go-Ichijo) and Crown Prince (later Go-Shujaku). This lord, without becoming a Consultant,[3] immediately became Acting Middle Counselor on the twenty-ninth day of the first moon of the second year of Eien[4] (988). His age [was then] twenty-three. . . . On the seventh day of the ninth moon of the second year of Shoryaku[4] (991), he became Great Counselor. On the twenty-seventh day of the fourth moon of the third year of Shoryaku (992), he received the Junior Second Rank. [At the time that] he was named Master of the Empress' House-

From Edwin O. Reischauer and Joseph K. Yamagiwa, *Translations from Early Japanese Literature*, Cambridge, Mass.: Harvard University Press, 1951, pp. 313-17, 328-33, 335-36. Reprinted by permission of Harvard University Press.

1. I.e., in 1025.
2. "Lay Priest" was a title indicating that its bearer had taken Buddhist vows without actually entering monastic life.
3. A "Consultant" was one of eight advisers to the throne, ranking below the four Great Counselors and the three Middle Counselors.
4. An era name—the designation for a period of years.

hold, his age [was] twenty-seven. . . . On the twenty-seventh day of the fourth moon of the first year of Chotoku (995), he acquired in addition the duties of the Commander of the Imperial Body Guards of the Left.

From before the festival[5] of [the year 994], the country had been greatly upset, and in the following year [conditions] became increasingly bad indeed. To begin with, Great Ministers and Nobles[6] died in great numbers.[7] On top of this, the number of those [who died] of the Fourth and Fifth Ranks was unknown. . . .

[Such a thing] is not likely to happen again. Even in ancient times, for seven or eight Great Ministers and Nobles to be thus swept away in a period of two or three months was a rare occurence. [But] this only seemed to bring to a peak the height of His Excellency, this Lay Priest's prosperity. If these lords had maintained themselves as they had been[8] for a long time, would he have been as extremely [prosperous] as he was? . . .

His Excellency the Lay Priest of whom we now [speak] was at that time referred to as Great Counselor-Master of the Empress' Household and was very young in years. He was at an age when he could [well] await [the honors that would come in] future years, but at [the age of] thirty, on the twenty-seventh day of the fourth moon, he became Commander.[9] On the eleventh day of the fifth moon, he received for the first time the Imperial decree [making him] the official in charge of the various affairs of the government, that is, Civil Examiner, and he began indeed to prosper. On the nineteenth of the sixth moon in the same year he became Great Minister of the Right, and on the twentieth day of the seventh moon in the second year of Chotoku (996) he next became Great Minister of the Left. In this way [the Chancellorship][10] became [his and his family's]

5. An annual festival held in honor of the patron deity of the capital.
6. A noble was technically a person holding the third rank or higher.
7. I.e., in an epidemic.
8. I.e., if they had preserved their lives and ranks.
9. Commander of the Imperial Bodyguards of the Left.
10. I.e., the office of *Kampaku* (Regent). In fact Michinaga never officially received this title, though he performed the functions of that office from 995 until 1016.

without passing to other lords. Even now[11] it seems as if it will probably remain the same. . . .

The children of this lord (Michinaga), sons and daughters, are twelve in all, and [this] number has remained constant.[12] As far as offices and ranks are concerned, both the sons and the daughters will probably [attain] whatever their hearts desire. Even [in] their temperaments and their characters there is nothing that is in the least insufficient or deserving of blame. The fact that each is well versed in ancient courtly practices is not at all extraordinary. It is due to the fact that the good fortune of His Excellency the Lay Priest appears to be beyond description. Although the lords that preceded him had possessed children, were they all so [superior] and as [their parents] wished? Though they were brothers and sisters, good and bad naturally seemed to be mixed together.

[Our lord Michinaga's] wives are both of the Minamoto clan. Thus it is assuredly said that the Minamoto clan will prosper in the future. Since this is so, the circumstances of these ladies [needed mentioning and] are as aforesaid.

But as far as the person of our lord is concerned: he has been Chancellor from the age of thirty, he has governed the country during the reigns of Retired Emperors Ichijo and Sanjo, and he has done as he has wished. Again, since the present Emperor (Go-Ichijo) came to the throne at the age of nine, in the year when [Michinaga] was fifty-one years old and when he was Regent, he himself became Prime Minister and passed over the Regency to the present Prime Minister (Yorimichi),[13] [but] when he became fifty-four, on the eighteenth day of the third moon in the third year of Kannin (1019), from about the middle of the night, he [began to] feel pains in his chest, and though it was not [a] sharp [pain], what must he have felt? For at about two o'clock in the afternoon of the twenty-first he suddenly got up, put on his headdress, and over an undergarment of glossed silk he put on an ordinary split skirt,[14] and after wash-

11. I.e., in 1025.
12. That is, none of them has died.
13. Michinaga's son, who held office as *Kampaku* from 1018 to 1069.
14. Trousers with strings passed through the cuffs, in place of the more formal split skirt worn in full court dress. (Tr.)

ing, while [all] the lords from the Chancellor (Yorimichi) down wondered what it was all about, he went out [of his quarters] to the corridor running to the west from his own apartment, and facing the south raised a prayer. This was to request of the deity enshrined at Kasuga[15] his surcease [from secular life]. The Assistant High Priest Kyomyo and the Master of Asceticism[16] Joki officiated [at the ceremony] when he took his tonsure. Beginning with the Lord Civil Dictator (Yorimichi), his children and the lords [all] thought that it was very extraordinary, but as it was something that he had determined upon and [then] had suddenly performed, each of them was dumbfounded, nor could they prevent him, and it is useless to say that it was unusual. The Priest of the First Rank[16] Ingen acted as initiating priest. The Assistant High Priest Shin'e presented him with his surplice, and [this was when he first] began [wearing one]. [Michinaga had become a priest so] suddenly [that] he had probably not prepared one. The [priest's] name Gyokan was given to him. Later, the second character [in writing it] was changed and [the name] became Gyokaku. After [Michinaga had] thus [become a priest], the facts were told to the Emperor (Go-Ichijo) and to the Crown Prince (later, Go-Shujaku). Needless to say, when these royal personages were told about him, they were astounded and deeply affected in their hearts. . . .

Even though he had left this world, still again on the eighth day of the same fifth moon he attained a rank equivalent to that of the Three Empresses[17] and received annual offices and annual ranks. He is the father of three Empresses, of the Chancellor and Great Minister of the Left (Yorimichi), of the Great Minister of the Center (Norimichi), and of many Counselors (Yorimune, Yoshimune, and Nagaie), and the grandfather of the Emperor (Go-Ichijo) and of the Crown Prince (later, Emperor Go-Shujaku). Thus he has continued to administer [this] country for almost thirty-one years. Because this year he has become a full

15. This was the patron deity of the Fujiwara clan.
16. The highest ranks in the Buddhist hierarchy were High Priest (first rank), Assistant High priest (second rank), and Master of Asceticism (third rank).
17. The three empresses who were Michinaga's daughters. In fact, Michinaga had received this rank prior to taking Buddhist orders.

sixty years,[18] men say that the celebration [on his attaining that age] will be held after [his daughter, the Imperial Concubine] Kan-no-tono has given birth to her child. How very happy [an occasion] it will be with so many different events! [Michinaga's prosperity] is something that probably will not be repeated in [this] country. That three daughters of a Great Minister should become Empresses in succession is an extraordinary and rare thing. In China in ancient times there were three thousand Empresses,[19] but their lineages were not inquired into. If only it was reputed that they were beautiful, they were selected and sent for even out of adjacent countries. . . . Since from His Excellency this Lay Priest's single family have come an Arch Empress Dowager, an Empress Dowager, and an Imperial Consort, it is indeed a rare good fortune [that he enjoys]. . . .

As for the Chinese poems and the Japanese poetry that this lord has composed on [various] occasions, even though one may mention Kyo-i [Po Chü-i],[20] Akahito[21] [and others], one feels that these are not to be thought of by way of comparison [with him]. . . . When those who have attained almost the highest fortune are inferior in the ways of poetry, the impression is that their estate is not [completely] prosperous. [But] this lord (Michinaga) on occasion invariably composes [a superb] poem and makes the occasion auspicious.

[The poem] he composed at [the celebration of] the sixtieth anniversary of his wife (Tomoko) was:

> The bonds, which we were used to, do not break
> And even now shall I say [in congratulation],
> "Long life [to you]," though it be a
> soiling of my heart.[22]

. . . .

18. This calculation is based upon the Japanese system of counting age. Since Michinaga was born in 966, in 1025 he had lived in 60 different years.
19. This piece of hyperbole comes from a poem by Po Chü-i about Yang Kuei-fei, the famous concubine who ruled the Chinese court for the twenty years prior to A.D. 756.
20. Po Chü-i was the most popular Chinese poet in Japan. For writings of Po Chü-i see above, pp. 109-13.
21. A leading poet of the *Collection of Myriad Leaves* (*Manyoshu*). Poems from the *Manyoshu* appear below, pp. 272-78.
22. Michinaga thus refers to his priestly state, which normally would prohibit any mention or thought of earthly ties. (Tr.)

The Founding of the Shogunate: Introduction

While the aristocracy of the capital during the Fujiwara period concerned itself with literary, artistic, and ceremonial pursuits, a very different type of society flourished in the provinces. Outside of Heian, life centered upon the activities of private agricultural estates (called *shoen*), whose owners or managers played the principal roles in local affairs. These estates were of diverse historical origin: some had been created through imperial grant, or given by an important lord to a relative or other retainer in return for services rendered or expected; others grew up through the practice of commendation, whereby weaker landowners assigned their property to a stronger neighbor in return for military protection. The larger *shoen* often comprised thousands of acres scattered through several provinces, though others might be no more than small farms. Income from the *shoen* was distributed proportionately according to a complex system of fixed rights, known as *shiki*, which varied from place to place according to circumstances. These rights were fully inheritable; they were ordinarily spelled out in written documents and given the sanction of local custom and law.

In the absence of effective centralized government, the enforcement of rights to land and the keeping of the peace inevitably devolved upon local leaders. Even in the heyday of the Chinese-style administrative system, officials appointed from the capital had tended to be clan chieftains, surrounded by their personal followers, rather than true bureaucrats in the Chinese style. With the growth of individual rights to land—a development fostered by the borrowed Chinese tax system—the hereditary basis of such authority was weakened. As the organs of the central government gradually ceased to function, the estate owners or managers who actually resided in the provinces assumed governmental powers. The resultant political and legal system, with its complex of mutual rights and obligations, bears many resemblances to the feudalism of medieval Europe.

Since hereditary prestige was important in Japan even in the countryside, the more important provincial leaders were generally members of collateral branches of the imperial family or court aristocracy who had settled for various reasons in the provinces. Separated from the elegant society of Heian and obliged to assume local police functions, they tended more and more to stress the military arts. Thus by the twelfth century the typical Japanese provincial lord was a warrior, proud of his courage and skill with weapons. He could boast of a noble pedigree; and he held important rights to land—for only wealthy persons could afford the price of a fine horse, armor, and sharp sword. The lord enrolled other fighting men as his vassals, supplying them with equipment and providing economic security in return for military services. In time the relationship of lord and vassal—originating in mutual dependence—assumed an ethical coloration and became idealized into a code of military honor (known as *bushi* or *bushido*). The principal virtues according to this code were personal bravery and total loyalty to one's lord—a loyalty outweighing any personal interests or family obligations. Such loyalties, whereby each vassal owed service to his immediate lord, who might in turn be the vassal of another, and so forth, formed a complex system of interrelationships, and provided the cement which held feudal society together.

The military prowess of the provincial lords was employed not only in keeping the peace, but also in conflicts over land and prestige. Such local warfare became increasingly common in the eleventh and early twelfth centuries; and ordinarily the government at Heian paid no attention to it. Indeed, since the emperor and the Fujiwara regents disposed of no military power of their own, they were forced to rely for protection upon one or another of the provincial military groups. Nonetheless, such local warfare gradually altered the balance of power in the provinces, making the strong lords stronger as they eliminated weaker rivals or enrolled them as their vassals. It was thus only a matter of time until the weak Heian government would be replaced by one of the provincial military groups. The occasion came in 1156-1160, when leaders of two great provincial families—the Taira and the Minamoto (known in their Chinese pronunciation as Heike and Genji respectively)—found themselves on opposing sides in a dispute over succession to the throne. The Taira-led group proved victorious and sent its opponents into exile in distant provinces. Although the emperor and the Fujiwara regents ostensibly continued to rule, the Taira leader, Kiyomori, was now the real head of state.

In the twenty-four years that Kiyomori dominated Heian, most of the Minamoto made their peace with him. Nonetheless the Taira, as a military family, exercised their power far more ruthlessly than the politically-minded Fujiwara had done; and their tactics inevitably aroused resentment and fear. In 1180 a leader of the Minamoto family, Yoritomo, rallied his supporters for an attack on the Taira supremacy. In the course of the ensuing war, which lasted intermittently from 1180 to 1185, the Minamoto displaced the Taira at Heian and also won a dominant military influence throughout most of the provinces. From their headquarters at Kamakura, three hundred miles east of Heian, Yoritomo and his successors provided Japan with a more effective centralized government than it had enjoyed since the Nara period. The real head of the government was no longer called Regent, but Shogun ("Generalissimo"). He exercised his authority not through the organs of civil government, but largely through the private family administration which had originated out of the need to manage great estates. The Shogunate was in fact a hereditary military dictatorship, whose authority was based on the loyalty of vassals to their lord. Known as the Bakufu or "tent government," it dominated Japan until the middle of the nineteenth century.

The following passages from the historical work known as the *Mirror of Eastern Japan* describe the origins of the civil war which ended in the establishment of the Shogunate. The conflict was precipitated in 1180 by two plotters with grievances against the Taira regime: Yorimasa, an aged Minamoto living at Heian who resented the insults he received from Taira partisans; and Mochihito, an imperial prince who had twice been by-passed for the succession, most recently in favor of Taira Kiyomori's infant grandson. Evidently the two conspirators had not consulted in advance with Minamoto leaders in the provinces; for no evidence exists to indicate that Yoritomo, the principal heir to Minamoto leadership, intended to lead a rebellion at this time. Discovery of the plot, however, forced his hand; he was obliged to take the initiative simply in order to forestall Taira revenge. Thus began, in almost accidental fashion, the war which ultimately made Yoritomo the military master of Japan.

Introduction to the Mirror of Eastern Japan

The *Mirror of Eastern Japan* (*Azuma Kagami*) is a work in diary form which constitutes the best extant source for the first century of the Kamakura Shogunate. Written in dry and straightforward style, it gives a chronological account of Japanese political events from 1180 to 1266. The various entries in the diary purport to have been composed shortly after the events they relate; but in fact the entire book dates from sometime between 1266 and 1301. Diverse sources went into its compilation: the house records of leading provincial families; the archives of religious orders; the diaries of court nobles; and even the popular war romances. Modelled after the official histories kept at the court at Heian, the *Mirror of Eastern Japan* evidently was intended to enhance the dignity and justify the existence of the Shogunate.

FROM THE MIRROR OF EASTERN JAPAN (AZUMA KAGAMI)

Chapter I

Jisho 4 [*1180*], fourth month, 9th day. The lay priest[1] and courtier, third rank, Minamoto Yorimasa had been planning for a long time to overthrow the lay priest and chancellor Taira Kiyomori. But realizing the difficulty of accomplishing this long-cherished ambition by his stratagem alone, he, together with his

From Minoru Shinoda, *The Founding of the Kamakura Shogunate, 1180-1185*, New York: Columbia University Press, 1960, pp. 149-55. Reprinted by permission of Columbia University Press.

Words in square brackets have been supplied by the present editors in order to reduce the number of Japanese names and terms.

1. This title denotes a man who has taken the Buddhist monastic vows but not actually entered a monastery.

son, the governor of Izu [province],[2] secretly called this evening on Prince Mochihito, the second son of the ex-sovereign, at [his] palace and urged him to join in the destruction of the Taira and to assume the rule of the country himself. He would be aided in the effort by Minamoto Yoritomo, the former assistant captain of the Military Guards, Right Division, and his followers of the Minamoto clan. The Prince instructed [one of his retainers] to issue a pronouncement[3] rallying the country against the Taira. As Minamoto Yukiie happened to be in the capital, he was ordered to take the pronouncement to Yoritomo and to the other members of the Minamoto clan in the eastern provinces. . . .

27th day. Prince Mochihito's pronouncement borne by Yukiie reached Yoritomo today at [his father-in-law's] residence in Izu Province. Wearing ceremonial robes and bowing respectfully toward distant [Mount] Otokoyama,[4] Yoritomo gave instructions to have the pronouncement opened and read. Meanwhile, Yukiie departed for [the provinces of] Kai and Shinano[5] to notify the Minamoto of the purport of the prince's directive.

It is twenty sad years since the 11th day of the Third Month of Eireki 1 [1160] when Yoritomo, involved in the disturbance created by the former captain of the Right Outer Palace Guards [Fujiwara] Nobuyori [against the Taira], was exiled to this province. During this period the lay priest and chancellor Kiyomori ruled the country despotically, meting out sentences on his ministers as he pleased, and even daring to confine the ex-sovereign in the Toba Detached Palace.[6] He has aroused the indigna-

2. Izu province occupied the peninsula just south of Yoritomo's later headquarters at Kamakura. Its distance from Heian made it a suitable location for launching a conspiracy undetected.

3. This was technically a *reishi*—a document which any imperial prince had the right to issue. Yoritomo based his alleged legal right to overthrow the Taira upon this document.

4. Otokoyama was a low mountain near Heian, the site of a shrine dedicated to Hachiman, the (Shinto) god of war. Through this ceremonial procedure, Yoritomo demonstrated his respect for the pronouncement of an imperial prince.

5. Northwest of Izu.

6. This was an example of the ruthlessness with which the Taira treated their opponents. The dispute between Kiyomori and the ex-sovereign (i.e., retired emperor) Go-Shirakawa had to do with the rights to a provincial estate.

tion of the reigning emperor and has caused him extreme anxiety. The prince's pronouncement, reaching Yoritomo at such a time, has caused him to resolve to raise an army of justice. This is the will of Heaven, and the destruction of the Taira will come to pass.

Now, Hojo Tokimasa . . . is a powerful lord of this reign. He is father-in-law to Yoritomo, to whom he has shown indisputable loyalty. Thus, on this occasion, it was he above all others who was invited by Yoritomo to open the pronouncement. It reads:

ORDERED: That the Genji [Minamoto] and bands of troops in the various provinces of the three circuits[7] of Tokai, Tosan, and Hokuriku proceed forthwith against the master of Buddhist Law[8] Taira Kiyomori, his partisans and rebels.

The foregoing is decreed by the former governor of Izu [the son of Yorimasa]. The pronouncement of His Excellency the prince [Mochihito] declares that Kiyomori and others, using the prestige of their office and their influence, have incited rebellion and have overthrown the nation. They have caused the officials and the people to suffer, seizing and plundering the five inner provinces and the seven circuits. They have confined the ex-sovereign, exiled public officials, and inflicted death and banishment, drowning and imprisonment. They have robbed property and seized lands, usurped and bestowed offices. They have rewarded the unworthy and incriminated the innocent. They have apprehended and confined the prelates of the various temples and imprisoned student monks. They have requisitioned the silks and rice of Mount Hiei[9] to be stored as provisions for a rebellion. They have despoiled the graves of princes and cut off the head of one, defied the emperor and destroyed Buddhist Law in a manner unprecedented in history. Now the country is saddened and the ministers and people alike grieve. In consequence thereof, I [Mochihito], the second son of the ex-sovereign, in

7. The circuit (*tao*) was an administrative unit borrowed from China: each circuit consisted of a number of provinces. The circuits mentioned here were located in northern and eastern Honshu.

8. This title—usually given to famous Buddhist clerics—is here used in lieu of "Lay Priest."

9. Mount Hiei was the site of a famous Buddhist monastery.

search of the ancient principles of Emperor Temmu,[10] and following in the footsteps of Prince Shotoku,[11] proclaim war against those who would usurp the throne and who would destroy Buddhist Law. We rely not on man's efforts alone but on the assistance of providence as well. If the temporal rulers, the Three Treasures,[12] and the native gods assist us in our efforts, all the people everywhere must likewise wish to assist us immediately. This being so, let those of the Minamoto, the Fujiwara, and the brave now living in the provinces of the three circuits add their efforts to the cause. If there be those who are not of like mind, they shall be regarded as partisans of Kiyomori and they shall suffer pain of death, exile, or imprisonment. If there be those who perform meritoriously, despatch missions to me and inform me of their names and deeds, I shall, without fail, following my enthronement, bestow rewards upon them according to their wishes. Proclaim this message in all the provinces and carry out the terms of this pronouncement.

Fifth month, 15th day. Cloudy. An imperial decree was issued banishing Prince Mochihito to Tosa [province] . . .[13] This action was the result of the disclosure of the granting of an imperial pronouncement by the prince exhorting the country to rise up in arms against the Heike [Taira]. Thus today, at 7 P.M., [several] imperial police, leading a guard of soldiers, went to [Prince Mochihito's] palace. However, the prince, forewarned by Yorimasa, had fled the palace, and thus the imperial police could find no trace of him despite a thorough search of the premises. . . .

16th day. Clear. This morning the imperial police surrounded the prince's palace and made a further search for the prince, tearing open the ceilings and removing the floors, but to no avail. However, [a Taira] Middle Councilor, on orders from the lay priest and chancellor [Kiyomori], proceeded to the [residence

10. Emperor Temmu (r. 668-86), a devout Buddhist, was known for having continued the Taika reforms begun in the reign of his predecessor.

11. Prince Shotoku, author of the famous Constitution (see above, pp. 207-12), was another reformer who was also a pious Buddhist.

12. The Buddha, the Dharma (Law), and the Sangha (order of monks).

13. In southern Shikoku—far removed from the main scene of events.

of the prince's young son] with picked troops and apprehended him . . . and removed him to Rokuhara.[14] It is impossible to say how great the confusion was within and without the capital.

19th day. Rain. On the 15th Prince Mochihito secretly entered Mii[15] Temple where quarters have been provided for him by the monks. Meanwhile, Minamoto Yorimasa set fire to his residence [in Heian] and with his children, nephews, and retainers left to join the prince.

26th day. Clear. Because of the inadequacy of forces at Mii Temple, the prince departed at 5 A.M. for Nara, to seek the protection of the monks there. He was escorted by Yorimasa's family and the monks of the temple. The sons of the lay priest and chancellor [Kiyomori] . . . leading a force of 20,000 government troops, pursued the prince to Uji, [16] where a battle ensued. Yorimasa [and three of] his sons were killed by the Heike and their heads pilloried. It is being said that the head purported to be that of Yorimasa is actually that of someone else. The prince [Mochihito] took his own life before the sacred gate of Komyozan. He was thirty years old.

27th day. Because the monks of Mii Temple had constructed defenses around Mimurodo at Uji, this building was burned and razed by the government troops. On the same day action was taken at the ex-sovereign's palace to proceed punitively against the Genji [Minamoto] in the provinces and the monks of the two temples of Kofuku-ji [at Nara] and Onjo-ji [near Uji] who had acknowledged the pronouncement of the late prince.

Sixth month, 19th day. A messenger [sent by] Yasunobu, [one of Yoritomo's sympathizers in Heian], arrived [in Izu province] and, meeting with Yoritomo in the seclusion of his residence, reported thus: "In the wake of the death of Prince Mochihito on the 26th of the past month, there has been a court action to proceed punitively against the Genji and all others who had endorsed the prince's pronouncement. This is of special

14. A district in Heian where Kiyomori had his palace.
15. Mii was a monastery on the shores of Lake Biwa, not far from Heian.
16. A spot near Heian.

concern to Your Lordship, the legitimate heir to the chieftainship of the Minamoto clan. It is suggested that Your Lordship flee immediately to Oshu." Yasunobu's mother is a younger sister of the woman who had been Yoritomo's wet nurse. Because of this close relationship between their families Yasunobu has always leaned toward the Minamoto. Through messengers who endure the dangers of the mountains and the rivers Yasunobu has been reporting on the details of the happenings in the capital three times a month. On this occasion he had sent his younger brother Yasukiyo because of the seriousness of the news of punitive action against the Genji. In order to bring the message to Yoritomo, Yasukiyo had taken leave of his court duties by pleading illness.

22nd day. [The messenger] Yasukiyo has departed for the capital. Yoritomo has entrusted him with a detailed letter to Yasunobu expressing his appreciation for his services. The scribe was [Yoritomo's] secretary. Included in the packet were His Lordship's brush and seal.

24th day. Since His Lordship [Yoritomo] does not regard as mere rumor the information contained in Yasunobu's letter that the Heike, following Minamoto Yorimasa's rout, were planning to attack the Genji in the provinces, he has summoned the hereditary vassals to his side that they might devise ways to check the Heike.

. . . .

Introduction to the Tale of the House of Taira

The *Tale of the House of Taira* (*Heike Monogatari*) is one of several popular romances inspired by the war between the Taira (Heike) and the Minamoto (Genji) clans. Poetic in form, it narrates the fall of the Taira from the position of supremacy it held under Kiyomori (1156-80) to the almost total destruction of its leadership (by 1185). While of lesser historical value than the *Mirror of Eastern Japan*,* which treats of the same events, it has much greater literary distinction, and in fact ranks as a masterpiece of Japanese literature. Accurate in broad outline, it includes many imaginative details, and must be used with caution as a historical source.

Though its authorship and exact date are uncertain, the *Tale* appears to have first been composed shortly after the end of the war and enlarged sometime in the thirteenth century. Its theme—showing the influence of popular Buddhism—is the vanity and impermanence of earthly power and glory. At the same time it glorifies the military virtues and the feudal code of loyalty. Like the other war romances, it proved enormously popular with the warrior class which now dominated Japanese society, and was chanted on festive occasions to the accompaniment of music.

The following excerpts describe the battle of Dan-no-Ura,† which brought the war to an end.

* See previous selection, pp. 229-34.
† At the far western end of the Inland Sea.

FROM THE TALE OF THE HOUSE OF TAIRA

Meanwhile Yoshitsune,[1] after his victory at Yashima,[2] crossed over to Suwo [province] to join his brother Noriyori . . . Just at this time Tanso, the [chief official] of Kumano, of the province of Kii, who was under great obligations to the Heike, suddenly changed his mind and hesitated as to which side he should support. So he went to the [Shinto] shrine of Ikumano at Tanabe and spent seven days in retirement there, having [sacred dances] performed, and praying before the [image of the god]. As a result of this he received an intimation from the deity that he should adhere to the white banner [of the Genji], but, being still doubtful, he took seven white cocks and seven red ones, and

From *The Heike Monogatari*, trans. by A. L. Sadler in *Transactions of the Asiatic Society of Japan*, Vol. XLIX, Part I (1921), pp. 242-46, 248-51.

1. Yoshitsune was Yoritomo's younger brother and the most capable military leader on the Genji side. His subsequent tragic end—precipitated by Yoritomo's jealousy—has made him a romantic hero in Japan and the subject of an extensive popular literature.
2. Place on the northern coast of Shikoku.

held a cock-fight before the [god]. As none of the red cocks were victorious but were all beaten and ran away, he at last made up his mind to join the Genji.

Assembling all his retainers to the number of some two thousand men, and embarking them on two hundred ships of war, he put the emblem of the deity of the shrine on board his ship and painted the name of [the guardian god] on the top of his standard. Accordingly when this vessel with its divine burden approached the ships of the Genji and Heike at Dan-no-ura, both parties saluted it reverently, but when it was seen to direct its course towards the fleet of the Genji, the Heike could not conceal their chagrin. Moreover, to the further consternation of the Heike, Shiro Michinobu of the province of Iyo also came rowing up with a hundred and fifty large ships and went over to the fleet of their enemies.

Thus the forces of the Genji went on increasing, while those of the Heike grew less. The Genji had some three thousand ships, and the Heike one thousand, among which were some of Chinese build; and so, on the twenty fourth day of the third month of the second year of Gen-ryaku [1185], at the Hour of the Hare (6 a.m.), at Ta-no-ura in the province of Bungo and at Dan-no-ura in the province of Nagato,[3] began the final battle of the Genji and the Heike. . . .

Now the two hosts of the Genji and Heike faced each other scarcely [half a mile] distant on the water; and as the tide was running strongly, the Heike ships were carried down by the current against their will, while the Genji were naturally able to advance on them with the tide. Kajiwara [a Genji leader], with his sons and retainers to the number of fourteen or fifteen, stuck close to the shore, and catching on with rakes to some ships of the Heike that went astray, they boarded them and sprang from one ship to the other, cutting their men down both at bow and stern and doing great deeds. And their merit that day has been specially recorded.

Thus both armies joined battle all along the line, and the roar of their war cries was such as to be heard even to the highest

3. Nagato province, on the extreme southwest tip of Honshu, and Bungo, in north Kyushu, lay almost directly opposite each other across the Inland Sea.

heavens of [the god] Brahma, and to cause the deity deep under the earth to start in amazement. Then [the Heike general] Tomomori, coming forth on to the deck-house of his ship, shouted to his men in a mighty voice: "Even in India and China and also in our own country, with the most renowned leader and the bravest warriors an army cannot prevail if fate be against it. Yet must our honour be dear to us, and we must show a bold front to these Eastern soldiers. Let us then pay no heed to our lives, but think of nothing but fighting as bravely as we may." [Another of the Heike], Kagetsune, again repeated this proclamation to the samurai.[4] "Ho! these Eastern fellows[5] may have a great name for their horsemanship," shouted [the warrior] Kagekiyo, "but they know nothing about sea-fights, and they will be like fish up a tree, so that we will pick them up one by one and pitch them into the sea!" . . .

So the Heike divided their thousand vessels into three fleets. . . . The fleet of the Genji was the more numerous with its three thousand ships, but as their men shot from various places here and there, their force did not show to advantage. Yoshitsune himself [the supreme commander of the Genji], who was fighting in the forefront of the battle, was greatly embarrassed by the arrows of the foe that fell like rain on his shield and armour. So, elated by their victory in the first attack, the Heike pressed onward, and the roar of their shouting mingled with the booming of their war-drums that continuously sounded the onset. . . .

After this both sides set their faces against each other and fought grimly without a thought for their lives, neither giving way an inch. But as the Heike had on their side an Emperor[6] endowed with the Ten Virtues[7] and the Three Sacred Treasures[8] of the Realm, things went hard with the Genji and their hearts were beginning to fail them, when suddenly something that they at first took for a white cloud, but which soon appeared to be a white banner floating in the breeze, came drifting over the

4. Military retainers.
5. The headquarters of the Genji were at Kamakura in the East.
6. This was Antoku, the child-grandson of Kiyomori.
7. Of Buddhism.
8. The Sword, the Jewel, and the Mirror—emblems of imperial authority.

two fleets from the upper air and finally settled on the stern of one of the Genji ships, hanging on by the rope.

When he saw this, Yoshitsune, regarding it as a sign from the great Bodhisattva Hachiman,[9] removed his helmet, and after washing his hands, did obeisance; his men all following his example. Moreover a shoal of some thousand of dolphins also made its appearance from the offing and made straight for the ships of the Heike. Then [the Heike general] Munemori called a diviner and said: "There are always many dolphins about here, but I have never seen so many as these before; what may it portend?" "If they turn back," replied the diviner, "the Genji will be destroyed; but if they go on then our own side will be in danger." No sooner had he finished speaking than the dolphins dived under the Heike ships and passed on.

Then, as things had come to this pass, [the lord] Shigeyoshi, who for three years had been a loyal supporter of the Heike, now made up his mind that all was lost, and suddenly forsook his allegiance and deserted to the enemy. Great was the regret of [the Heike general] Tomomori that he had not cut off the head of "that villain Shigeyoshi," but now it was unavailing.

Now the strategy of the Heike had been to put the stoutest warriors on board the ordinary fighting ships and the inferior soldiers on the big ships of Chinese build, so that the Genji should be induced to attack the big ships, thinking that the commanders were on board them, when they would be able to surround and destroy them. But when Shigeyoshi went over and joined the Genji he revealed this plan to them, with the result that they immediately left the big ships alone and concentrated their attacks on the smaller ones on which were the Heike champions. Later on the men of Shikoku and Kyushu all left the Heike in a body and went over to the Genji. Those who had so far been [the Heike's] faithful retainers now turned their bows against their lords and drew the sword against their own masters. On one shore the heavy seas beat on the cliff so as to forbid any landing, while on the other stood the serried ranks of the enemy waiting with levelled arrows to receive them. And so on

9. Hachiman, the Shinto god of war, was also regarded as a Buddha incarnate.

this day the struggle for supremacy between the Genji and the Heike was at last decided.

Meanwhile the Genji warriors sprang from one Heike vessel to the other, shooting and cutting down the sailors and helmsmen, so that they flung themselves in panic to the bottom of the ships unable to navigate them any longer. Then Tomomori rowed in a small boat to the Imperial Vessel and cried out: "You see what affairs have come to! Clean up the ship, and throw everything unsightly into the sea!" And he ran about the ship from bow to stern, sweeping and cleaning and gathering up the dust with his own hands. . . .

Then the Lady Nii, who had already resolved what she would do, donning a double outer dress of dark grey mourning colour, and tucking up the long skirts of her glossy silk garment, put the Sacred Jewel under her arm, and the Sacred Sword in her girdle, and taking the Emperor in her arms, spoke thus: "Though I am but a woman I will not fall into the hands of the foe, but will accompany our Sovereign Lord. Let those of you who will, follow me." And she glided softly to the gunwale of the vessel.

The Emperor was eight years old that year, but looked much older than his age. His appearance was so lovely that he shed as it were a brilliant radiance about him, and his long black hair hung loose far down his back. With a look of surprise and anxiety on his face he enquired of the Lady Nii: "Where is it that you are going to take me?" Turning to her youthful Sovereign with tears streaming down her cheeks, she answered: "Perchance our Lord does not know that, though through the merit of the Ten Virtues practised in former lives you have been reborn to the Imperial Throne in this world, yet by the power of some evil karma destiny now claims you. So now turn to the east and bid farewell to the deity of the Great Shrine of Ise, and then to the west and say the Nembutsu[10] that Amida Buddha and the Holy Ones may come to welcome you to the Pure Western Land. Japan is called small as a grain of millet, but yet is it now but a vale of misery. There is a Pure Land of happiness beneath the waves, another Capital where no sorrow is. Thither it is that I

10. Declaration of faith in the Buddha Amida.

am taking Our Lord." And thus comforting him, and binding his long hair up in his dove-coloured robe, blinded with tears the child-Sovereign put his beautiful little hands together and turned first to the east to say farewell to the deity of Ise and to [the god] Hachiman, and then to the west and repeated the Nembutsu. Then the Lady Nii, holding him tightly in her arms and saying consolingly: "In the depths of the Ocean we have a Capital" sank with him at last beneath the waves.

Ah, the pity of it! That the gust of the spring wind of Impermanence should so suddenly sweep away his flower form. That the cruel billows should thus engulf his Jewel Person. Since his Palace was called the Palace of Longevity, he should have passed a long life therein; its gate was called the Gate of Eternal Youth, the barrier that old age should not pass; and yet, ere he had reached the age of ten years, he had become like the refuse that sinks to the bottom of the sea. How vain it was to proclaim him as one who sat on the Throne as a reward of the Ten Virtues! It was like the Dragon that rides on the clouds descending to become a fish at the bottom of the ocean. He who abode in a Palace fair as the terraced pavilions of the highest heaven of Brahma, or the paradise where Shakya Muni dwells among his Ministers and Nobles . . . thus came to a miserable end beneath the ocean waves.

Religion

Introduction to Shinto

The indigenous religion of Japan is a form of nature-worship dating back to an unrecorded antiquity. Originally nameless, this faith was later termed "Shinto" (i.e., "The Way of the Gods") in order to distinguish it from the imported Chinese thought-systems—Buddhism and Confucianism. The objects of Shinto-worship were the spirits of dead ancestors and of certain powerful living men as well as a large variety of deities thought to inhabit natural phenomena, e.g. rocks, streams, birds, animals, trees, mountains. Called *kami*—a broad term which originally meant merely "superior"—these Shinto deities were all felt to represent powerful, awesome, mysterious natural forces. Associated with Shinto was an involved mythology tracing the creation of the Japanese islands and the birth of the imperial ancestors to a series of godly acts in Heaven. With the passage of time the various cults of local deities became integrated through an official mythology which proclaimed the descent of the imperial dynasty from the Sun Goddess. The most important *kami* were thus the emperor's ancestors; and Shinto-worship served to unite the Japanese nation under imperial rule.

Shinto is a ritualistic rather than an ethical religion, lacking either a moral code or a body of sacred scriptures. Through appropriate ceremonies the believer seeks the aid and protection of the gods or the removal of ritual impurities incurred, for example, through the touching of unclean objects, eating forbidden food, or through contact with childbirth or death. Shinto shrines were places where the *kami* were believed to reside, or to which they might be summoned through proper performance of ceremonies. A typical shrine was a plain wooden building covered with thatch, its entrance guarded by a gateway supposed to guard it against evil and contamination. Worship ordinarily was simple: the devotee bowed and clapped his hands in front of the shrine, rang a bell to attract the god's attention, and deposited his offering of food or money. On special festival-days, ceremonies on behalf of the whole community were held before the shrines. Presiding at such ceremonies were members of the hereditary priesthood, who were classified into four groups: Ritualists (Nakatomi clan), Abstainers (Imbe clan), Diviners (Urabe clan), and Musicians and Dancers (Sarume clan). In early historical times the most important Shinto festivals were associated with agriculture, and designed to secure divine protection for crops and the avoidance of natural disasters.

With the wide dissemination of Chinese culture in Japan beginning in the seventh century A.D., Shinto was forced to adjust itself to the far more complex religions of the mainland. Confucianism, for example, possessed a highly developed code of ethics; Buddhism could boast of a subtle and profound doctrine, impressive ceremonies, and sophisticated art-forms—all of which tended to overwhelm the more primitive Shinto. As a result, by the ninth century Shinto had largely lost its unique characteristics and become assimilated to Buddhism. The first efforts at amalgamation were made by Buddhist monks of the Tendai sect, who taught that the native gods were local manifestations of Buddhist divinities (the Bodhisattvas), who in turn were manifestations of the one transcendent Buddha. But a more practical type of assimilation—later known as "Dual" Shinto—was later developed by Buddhist monks of the Shingon sect, and became especially prominent under the Kamakura Shogunate. Joint Shinto-Buddhist sanctuaries arose, and a joint priesthood evolved. Buddhist ceremonies and ritual objects came to be employed in Shinto worship; Buddhist sutras were read to Shinto gods; and Shinto deities were officially proclaimed to be incarnations of the supreme and universal Buddha-principle. Thereby Shinto largely ceased to exist as an independent religion until the nineteenth century, when representatives of the new nationalism attempted to free it of all foreign accretions and to equate the worship of the native gods with Japanese patriotism.

Introduction to Gleanings from Ancient Stories

The myths of the native gods of Japan—though dating back to a high antiquity—possessed far more than antiquarian interest for the

Japanese of later times. Not only did the descent of the emperor from the Sun Goddess serve to legitimize his government; the events of the legendary "Age of the Gods" were believed to have established the proper relationships to be observed in contemporary society.

According to the myth, the divine ancestors of the Imbe and the Nakatomi—two clans of hereditary Shinto ritualists—had been of equal importance in the Age of the Gods. With the passage of time, however, the Nakatomi (of whom the Fujiwara regents were an offshoot) became all-powerful at court, eclipsing all their rivals. This state of affairs naturally aroused the Imbe family's indignation, since participation in the religious ceremonies performed at court conferred high social prestige. Therefore in the year 807, prompted by an acute sense of having been wronged, Imbe Hironari penned his *Gleanings from Ancient Stories* (*Kogoshui*) as a formal protest to the emperor. Therein he sets forth some of the more important Shinto traditions, interpreting them so as to justify his family's claim to equal status with the Nakatomi.

FROM GLEANINGS FROM ANCIENT STORIES (KOGOSHUI)

It was in the Taiho Era [A.D. 697-707] that Japan first possessed official records of the Shinto Gods. Even then, however, a complete list of the names of Shinto Gods and Shrines was lacking and the national Shinto rites were not well established. When the Government Authorities began to compile a book on the Shinto Shrines officially registered during the Tempyo Era [A.D. 724-749], the Nakatomi family, being then most influential at court in religious affairs, took arbitrary measures and strictly superintended the compilation. Consequently the shrines, no matter how insignificant, were all recorded in the registry if they had any connection with the Nakatomi, whilst on the contrary even the greater, more renowned shrines, if not related to that house, were omitted from all mention therein. Thus the Nakatomi family, being then all-powerful, made an unwar-

From Genchi Kato and Hikoshiro Hoshino, trans., *Kogoshui, Gleanings from Ancient Stories*, Tokyo: Meiji Japan Society, 1925, pp. 44-48, 50, 52-54.

ranted use of its authority in Shinto matters to the detriment of the other families. The Nakatomi alone enjoyed the large income derived from the public tributes paid by the people attached to each shrine. All the names of the divine attendants who escorted the Heavenly Grandson to earth or those who accompanied the first human Emperor [Jimmu] on his eastern expedition[1] mentioned in our old historical books are familiar to us. Some of them served by guarding His Majesty against his foes in obedience to the command of the celestial deities, whilst the rest rendered distinguished services to the Emperor in aiding him to carry out his plans for establishing Imperial rule and thus assure the prosperity of the Empire. Therefore, each one of them should have been justly and impartially rewarded with posthumous divine honours in recognition of those past meritorious services. Yet, to my profound regret, the opposite has occurred, for in these days they do not all receive the same divine honour of homage from the Imperial Government. Permit me, gracious Sovereign, to mention those things which the Authorities concerned have unfairly omitted. . . .

From the beginning in Heaven, Amaterasu [the Sun Goddess], symbolized by the Sacred Mirror, remained in the same house with the Emperor,[2] so both the Deity and the Emperor were waited upon exactly in the same manner by the attendants, there being no discrimination between the Deity and the Sovereign at all. [Moreover], Imbe and Nakatomi conjointly prayed the Sun-Goddess graciously to re-appear from the Heavenly Rock-Cave,[3] and it was the ancestress of the Sarume family[4] who succeeded in propitiating the incensed Goddess. The Government, therefore, should appoint the descendants of the

1. Jimmu, the Heavenly Grandson's great-grandson, allegedly moved with his followers from his original residence on Kyushu to central Honshu, where he is supposed to have founded the first Japanese state (Yamato) in 660 B.C.

2. Until the first century B.C. the Mirror remained under the same roof with the Emperor in the imperial palace. This sacred Mirror, Sword, and Jewel—all allegedly brought to earth by the Heavenly Grandson—remain to this day the three symbols of imperial authority in Japan.

3. Where she had retreated in anger at her brother, the god Susa-no-o. As a result, the entire world was plunged in darkness.

4. Clan whose members served as musicians and dancers at divine services.

three families conjointly to the office of Shinto service. Yet nevertheless the Nakatomi family alone nowadays enjoys the exclusive privilege of holding the priestly office of the Ise Shrine,[5] the two other families being utterly ignored.

Ever since the Divine Age it had been the sacred prerogative of the Imbe family to be entrusted with the official work of constructing Shinto shrines. Thus the official head of the Imbe family, with his kinsfolk, began the work by cutting down forest trees with consecrated axes, turning the sod with consecrated mattocks, and finished the entire structure with the aid of craftsmen. When completed, the shrines and their gates were consecrated by the Imbe family with the prescribed ceremonial rites of Shinto, and thus became actually fit for divine abodes. In violation of these dear old Shinto customs and usages, the services of the Imbe family are today wholly dispensed with, whether for re-building the Ise Shrine or erecting the sacred tabernacles or pavilions for the Great Harvest Festival at the enthronement of a new Emperor. Is this not a gross injustice to the time-honoured privilege of the Imbe family?

Also the Shinto Ceremony for Blessing the Great Palace and the Religious Service for the Guardian Gods of the Imperial Gates were both originally entrusted to [an ancestor of the Imbe], so it is beyond dispute that the Imbe family alone should enjoy the time-honoured hierarchic privilege in both cases of Shinto worship. As the Nakatomi and the Imbe, who are the officially commissioned priests of the Shinto Bureau,[6] used to attend to the Shinto rites and ceremonies conjointly, an officer of the Imperial Household Department was accustomed to report himself in the following words: "Both Nakatomi and Imbe are present at the August Gates in order that they may solemnize the Shinto Ceremony for Blessing the Great Palace." In the Hoki Era [A.D. 770-780], however, it was a Nakatomi who arbitrarily changed the words in the report to the Emperor, saying, "Nakatomi with Imbe *under him* is now at the August Gates." In this way the Imbe, once placed in a position inferior to that of the Nakatomi, have, owing to the procrastination and negligence of

5. The most important Shinto shrine in all Japan.
6. A government office.

the officials of the Imperial Household Department, never been restored to their former rightful place all this time. This is a thing that I feel keenly regrettable. . . .

In preparing the great offerings for the divine service, the chieftain of the Imbe family should be entrusted as formerly with the charge of making them up, and lead all the other families to whom hereditary [religious] callings respectively belonged. Hence, among those serving in the Shinto Bureau there should be officials related to such families, as the Nakatomi, the Imbe, the Sarume, [and others] . . . Yet, in the present state of things, we do not find any in the same Bureau except the Nakatomi, the Imbe, and some few others. Those families unrelated to the Nakatomi and the Imbe are not admitted into the service of the Shinto Bureau. All their descendants, not excepting even those of divine origin, have been reduced to poor and miserable circumstances and are greatly decreasing in number. Is this not a cause for deep regret? . . .

Nowadays people discredit the above traditions handed down from the Divine Age, just as a summer insect does not credit the existence of winter ice. Yet things divine or miraculous, however incredible they may appear, are often revealed for the benefit of a nation even in the present age of unbelief—a proof of their actual existence. And in the ages prior to our own, the Japanese civilization not being in an advanced condition, State ceremonies were not then perfected, and the national institutions were irregular and unsatisfactory. [However,] now Your Imperial Majesty has inaugurated over our Eight-Islands the present glorious rule which embodies the ideal of the ancient Chinese Emperor Yao,[7] and this New Era has brought peace such as that which prevailed all over the Four Seas under the venerable Chinese Emperor Shun.[7] Your Imperial Majesty is endeavouring to bring the people back from the present deteriorated manners and customs to the purity of the good old past, and reform the imperfect system of Government by establishing Government institutions such as the circumstances now require. By restoring the dear old customs and usages that have now lapsed almost into oblivion, [Your Majesty is attempting] thereby to preserve

7. Legendary figures known as paragons of wise rule.

and propagate the essence of the fine customs of the past among your subjects in the hope of perfecting the observance of the ancient laws and State ceremonies.

[Therefore] I [Imbe Hironari], Your Imperial Majesty's humble servant, sincerely pray that Your Imperial Majesty will be pleased to promulgate the ceremonial rules and regulations for worshipping the Shinto gods, utilizing this opportunity wherever the State institutions are to be re-established. Otherwise I dread that our posterity will have cause to complain of us just as we now do of our own forefathers. I, Your Majesty's humble servant Hironari, instinctively loyal to the Imperial Court and deeply revering my cherished old traditions, being now over eighty years of age and having idled my time away to such an advanced age,—if I should ever die suddenly without publishing all the traditions preserved in my family, my poor soul would be restless in its tomb. . . . Your Imperial Majesty having deigned to enquire about my family traditions, I . . . am overjoyed by the thought that the occasion will enable me to submit all my family traditional documents to the Imperial throne. I trust most sincerely that this appeal will be honoured by Your Majesty's gracious inspection.

Introduction to the Diary of a Pilgrim to Ise

From very ancient times the chief shrine (actually, group of shrines) dedicated to the Japanese Sun Goddess has been located on a promontary east of Yamato in Ise province. According to tradition, the sacred Mirror from Heaven—a prime symbol of the emperor's sovereignty—was removed from court in 5 B.C. and installed at Ise under the supervision of an imperial princess appointed as High Priestess. Each year numerous pilgrims visited the place, which was then and still remains the holiest spot in all Japan.

One such visitor was Saka, a Buddhist monk and physician who was also deeply attached to the Shinto deities. A man highly learned in both Chinese and Japanese literature, and skillful at verse-making as well, he recorded his impressions of the shrine in a diary (the *Ise Daijingu Sankeiki*) which ranks as an important work of Japanese literature. Saka made his pilgrimage in the year 1342—not long after the civil disturbances which had culminated six years previously in the overthrow of the Kamakura Shogunate; and he remarks on the devastation of the countryside. His observations also plainly indicate the degree to which the Shinto and Buddhist religions had become amalgamated by the fourteenth century. Saka stresses the "inner purity" of the spirit far more than the characteristic "outer purity" of Shinto, and treats the sacred Mirror less as an object divine in itself than as a symbol of spiritual illumination.

FROM THE DIARY OF A PILGRIM TO ISE

About the tenth day of the tenth month of the first year of the era Koei [i.e., 1342] I arrived at the port of Anonotsu in Ise with the intention of making a pilgrimage to the great Shrines. I stayed here for some three days with someone I had once met at home in order to beguile myself and stimulate my interest in the further journey. . . .

As I left Anonotsu and passed by Akogi Beach the smoke of the salt-burners had a dreary look and rose to the sky overhead and it too made me feel restless, as the cry of the solitary seabird falling on my ear reminded me how uncertain and full of vicissitudes is this life of ours. . . . And the sinking of the sun in the west naturally reminds us of our latter end that it too is not far off, while the ebbing and flowing of the tide suggests that there is, as it were, a life and death even in the waters, as the ancient poem says. So I composed a poem:

In this troublous life,
Now we float and now we sink;
Just so in the sea,
In the ever moving tide,
You may see a great wave break.

From A. L. Sadler, trans., *Saka's Diary of a Pilgrim to Ise* (*Ise Daijingu Sankeiki*), Tokyo: The Meiji Japan Society, 1940, pp. 27-36, 44-45, 47-49, 57-60.

Now we go on past the lustration place[1] by the Kushida River and it is very evident how terribly the southern part of this province has been devastated through the chaotic state of the country of recent years. There are plenty of plantations of bamboos and thickets of trees and the like but when we approach we see no habitations. In a space between the eulalia and anthistirea bushes[2] there is a newly-made path full of dead tree-stumps, and when we asked a passer-by about it he said it was just a place where there had been rice-fields before; and I thought how sad it was that things had come to this pass.

I went on to the residence of the Imperial Princess.[3] I saw what was evidently the remains of the ancient walls where there were a lot of tall trees and shrubs. The Shinto gateway [*torii*] had fallen and its decayed pillars were lying in the road, and you might easily mistake them for fallen trees if you did not look carefully. There have been very laudable intentions of late of restoring this long disused building, but the cherries of Yoshino[4] have been snatched away by the blast of impermanence as the patrinias of Sagano[5] have withered in the dew of enmity, and so only the name of the "Rustic Palace" remains and there is no Imperial Vestal to come and live in her residence in Ise. And we must reflect how little consideration for the sanctity of the deities there is in the present government—the administration is not obedient to the Divine Will. And this is a recent matter. . . .

Crossing the Miya River and viewing the scene at the feet of hills high and low the road widens on this side and that and there is what looks quite like a city. This is the place called Yamada where are many thick groves of pines. And here is the Outer Shrine [*Gegu*]. I lodged at a Buddhist temple called Samboin, and as there was some talk about "Verse-capping"[6]

1. The spot where the purification ceremony was performed.
2. Flowering herbaceous plants.
3. The High Priestess of the shrine—a sort of vestal virgin who was kept apart from all impurity.
4. Literary reference to the late emperor Go-daigo (r. 1318-39), whose attempt to depose the Kamakura Shoguns and restore imperial power had precipitated the recent civil war.
5. Reference to the High Priestess. The patrinia is a perennial herb with yellow flowers.
6. Literary game whereby one person invents the first half of a verse, another the second half.

the Chief Shinto Ritualist of the Shrine came to hear about me. As he seemed to want to hear the latest news of the Capital I was asked to go and visit him, so I betook myself to his official residence. He was the Lord Ieyuki of the Lower Third Court Rank. He received me and asked me about veteran teachers of verse-capping but I was unfortunately incompetent to give him any information. He was able to answer all our enquiries about the primeval deities and their incarnations without referring to any records, so that our former difficulties and doubts were dissolved like mist in the breeze. He seemed indeed an ideal Chief of the Great Shrine with his hoary eye-brows and snow-white beard that matched the hoar-frost outside, his expression of countenance always adapted to the occasion and his pellucid mind always the source of a well-spring of speech. So by his eloquence the past lived again before our eyes. So thankful was I for such an opportunity that after talking all the evening I hastened to write down all I had heard without any revision before I had time to forget any of it.

Now it was in the days of the Emperor Suinin[7] that the Deity took up her abode in the Inner Shrine, while the manifestation in the Outer Shrine took place in the time of the Emperor Yuryaku [5th century A.D.]. There may be some centuries between them but I will begin with the manifestation of the Outer Shrine according to the order of the pilgrimage. The Deity of this Shrine is the Moon-Deity. About this matter there are many opinions, but taking that of the *Nihongi* it says that [the primal pair] Izanagi and Izanami gave birth to the Sun-Deity and the Moon-Deity and sent them up to the Plain of High Heaven and that these two Deities are those of the Inner and Outer Shrines. And this is what most people believe . . .

When on the way to these Shrines one does not feel like an ordinary person any longer but as though reborn in another world. How solemn is the unearthly shadow of the huge groves of ancient pines and cypresses, and there is a delicate pathos in the few rare flowers that have withstood the winter frosts so gaily. The cross-beam of the Shinto gateway is without any

7. According to the *Nihongi*, the Emperor Suinin reigned from 29 B.C. until A.D. 70, dying at the age of 140 years.

curve, symbolizing by its straightness the sincerity of the direct beam of the Divine promise. The shrine-fence is not painted red nor is the Shrine itself roofed with cedar shingles. The eaves, with their rough reed-thatch, recall memories of the ancient days when the roofs were not trimmed. So did they spare expense out of compassion for the hardships of the people. Within the Shrine there are many buildings where the festival rites are performed, constructed just like those in the Imperial Palace. Buddhist monks may go only as far as the Sacred Tree known as the Pine of the Five Hundred Branches. They may not go to the Shrine. This, too, is a ceremonial rule of the Imperial Court.

The Divine Descendants received the Sovereignty and were proclaimed Emperors and the Imperial Ancestress was venerated and called the Great Deity. And the benevolent grace that gives to this land peace and security is that which radiates from the all-protecting Ancestral Shrine. And thinking over this I wrote:

> When we consider
> The forbear of our Sovereigns,
> Deity of ancient Ise,
> We see then how this place is
> The Capital of the Deity.

. . . .

To the south-east of the Shrine beyond the sacred pool on a high hill there is a shrine called Taka. If, when praying to the Shrine, one first informs the Deity here of it, he will forward the petition to the Great Shrine, he being as it were Regent to the Son of Heaven. And there is no example of this indirect communication in any other shrine.

Moreover, behind this Shrine is a wondrous great crag where all the deities assemble and here supernatural visitants are always present, it is said. It is believed too that there are forty-eight caves,[8] and there are some places on the stones that are quite warm, so that it is evident that someone has just been sitting on them. And sometimes people meet a strange unearthly

8. Probably Saka had in mind the forty-eight vows of the Bodhisattva Amida.

old man here. Chinese scholars speak of the thirty-six heavenly caves.[9] These are the ancient ones where the Taoist magicians perform their rites, but in this mountain there are forty-eight of them, and hallowed resorts and fairy confines where the deities and spirits hold their revels. . . .

When I entered the second Shinto Gateway to worship it was dark under the pines at the foot of the hill and the branches were so thick-matted that one could hardly discern the Pine of One Hundred Branches. The pines within the Shrine precincts were so dense that even the oblique projecting roof-beams could hardly be made out. When I come to reflect on my condition my mind is full of the Ten Evils[10] and I felt shame at so long forsaking the will of Buddha, yet as I wear one of the three monkish robes I must feel some chagrin at my estrangement from the Way of the Deities.[11]

And particularly is it the deeply-rooted custom of this Shrine that we should bring no Buddhist rosary or offering, or any special petition in our hearts. This is called "Inner Purity." Washing in sea water and keeping the body free from all defilement is called "Outer Purity." And when both these Purities are attained there is then no barrier between our mind and that of the Deity. And if we feel to become thus one with the Divine, what more do we need and what is there to pray for? When I heard that this was the true way of worshipping at the Shrine, I could not refrain from shedding tears of gratitude.

That which embodies the Deity in the Inner Shrine is the Sacred Mirror. It was cast in the heavens by the eight million deities. And it is written that when Amaterasu [the Sun Goddess] secluded herself in the Heavenly Rock Cave utter darkness took possession of the world. Then the deities assembled, and on the uprooted sacred tree of Mount Kagu they hung a mirror and jewels and the blue and white soft hempen cloths. And when

9. In Hangchow (China) there were thirty-six caves where Taoist immortals were believed to reside.

10. I.e., the ten Buddhist sins: of the body (murder, theft, adultery); of the mouth (lying, boastfulness, abuse, ambiguity); and the mind (covetousness, malice, scepticism).

11. As a Buddhist monk, Saka could only worship at a certain distance from the shrine.

they sang and danced the divine dance [*Kagura*] and the Sun-Goddess opened the door of the cave a little to look out, the Deity Tajikarao pushed it back and drew her forth so that her August Figure was reflected in the mirror. . . .

And as to the Way of the Deities, in primeval days they reached out from on high and created land and gave it the name of Onokoro Island, and on to it the two Deities descended from Heaven. And so the land was made and trees and herbs came into being on it. And when the country was thus constituted mankind came into existence . . . During this period the deities alone protected the land and dealt graciously with the people, for the virtuous assistance of Buddhism in governing the country was not yet.

But after many years, when people had ceased to trust in the Way of the Deities, Prince Shotoku appeared and not only spread the knowledge of Buddhism but was also [himself] a manifestation of this Way. After him came Dengyo-daishi and founded his temple on the northern Mount[12] where he made the essential doctrine shine forth in great effulgence under the divine protection of the Seven Shrines [of the Bodhisattvas]. Another great establishment was that which Kobo set up on the southern Mount[13] where he taught the doctrine of the Three Mysteries[14] by the virtuous aid of the Four Tutelary [Shinto] Deities. So Buddhism did not remain an exclusive faith: it made friends with the Way of the Deities. And though its sects have various doctrines they all have the one principle of perfecting the intuitive soul and revealing the jewel of the enlightened mind. When our mind is interpreted as fixed on Buddha's teaching it is called the Supreme Mind, and when it is seen in the light of the Shinto writings it is called the Invisible Mind. It may be so described because our mind is stupid, but after a while when it becomes inwardly true to itself it may be possible that it is a partaker of

12. Mount Hiei near Heian (Kyoto). Dengyo-daishi (*daishi* means "Great Teacher") was the monk Saicho (767-822), who introduced the T'ien-t'ai (Tendai) sect of Buddhism from China into Japan.

13. Mount Koya in Kii province. Kobo-daishi was the monk Kukai (744-835), who founded the Shingon sect of Buddhism.

14. The Three Mysteries of the body, speech, and mind through which the believer can attain Buddhahood.

the divine nature. For, though one's inward conviction may have a profound assurance of the reality of the Nirvana state, it is difficult for those born in folly and delusion to be saved. Whereas these deities manifest themselves outwardly among the unsaved worldly minded and it is easy for the unenlightened to profit by them. And when I thought over what we had discussed all the evening I realized how truly profound is the meaning of the character for "Heart" or "Mind" qualifying the word pillar. And as I regretted that I was not so pure as I might be, I felt how much I should like to visit the Shrine frequently; yet as I am in the sixth decade of my life I can hardly be very certain of being able to come here again. I must grieve for this loss of the divine grace, for the sanctity of this place moves me very deeply.

Introduction to Japanese Buddhism

Like so many other elements in the early culture of Japan, Buddhism was an import from China, though it first entered the islands by way of Korea. According to Japanese sources, this alien religion first attracted official notice in the middle of the sixth century A.D., when the king of one of the Korean states presented some Buddhist sutras and a statue of the Buddha to the court of Yamato. The gift precipitated a sharp controversy over whether Buddhism should be permitted in Japan—a debate which reflected the existing political rivalries at court. However, no Japanese at that time had any inkling of the philosophical complexities of Buddhist doctrine. Rather, the Buddha was regarded as a powerful foreign deity whose magic might prove superior to that of the native gods. The acceptance of Buddhism by the emperor and many leading families toward the end of the sixth century was a direct result of clan strife, in which the Soga (who favored Buddhism) displaced their rivals, the Nakatomi, as the principal influence at court. From that time onward, Buddhism acquired an ever-increasing influence in Japan, though worship of the Shinto deities was not abandoned.

All the early divisions within Japanese Buddhism were derived from Chinese prototypes. The so-called "Six Sects" which flourished during the Nara period aspired faithfully to imitate their Chinese counterparts; and the two most popular Buddhist sects of the ninth and tenth centuries—Shingon and Tendai—were introduced into Japan by monks who had accompanied the Japanese embassy to China in the year 804. In Japan, as in China, popular Buddhism tended to absorb the cults of the native gods; and the deities of Shinto gradually came to be regarded as local incarnations of the Buddhas and Bodhisattvas. However, in the tenth century the history of Buddhism in Japan began to diverge from that of the mainland. While in China Neo-Confucianism replaced Buddhism as the principal religious inspiration of the upper classes, in Japan Buddhism became more and more popular. Henceforth, the important leaders of Japanese Buddhism were native monks who had never visited China.

In its varying forms, Buddhism appealed to people of every class within Japanese society. Most of the emperors from the seventh century onward were devout believers, while members of the imperial family and aristocracy joined in providing generous financial support for Buddhist institutions. It was not unusual for high-ranking personages to take Buddhist monastic vows in middle or old age. At court the most influential Buddhist sect was the Tendai (Chinese: T'ien-t'ai), which had its headquarters on Mount Hiei near Heian. Using the *Lotus Sutra* as its principal text, Tendai Buddhism sought to harmonize the divergent doctrines of various Buddhist sects by classifying them as different (but equally valid) levels of truth. In practice, Tendai laid heavy emphasis upon magical prayers and elaborate ritual, thereby providing a religious counterpart to the complex ceremonial functions of the court itself. By contrast, the Zen (Chinese: Ch'an) sect appealed particularly to the provincial warriors who formed the most powerful element of society under the Kamakura Shogunate. The rigorous meditative practices of Zen, its stress upon personal probity, a simple life close to nature, and direct (sometimes wordless) communication between teacher and pupil (as contrasted with book-learning) provided an appropriate religious underpinning for the military code of honor, which stressed personal bravery, austerity, uncomplaining endurance of hardship, and the total loyalty of vassal to lord.

Those Buddhist sects which appealed most to the peasant and artisan classes, however, were those that emphasized salvation through faith in one of the Buddhas or Bodhisattvas. In this popular Buddhism the oustanding personality was Genshin (942-1017), a Tendai monk from Mount Hiei. Genshin believed that mankind had now entered the degenerate "latter period of the Law," when the severe discipline of the older Buddhism must give way to simpler doctrines and easier methods of salvation. He taught that rebirth in Paradise could be achieved solely through the grace of the Buddha Amida, and that a believer needed only to demonstrate his faith by calling upon Amida's name (the so-called *nembutsu*).* Genshin also wrote a book which depicts in vivid terms the joys of Paradise and the horrors of Hell. Entitled *The Essentials of Salvation* (*Ojo Yoshu*), it became enormously popular in Japan and eventually went through many reprintings.

Genshin's book also provided the greatest single inspiration for two of the best-loved figures in the history of Japanese Buddhism—Honen Shonin (*shonin* means "saint") and his principal disciple, Shinran Shonin. Honen (1133-1212) was the founder of the Pure Land sect in Japan. He taught that salvation could be achieved simply by calling upon the name of Amida, without benefit of temples, priests, or rituals. His successor Shinran then carried these ideas to their logical conclusion, arguing that the continual invocation of Amida's name was not necessary. According to him, a single *nembutsu*, if made sincerely and with true faith, suffices to assure the believer of a place after death in Amida's Pure Land. Shinran was the author of many popular devotional hymns; and the branch of the Pure Land sect which he founded remains influential in Japan to this day.

* Shortened form of *Namu Amida Butsu*, which translates as "Hail to the Buddha Amida!"

FROM THE CHRONICLES OF JAPAN (NIHONGI)*

The Introduction of Buddhism into Japan

[A.D. 552],[1] Winter, 10th month. King Syong of Paekche[2] sent [two envoys] with a present to the Emperor of an image of

* On the *Chronicles* see "The Sources of Early Japanese History," above, pp. 206-7.

From W. G. Aston, trans., *Nihongi. Chronicles of Japan from the Earliest Times to A.D. 697*, London: George Allen & Unwin Ltd., 1896, 1956, pp. 65-67, 101-102. Reprinted by permission of George Allen & Unwin, Ltd.

Words in square brackets have been added by the present editors to replace Japanese names and terms.

1. The correct date is probably A.D. 538.
2. Paekche was one of the three main Korean kingdoms.

[Shakyamuni, the Buddha] in gold and copper, several flags and umbrellas, and a number of volumes of Sutras. Separately he presented a memorial in which he lauded the merit of diffusing abroad religious worship, saying:—"This doctrine is amongst all doctrines the most excellent. But it is hard to explain, and hard to comprehend. Even the Duke of Chou and Confucius[3] had not attained to a knowledge of it. This doctrine can create religious merit and retribution [karma] without measure and without bounds, and so lead on to a full appreciation of the highest wisdom. Imagine a man in possession of treasures to his heart's content, so that he might satisfy all his wishes in proportion as he used them. Thus it is with the treasure of this wonderful doctrine. Every prayer is fulfilled and naught is wanting. Moreover, from distant India it has extended hither to the three [kingdoms of Korea], where there are none who do not receive it with reverence as it is preached to them.

"Thy servant, therefore, Syong, King of Paekche, has humbly despatched a retainer to transmit it to the Imperial Country [of Japan], and to diffuse it abroad throughout the home provinces, so as to fulfil the recorded saying of Buddha: 'My law shall spread to the East.' "

This day the Emperor, having heard to the end, leaped for joy, and gave command to the Envoys, saying:—"Never from former days until now have we had the opportunity of listening to so wonderful a doctrine. We are unable, however, to decide of ourselves." Accordingly he inquired of his Ministers one after another, saying:—"The countenance of this Buddha which has been presented by the Western frontier State is of a severe dignity, such as we have never at all seen before. Ought it to be worshipped or not?" The Oho-omi[4] [who was chief of the Soga clan] addressed the Emperor, saying:—"All the Western frontier lands without exception do it worship. Shall [our land of] Yamato alone refuse to do so?" [The chiefs of the Mononobe and Nakatomi clans] addressed the Emperor jointly, saying:—

3. Confucius was an approximate contemporary of the Buddha (sixth century B.C.); the Duke of Chou lived in the twelfth or eleventh century B.C.

4. *Omi* is a title identifying its bearer as an offshoot of the imperial house. A Great Omi (*Oho-omi* or *O-omi*) was appointed in each reign to oversee the activities of the families related to the emperor.

"Those who have ruled the Empire in this our State have always made it their care to worship in Spring, Summer, Autumn, and Winter the 180 [Shinto] Gods of Heaven and Earth, and the Gods of the Land and of Grain. If just at this time we were to worship in their stead foreign Deities, it may be feared that we should incur the wrath of our National Gods."

The Emperor said:—"Let [the image] be given to [the Oho-omi], who has shown his willingness to take it, and, as an experiment, make him to worship it."

The Oho-omi knelt down and received it with joy. He enthroned it in his house at Oharida, where he diligently carried out the rites of retirement from the world, and on that score purified his house at Muku-hara and made it a Temple. After this a pestilence was rife in the Land, from which the people died prematurely. As time went on it became worse and worse, and there was no remedy. [The chiefs of the Mononobe and Nakatomi clans] addressed the Emperor jointly, saying:—"It was because thy servants' advice on a former day was not approved that the people are dying thus of disease. If thou dost now retrace thy steps before matters have gone too far, joy will surely be the result! It will be well promptly to fling it away, and diligently to seek happiness in the future."

The Emperor said:—"Let it be done as you advise." Accordingly officials took the image of Buddha and abandoned it to the current of the Canal of Naniha. They also set fire to the Temple, and burnt it so that nothing was left. Hereupon, there being in the Heavens neither clouds nor wind, a sudden conflagration consumed the Great Hall (of the Palace).

. . . .

[A.D. 584], Autumn, 9th month. [A man] who had come from Paekche had a stone image of [the Bodhisattva Maitreya] and an image of Buddha. This year [a Soga clansman named] Mumako Sukune, having asked for these two Buddhist images, sent [three retainers] in all directions to search out persons who practised (Buddhism). Upon this he only found in the province of Harima a man [of Korean origin], who from a Buddhist priest had become a layman again. So the Oho-omi made him teacher, and caused him to receive [three young women] into religion . . . Mumako Sukune, still in accordance with the Law of Buddha, reverenced the three nuns, and gave orders to provide them with food and clothing. He erected a Buddhist Temple on the east side of his dwelling, in which he enshrined the stone image of [the Bodhisattva Maitreya]. He insisted on the three nuns holding a general meeting to partake of [a vegetarian meal].[5] At this time [the father of one of the nuns] found a Buddhist relic on [top of] the food, and presented it to Mumako Sukune. Mumako Sukune, by way of experiment, took the relic, and placing it on the middle of a block of iron, beat it with an iron sledge-hammer, which he flourished aloft. The block and the sledge-hammer were shattered to atoms, but the relic could not be crushed. Then the relic was cast into water, where it floated on the water or sank as one desired. In consequence of this, Mumako Sukune held faith in Buddhism and practised it unremittingly. [He] built another Buddhist Temple at his house in Ishikaha. From this arose the beginning of Buddhism.

5. The Buddhists forbade meat-eating.

GENSHIN: FROM THE ESSENTIALS OF SALVATION

The teaching and practice which leads to birth in Paradise is the most important thing in this impure world during these degenerate times. Monks and laymen, men of high or low station, who will not turn to it? But the literature of the exoteric and the esoteric teachings of Buddha are not one in text, and the practices of one's work in this life in its ritualistic and philosophical aspects are many. These are not difficult for men of keen wisdom and great diligence, but how can a stupid person such as I achieve this knowledge? Because of this I have chosen the one gate to salvation of *nembutsu*.[1] I have made selections from the

Translated by Philip Yampolsky in Ryusaku Tsunoda, ed., *Sources of Japanese Tradition*, New York: Columbia University Press, 1958, pp. 198-203. Reprinted by permission of Columbia University Press.

1. I.e., meditation on or repetition of the invocation *Namu Amida Butsu* ("Hail to the Buddha Amida!").

important sutras and shastras[2] and have set them forth so that they may be readily understood and their disciplines easily practiced. In all there are ten divisions [of the teaching], divided into three volumes. The first is the corrupt life which one must shun, the second is the Pure Land for which one should seek, the third is the proof of the existence of the Pure Land, the fourth is the correct practice of *nembutsu*, the fifth is the helpful means of practicing the *nembutsu*, the sixth is the practice of *nembutsu* on special occasions, the seventh is the benefit resulting from *nembutsu*, the eighth is the proof of the benefit accruing from *nembutsu* alone, the ninth is the conduct leading to birth in Paradise, and the tenth comprises questions and answers to selected problems. These I place to the right of where I sit lest I forget them.

The first division, the corrupt land which one must shun, comprises the three realms [i.e., past, present, and future] in which there is no peace. Now, in order to make clear the external appearances of this land, it is divided into seven parts: 1) hell; 2) hungry demons; 3) beasts; 4) fighting demons; 5) man; 6) gods; and 7) a conclusion.

The hell of repeated misery is one thousand yojanas[3] beneath the Southern Continent[4] and is ten thousand yojanas in length and breadth. Sinners here are always possessed of the desire to do each other harm. Should they by chance see each other, they behave as does the hunter when he encounters a deer. With iron claws they slash each other's bodies until blood and flesh are dissipated and the bones alone remain. Or else the hell-wardens, taking in their hands iron sticks and poles, beat the sinners' bodies from head to foot until they are pulverized like grains of sand. Or else, with a sword of awful sharpness, they cut their victims' bodies in regular pieces as the kitchen worker slices the flesh of fish. And then a cool wind arises, and blowing, returns the sinners to the same state in which they were at the outset.

2. In Buddhist terminology, a Sutra is supposed to record the exact words of the historical Buddha (Shakyamuni); a Shastra is a work composed by someone else, often as an explanation of the Buddhist teaching.

3. The distance an army can march in one day. (Tr.)

4. India and adjoining regions. (Tr.)

Thereupon they immediately arise and undergo torment identical to that which they had previously suffered. . . .

Outside the four gates of this hell are sixteen separate places which are associated with this hell. The first is called the place of excrement. Here, it is said, there is intensely hot dung of the bitterest of taste, filled with maggots with snouts of indestructible hardness. The sinner here eats of the dung and all the assembled maggots swarm at once for food. They destroy the sinner's skin, devour his flesh and suck the marrow from his bones. People who at one time in the past killed birds or deer fall into this hell. Second is the place of the turning sword. It is said that iron walls ten yojanas in height surround it and that a terrible and intense fire constantly burns within. The fire possessed by man is like snow when compared to this. With the least of physical contact, the body is broken into pieces the size of mustard-seeds. Hot iron pours from above like a heavy rainfall, and in addition, there is a forest of swords, with blades of exceptional keenness, and these swords, too, fall like rain. The multitude of agonies is in such variety that it cannot be borne. Into this place fall those who have killed a living being with concupiscence. Third is the place of the burning vat. It is said that the sinner is seized and placed in an iron vat, and boiled as one would cook beans. Those who in the past have taken the life of a living creature, cooked it, and eaten of it, fall into this hell. . . .

The second division [of the teaching] is the Pure Land towards which one must aspire. The rewards of Paradise are of endless merit. Should one speak of them for a hundred kalpas[5] or even for a thousand kalpas, one would not finish describing them; should one count them or give examples of them, there would still be no way to know of them. . . .

[The] first [reward] is the pleasure of being welcomed by many saints. Generally when an evil man's life comes to an end, the elements of wind and fire leave first, and as they control movement and heat, great suffering is felt. When a good man dies, earth and water depart first, and as they leave gently, they cause no pain. How much less painful then must be the death of a man who has accumulated merit through *nembutsu!* The man

5. A kalpa is reckoned as 4320 million earthly years.

who carries this teaching firmly in his mind for a long time feels a great rejoicing arise within him at the approach of death. Because of his great vow, [the Buddha] Amida, accompanied by many bodhisattvas and hundreds of thousands of monks, appears before the dying man's eyes, exuding a great light of radiant brilliance. And at this time the great compassionate [bodhisattva] Kannon,[6] extending hands adorned with the hundred blessings and offering a jeweled lotus throne, appears before the faithful. The Bodhisattva Seishi and his retinue of numberless saints chant hymns and at the same time extend their hands and accept him among them. At this time the faithful one, seeing these wonders before his eyes, feels rejoicing within his heart and feels at peace as though he were entering upon meditation. Let us know then, that at the moment that death comes, though it be in a hut of grass, the faithful one finds himself seated upon a lotus throne. Following behind Amida Buddha amid the throng of bodhisattvas, in a moment's time he achieves birth in the Western Paradise. . . .

[The] second [reward] is the pleasure of the first opening of the Lotus. After the believer is born into this land and when he experiences the pleasures of the first opening of the lotus, his joy becomes a hundred times greater than before. It is comparable to a blind man gaining sight for the first time, or to entering a royal palace directly after leaving some rural region. Looking at his own body, it becomes purplish gold in color. He is gowned naturally in jeweled garments. Rings, bracelets, a crown of jewels, and other ornaments in countless profusion adorn his body. And when he looks upon the light radiating from the Buddha, he obtains pure vision, and because of his experiences in former lives, he hears the sounds of all things. And no matter what color he may see or what sound he may hear, it is a thing of marvel. Such is the ornamentation of space above that the eye becomes lost in the traces of clouds. The melody of the wheel of the wonderful Law as it turns, flows throughout this land of jeweled sound. Palaces, halls, forests, and ponds shine and glitter everywhere. Flocks of wild ducks, geese, and mandarin

6. Kannon or Kwannon (Avalokita) is a Bodhisattva associated with Amida. In Japan she was worshipped as a goddess of mercy.

ducks fly about in the distance and near at hand. One may see multitudes from all the worlds being born into this land like sudden showers of rain. And one may see a throng of saints, numerous as the grains of sand in the Ganges, arriving from the many Buddhalands.

SHINRAN SHONIN: SONGS IN PRAISE OF AMITABHA*

1. Since the attainment of Buddhahood by Amitabha,
Ten kalpas[1] have now passed away;
The Light radiating from the Dharmakaya[2] has no limits:
It illuminates the world's blindness and darkness.
2. The Light of [Amida's] wisdom is measureless,
All conditional forms[3] without exception
Are enveloped in the dawning Light;
Therefore take refuge in the True Light.
3. Amida's Light is like a wheel radiating without bounds.
Buddha[4] declared that all things illumined by [Amida's] Light
Are freed from all forms of being and not-being.
Take refuge in the One who is universally enlightened.
4. The clouds of Light have, like space, no hindrances;
All [beings] that have obstructions are not impeded by them;
There is no one who is not embraced in His Soft Light:
Take refuge in Him who is beyond thought.

From D. T. Suzuki, *A Miscellany on the Shin Teaching of Buddhism*, Kyoto: Shinshu Otaniha Shumusho, 1949, pp. 122-28. Reprinted by permission of Shinshu Otaniha Shumusho (Eastern Buddhist Society).

* Amitabha is the Sanskrit term for the Buddha who is known in Chinese as O-mi-t'o-fo, in Japanese as Amida.

1. The kalpa is the basic cycle of Indian cosmology, calculated as 4320 million earthly years.
2. The Dharmakaya ("Body of the Law") is the system of universal Nature.
3. I.e., phenomena subject to earthly limitations, as contrasted with the universal Buddhas and Bodhisattvas.
4. I.e., Gautama Shakyamuni, the Buddha who lived in India in the sixth century B.C.

7. The radiance of [Amida's] Light of Truth surpasses all,
So He is called the Buddha of Pure Light:
Those who are embraced in the Light
Are cleansed from the dirt of karma and attain enlightenment.

10. As there is a constant flow of Light,
[Amida] is known as the Buddha of Increase;
Because of perceiving the power of light with uninterrupted faith,
We are born into the Pure Land.

14. At the first discourse given by Amida
The holy multitudes were beyond calculation;
Those who wish to go to the Pure Land
Should take refuge in the Buddha who commands great numbers.

15. The numberless great Bodhisattvas in the Land of Bliss
After one birth more will become Buddhas;
When they have taken refuge in the virtues of [the Bodhisattva] Fugen[5]
They will come back to this world in order to teach beings.

18. Those [beings] who reach the Land of Purity and Happiness,
When they return to this world of five defilements,[6]
Like Buddha Shakyamuni work without cessation
For the welfare of all beings.

19. The miraculous power and self-mastery
Enjoyed by them is beyond calculation;
They have accumulated virtues beyond thought:
Take refuge in the Honoured One who is peerless.

23. When all beings in every condition within the ten quarters,
Endowed with all excellent virtues,
Hearing the name of Amida with sincerity of heart,
Attain faith; how they will rejoice at what they hear!

24. "Because of my Vow if they should not be born [in the Pure Land]

5. Samantabhadra, a Bodhisattva engaged in the work of salvation.

6. Defilements relating to age, philosophical insight, morality, physical existence, and length of life.

I will not attain enlightenment."[7]
When the right moment for faith arises, joy is instantly felt,
And rebirth is definitely confirmed, once for all.

27. Rebirth [in the Pure Land] for all the periods of time
Not only is assured for beings of this world
But for all in the Buddha-lands of the ten quarters:
Their number is indeed measureless, numberless, and incalculable.

28. Those beings who hearing the Holy Name of Amitabha Buddha
Feel joyous and adore him,
Will be given treasures of merit
And benefits great and incomparable.

29. Although the great chiliocosm[8] may be filled with flames,
Yet he who hears the Holy Name of the Buddha,
Always in accord with steadfastness,
Will freely pass [to the Pure Land].

30. Amida's mysterious limitless Power
Is praised by innumerable Buddhas;
From the Buddha-lands in the East
As many as the sands of the Ganges, numberless Buddhas come.

31. From the Buddha-lands in the remaining nine quarters,
Come the Bodhisattvas to see him;
Shakyamuni the Tathagata[9] composing songs
Praises his virtues infinite.

32. All the countless Bodhisattvas of the ten quarters
In order to plant the root of merit
Pay homage to the Lord [Amida] and praise him in song:
Let all beings take refuge in Him.

7. Amida had vowed not to accept salvation for himself until all other beings had been saved.
8. The universe filled with myriad beings.
9. The universal, spiritual Buddha.

Introduction to An Account of My Hut

The Buddhist ethic always encouraged a simple, ascetic life far from the centers of civilization; and especially in times of political and social upheaval many Buddhists adopted this mode of existence. Kamo Chomei (1151-1213) was one of these. In his youth he had belonged to the court society of Heian; but the middle years of his life coincided with the wars of the Taira and Minamoto clans for supremacy in Japan. His decision to retire to the countryside apparently was prompted both by the desolation resulting from these wars and by a series of natural disasters. Eventually Kamo took Buddhist orders and became a recluse, living in a remote rural area in a hut only ten feet square. In *An Account of My Hut* (*Hojoki*), written in the year 1212, he describes his hermit's existence, expressing calm satisfaction with this mode of life and incidentally giving testimony to his own deep Buddhist piety.

FROM AN ACCOUNT OF MY HUT (HOJOKI)

About 1181[1]—it is so long ago that I cannot remember for certain—there was a famine in the country which lasted two years, a most terrible thing. A drought persisted through the spring and summer, while the autumn and winter brought storms and floods. One disaster followed another, and the grains failed to ripen. All in vain was the labor of tilling the soil in spring or planting in summer, for there was none of the joy of the autumn reaping or winter harvest. Some of the people as a result abandoned their lands and crossed into other provinces; some forgot their homes and went to live in the mountains. All manner of prayers were begun and extraordinary devotions performed, but without the slightest effect.

From Donald Keene, ed., *Anthology of Japanese Literature*, New York: Grove Press, 1955, pp. 201-06, 209-11. Reprinted by permission of Grove Press.

1. The Taira-Minamoto war broke out in 1180.

The capital had always depended on the countryside for its needs, and when supplies ceased to come it became quite impossible for people to maintain their composure. They tried in their desperation to barter for food one after another of their possessions, however cheaply, but no one desired them. The rare person who was willing to trade had contempt for money and set a high value on his grain. Many beggars lined the roads, and their doleful cries filled the air.

Thus the first year of the famine at last drew to a close. It was thought that the new year would see an improvement, but it brought instead the additional affliction of epidemics, and there was no sign of any amelioration. The people were starving, and with the passage of days approached the extremity, like fish gasping in insufficient water. Finally, people of quality, wearing hats and with their legs covered,[2] were reduced to going from house to house desperately begging. Overwhelmed by misery, they would walk in a stupor, only presently to collapse. The number of those who died of starvation outside the gates or along the roads may not be reckoned. There being no one even to dispose of the bodies, a stench filled the whole world, and there were many sights of decomposing bodies too horrible to behold. Along the banks of the Kamo River there was not even room for horses and cattle to pass.

The lower classes and the wood-cutters were also at the end of their strength, and as even firewood grew scarce those without other resources broke up their own houses and took the wood to sell in the market. The amount obtainable for all that a man could carry, however, was not enough to sustain life a single day. Strange to relate, among the sticks of firewood were some to which bits of vermilion or gold and silver leaf still adhered. This, I discovered, came about because people with no other means of living were robbing the old temples of their holy images or breaking up the furnishings of the sacred halls for firewood. It was because I was born in a world of foulness and evil that I was forced to witness such heartbreaking sights. . . .

Then there was the great earthquake of 1185, of an intensity not known before. Mountains crumbled and rivers were buried,

2. Ordinary beggars would have been bareheaded and barelegged. (Tr.)

the sea tilted over and immersed the land. The earth split and water gushed up; boulders were sundered and rolled into the valleys. Boats that rowed along the shores were swept out to sea. Horses walking along the roads lost their footing. It is needless to speak of the damage throughout the capital—not a single mansion, pagoda, or shrine was left whole. As some collapsed and others tumbled over, dust and ashes rose like voluminous smoke. The rumble of the earth shaking and the houses crashing was exactly like that of thunder. Those who were in their houses, fearing that they would presently be crushed to death, ran outside, only to meet with a new cracking of the earth. They could not soar into the sky, not having wings. They could not climb into the clouds, not being dragons. Of all the frightening things of the world, none is so frightful as an earthquake.

Among those who perished was the only child of a samurai family, a boy of five or six, who had made a little house under the overhanging part of a wall and was playing there innocently when the wall suddenly collapsed, burying him under it. His body was crushed flat, with only his two eyes protruding. His parents took him in their arms and wailed uncontrollably, so great was the sorrow they experienced. I realized that grief over a child can make even the bravest warrior forget shame—a pitiable but understandable fact. . . .

All is as I have described it—the things in the world which make life difficult to endure, our own helplessness and the undependability of our dwellings. And if to these were added the griefs that come from place or particular circumstances, their sum would be unreckonable. . . .

Those who are powerful are filled with greed; and those who have no protectors are despised. Possessions bring many worries; in poverty there is sorrow. He who asks another's help becomes his slave; he who nurtures others is fettered by affection. He who complies with the ways of the world may be impoverished thereby; he who does not, appears deranged. Wherever one may live, whatever work one may do, is it possible even for a moment to find a haven for the body or peace for the mind?

I inherited the house of my father's grandmother and for a long time lived there. Afterward I lost my position and fell on hard times.[3] Many things led me to live in seclusion, and finally, unable longer to remain in my ancestral home, in my thirties I built after my own plans a little cottage. It was a bare tenth the size of the house in which I had lived, and being intended just as a place where I might stay it had no pretensions about it. An earthen wall was, it is true, raised around it, but I lacked the means to put up an ornamental gate. I also built a rough shed of bamboo posts for my carriage. I must confess that when the snow fell or gales blew, I could not but feel alarmed; and since the house was near the Kamo River, there was considerable danger of flooding as well as the threat of bandits.

For over thirty years I had tormented myself by putting up with all the things of this unhappy world. During this time each stroke of misfortune had naturally made me realize the fragility of my life. In my fiftieth year, then, I became a [Buddhist] priest and turned my back on the world. Not having any family, I had no ties that would make abandoning the world difficult. I had no rank or stipend—what was there for me to cling to? How many years had I vainly spent [in my cottage] among the cloud-covered hills of Ohara?[4]

Now that I have reached the age of sixty, and my life seems about to evaporate like the dew, I have fashioned a lodging for the last leaves of my years. It is a hut where, perhaps, a traveler might spend a single night; it is like the cocoon spun by an aged silkworm. This hut is not even a hundredth the size of the cottage where I spent my middle years.

Before I was aware, I had become heavy with years, and with each remove my dwelling grew smaller. The present hut is of no ordinary appearance. It is a bare ten feet square and less than seven feet high. I did not choose this particular spot rather than another, and I built my house without consulting any diviners.[5] I laid a foundation and roughly thatched a roof. I fastened hinges to the joints of the beams, the easier to move else-

3. Kamo Chomei's family enjoyed a hereditary position as Shinto priests at the Kamo Shrine; but in his generation this privilege was rescinded. (Tr.)

4. Chomei felt that even the simplicity of his cottage was still not a suitable life; he had to become a true hermit. (Tr.)

5. Normally the site of a house was selected after consulting *yin-yang* diviners; but for a Buddhist priest one place was as good as another. (Tr.)

where should anything displease me. What difficulty would there be in changing my dwelling? A bare two carts would suffice to carry off the whole house, and except for the carter's fee there would be no expenses at all. . . .

When I first began to live here I thought it would be for just a little while, but five years have already passed. My temporary retreat has become rather old as such houses go: withered leaves lie deep by the eaves and moss has spread over the floor. When, as chance has had it, news has come to me from the capital, I have learned how many of the great and mighty have died since I withdrew to this mountain. And how to reckon the numbers of lesser folk? How many houses have been destroyed by the numerous conflagrations? Only in a hut built for the moment can one live without fears. It is very small, but it holds a bed where I may lie at night and a seat for me in the day; it lacks nothing as a place for me to dwell. The hermit crab chooses to live in little shells because it well knows the size of its body. The osprey stays on deserted shores because it fears human beings. I am like them. Knowing myself and the world, I have no ambitions and do not mix in the world. I seek only tranquillity; I rejoice in the absence of grief. . . .

I do not prescribe my way of life to men enjoying happiness and wealth, but have related my experiences merely to show the differences between my former and present life. Ever since I fled the world and became a priest, I have known neither hatred nor fear. I leave my span of days for Heaven to determine, neither clinging to life nor begrudging its end. My body is like a drifting cloud—I ask for nothing, I want nothing. My greatest joy is a quiet nap; my only desire for this life is to see the beauties of the seasons.

The Three Worlds[6] are joined by one mind.[7] If the mind is not at peace, neither beasts of burden nor possessions are of service, neither palaces nor pavilions bring any cheer. This lonely house is but a tiny hut, but I somehow love it. I naturally

6. Past, present, and future.

7. Quotation from the *Avatamsaka Sutra* (in Japanese: *Kegon Sutra*). The Kegon school of Buddhism taught that the universe is a harmony ruled by the universal Buddha, Vairocana (Jap.: Roshana).

feel ashamed when I go to the capital and must beg, but when I return and sit here I feel pity for those still attached to the world of dust. Should anyone doubt the truth of my words, let him look to the fishes and the birds. Fish do not weary of the water, but unless one is a fish one does not know why. Birds long for the woods, but unless one is a bird one does not know why. The joys of solitude are similar. Who could understand them without having lived here?

Now the moon of my life sinks in the sky and is close to the edge of the mountain. Soon I must head into the darkness of the Three Ways:[8] why should I thus drone on about myself? The essence of the Buddha's teaching to man is that we must not have attachment for any object. It is a sin for me now to love my little hut, and my attachment to its solitude may also be a hindrance to salvation. Why should I waste more precious time in relating such trifling pleasures?

8. The three paths in the afterworld leading to different types of hells. (Tr.)

Society

Introduction to the Collection of Myriad Leaves

The *Collection of Myriad Leaves* (*Manyoshu*) is an anthology of 4,516 poems in the Japanese language, all composed in the century prior to A.D. 760. Of the *c.* 450 different authors represented, nearly all were members of the court aristocracy of Heian, so that the poems inevitably reflect the attitudes and interests of this social class. More than four thousand of the poems belong to the genre known as *tanka*, consisting of five short lines of 5-7-5-7-7 syllables respectively, though some longer poems are likewise included. The brevity and delicacy of the *tanka*—which remains the favorite poetic form in Japan even nowadays—makes the true quality of these poems difficult to capture in translation. They are lyric and impressionistic, using parallelism and alliteration but not rhyme. A frequent technique is the setting of a mood by describing a scene from nature, then expertly transforming it into an emotion.

The paramount influence of Chinese culture upon upper-class Japan in the seventh and eighth centuries has unquestionaly left its mark upon the *Collection of Myriad Leaves*. Poetry was of high importance in the Chinese literary tradition; and many poetic anthologies were compiled in China. Images and figures of speech in the Japanese poems frequently demonstrate the poet's acquaintance with Confucian, Buddhist, or Taoist ideas. The entire anthology is written in Chinese characters employed to represent Japanese ideas or sounds. Indeed, compared to the rather simple verses included in the early Japanese historical chronicles, the poems of the *Collection* exhibit an astonishing increase in sophistication—a change almost certainly attributable to the Japanese study and cultivation of Chinese literature in the intervening period.

FROM THE COLLECTION OF MYRIAD LEAVES

LOVE*

244 Ah, that rascal love
I have put away at home,
Locked in a coffer—
Here he comes, pouncing on me!

262 I have not met her for so long
That the street-trees at the Eastern Market
Let droop their branches low—
Well may I languish for love of her!

269 The sheaves of my love-thoughts
Would fill seven carts—
Carts huge and heavy-wheeled.
Such a burden I bear
Of my own choice.

316 Oh how steadily I love you—
You who awe me
Like the thunderous waves
That lash the sea-coast of Ise!

351 My very soul, it seems,
Has stolen into every stitch
Of the robe you wear.

860 I will think of you, love,
On evenings when the grey mist
Rises above the rushes,

From Nippon Gakujutsu Shinkokai, *The Manyoshu,* New York: Columbia University Press, 1965. Reprinted by permission of Columbia University Press.

* These classifications were provided by the present editors; they do not appear in the Japanese text.

And chill sounds the voice
Of the wild ducks crying.

887 Come to me, my dearest,
Come in through the bamboo-blinds!
Should my mother ask me,
I'll say, 'Twas but a gust of wind.

RELIGION

367 If I could but be happy in this life,
What should I care if in the next
I became a bird or a worm!

[The following poem was chanted at a religious service to the author's ancestral god.]

386 Oh, our heaven-born god,
Descended from the heavenly plains—
With the evergreen branch
Fresh from the inmost hill,
Tied with white paper and mulberry cloth,
With a wine-jar set in the purified earth,
With a cord of many bamboo-rings
Hanging from my neck,
With my knees bent like the deer's,
With my maiden's scarf flung over me,—
Thus I entreat thee, our god,
Yet can I not meet him?

543 I know well this body of mine
Is insubstantial as foam;
Even so, how I wish
For a life of a thousand years!

828 Loathing both seas of Life and Death,
How deeply I long
For the upland of Nirvana,
Untouched by the tides of Change!

WARRIORS

306 In the great ship, full-oared,
I sail along the coast,
Obedient to our Sovereign's word.

502 Am I the son my father and mother cherish
With common love and care?
Can it be well that I, a man,
Live but an idle life?
Lifting up the bow-end,
Shooting arrows a thousand fathoms far,
Bearing my sword by my side,
Scaling the many-peaked mountains—
Betraying not our Sovereign's trust—
I ought to win a name
To echo from age to age!

764 The dread imperial command
I have received: from to-morrow
I will sleep with the grass,
No wife being by me.

784 Praying to the gods of heaven and earth,
And thrusting hunting arrows in my quiver,
For the far isle of Tsukushi[1]
Now I depart—yes, I!

DEATH

416 Such a fleeting life though we shared together,
We both had trusted that our love
Would last a thousand years.

497-8 Alhough I wished him health,
He rose into white-trailing clouds,
How sad I am to hear!

Had I known him destined thus,

1. Ancient name for Kyushu.

I had shown him the breakers on the jutting rocks
Of the sea of Koshi!

716 To what shall I liken this life?
It is like a boat,
Which, unmoored at morn,
Drops out of sight
And leaves no trace behind.

897 When I take the lute, sobs break forth;
Can it be that in its hollow space
The spirit of my wife is hiding?

DRINKING

357 Instead of wasting thoughts on unavailing things,
It would seem wiser
To drink a cup of raw sake.[2]

360 Far better, it seems, than uttering pompous words
And looking wise,
To drink sake and weep drunken tears.

362 Ceasing to live this wretched life of man,
O that I were a sake-jar;
Then I should be soaked with sake!

CLAN HONOR

538 In the remote age of the gods
When the Imperial Ancestor, opening heaven's
gate,
Descended upon the Peak of Takachiho,
It was the founder of our clan,
Who, gripping in his hand a wax-tree bow
And grasping withal arrows for the deer hunt,
Made advance the brave troops
Of Okume with quivers on their backs;
Forced his way across mountains and rivers,

2. An alcoholic drink made from fermented rice.

Trampling under foot rocks and stones;
And who, seeking for a good habitable land,
Subdued the fierce gods
And pacified the unruly tribes—
Sweeping and cleansing thus the country,
He rendered a loyal service to his lord.

Thereafter, under the successive reigns
Of the sovereigns on the Celestial Throne,
Descended from that First Emperor
Who, raising the stout-pillared Unebi Palace
Of Kashihara in the land of Yamato,
Ruled the under-heaven,
Our forefathers served the Imperial House
With all their hearts faithful and true.

Ours is the ancestral office of the clan,
So proclaimed and bestowed upon us,
To be handed down from father to son,
Generation after generation—
Those who see will tell of it from mouth to mouth;
Those who hear will hold it up as a mirror.

So cherished and clean is the name of our clan.
Neglect it never, lest even a false word
Should destroy this proud name of our fathers,
You clansmen all, who bear the name of Otomo.

ADULTERY

477 Since the time of the gods
Of Onamuchi and Sukunahikona[3]
It has been said from age to age:
"To see one's parents is to revere them,
To see one's wife and children is to love them:
This is the law of the world of man."
And so has it been told unto these days.

3. Deities supposed to have ruled over Izumo (an area of northwest Honshu) in ancient times.

You who are a man of this world—
Have you not declared—did you not sighing say
In that full-flowering time of the *chisa*-trees,[4]
While talking with your dear wife,
Morning and evening, 'mid smiles and tears:
"It will not be thus for ever.
The gods of heaven and earth helping us,
Some day we may prosper like spring flowers."
Now that prosperity has come which you longed
for,[5]
Your wife far away[6] is waiting
In sorrow and in solitude,
Wondering when you will send for her.
Yet to that Saburu[7] girl, who drifts
With no place to settle in like the foam
That floats on the swelling stream of the Imizu[8]
When the south wind blows and melts the snow,
You cling inseparably like tangled twine.
Paired with her like the grebes,
You plunge into the depths of folly
Deep as the gulf of Nago,[9] hopeless man!

4. The *chisa* is a tall tree whose white flowers appear in July and August.
5. Reference to the man's appointment as an official of Etchu province.
6. The wife remained at Nara.
7. The name of a wandering woman of pleasure. (Tr.)
8. A river flowing by the capital of Etchu province.
9. Part of Etchu Bay, lying to the east of the provincial capital.

Introduction to the Diary of Lady Murasaki

Murasaki Shikibu (978-1015?) is the pen-name of the lady whose multi-volume novel, *The Tale of Genji* (*Genji Monogatari*), is generally conceded to be the greatest achievement of Japanese classical literature. Completed ca. A.D. 1004, the story centers about the numerous romantic escapades of one Prince Genji, a son of the emperor of Japan by a favorite concubine. With great aesthetic charm, psychological penetration, and a wealth of realistic detail, it describes the everyday life and pursuits of members of the elegant high society of Heian.

Lady Murasaki (her true name is unknown) belonged to a junior branch of the powerful Fujiwara clan. Several male members of her immediate family were scholars or poets of some note; she herself was well-versed in both Chinese and Japanese literature—an unusual achievement for a woman of that time. Following the early death of her husband—also a Fujiwara and a scholar—she appears to have joined the entourage of the empress Akiko, who shared her scholarly interests. In any event, Murasaki was thoroughly familiar with the institutions and ceremonies of the court at Heian and the activities and intrigues of its members.

The following excerpts from Lady Murasaki's *Diary* give an indication of her literary style and of various attitudes of the aristocrats among whom she lived.

FROM THE DIARY OF LADY MURASAKI

[The following are portraits of prominent ladies of the court.]

Lady Dainagon is very small and refined, white, beautiful, and round, though in demeanor very lofty. Her hair is three inches longer than her height. She uses exquisitely carved hairpins. Her face is lovely, her manners delicate and charming.

Lady Senji is also a little person, and haughty. Her hair is fine and glossy and one foot longer than the ordinary. She puts us to shame, her carriage is so noble. When she walks before us we feel so much in the shade that we are uncomfortable. Her mind and speech make us feel that a really noble person ought to be like her.

—If I go on describing ladies' manners I shall be called an old gossip, so I must refrain from talking about those around me. I will be silent about the questionable and imperfect.

From *Diaries of Court Ladies of Old Japan*, trans. by Annie Shepley Omori and Kochi Doi with an introduction by Amy Lowell, Tokyo: Kenkyusha Ltd., 1961. Reprinted from Donald Keene, ed., *Anthology of Japanese Literature*, pp. 149-55, by permission of Kenkyusha Ltd.

Lady Koshosho, all noble and charming. She is like a weeping willow tree at budding time. Her style is very elegant and we all envy her her manners. She is so shy and retiring that she seems to hide her heart even from herself. She is of childlike purity even to a painful degree—should there be a low-minded person who would treat her ill or slander her, her spirit would be overwhelmed and she would die. Such delicacy and helplessness make us anxious about her. . . .

Among the younger ladies I think Kodayu and Genshikibu are beautiful. The former is a little person quite modern in type. Her pretty hair is abundant at the roots, but gets too thin at the end, which is one foot longer than she is. Her face is full of wit. People will think her very pretty, and indeed there is no feature one would wish to improve. The latter is tall and rather superior. Her features are fine; she is smile-giving and lovable. She is very refined and seems to be a favorite daughter of some person of dignity. . . .

So much for their appearance and now for their dispositions. Here few can be selected, though each has some good points and few are entirely bad. It is very difficult to possess such qualities as prudence, wit, charm, right-mindedness, all at once. As to many ladies, the question is whether they excel most in charms of mind or person. It is hard to decide! Wicked, indeed, to write so much of others!

There is Lady Chujo who waits upon the Princess dedicated to the service of the Kamo Shrine. I had heard of her and secretly managed to see her letters addressed to other persons. They were very beautifully written but with such an exalted opinion of herself; in the whole world she is the person of profoundest knowledge! None to compare with her, it seems she is thinking. On reading them my heart beat faster, I was furiously indignant for every one here [the ladies of her own Queen's court], although it may be it is wrong to feel so . . .

In our Queen's court we rather neglect to adorn ourselves, for our Queen has no rivals now. Moreover, she thinks unfavorably of frivolous women, so those who wish to serve her and remain in favor keep from association with men. Of course everywhere there are lighthearted, unashamed, thoughtless women, and men who visit our court to find them say we are awkward and unversed in social usage. Our ladies of the higher ranks are, indeed, much too reserved and haughty; it is not in this way that they can bring honor to our Queen. It is painful to see them . . .

Our Queen of perfect mind, enviably lovely, is reserved and never obtrusive, for she believes that few who are forward can avoid blunders. In fact, imperfect wit is worse than reserve. Our Queen when she was very young was much annoyed to hear persons of shallow culture saying vulgar, narrow things with conceit, so she favored ladies who made no mistakes, and childlike persons pleased her very well. This is why our ladies have become so retiring. As Her Majesty grows older, she begins to see the world as it is, the bad and good qualities of the human heart. Reserve or boldness—she knows neither is good. The court nobles rather look down on us—"Nothing interesting here!" they seem to say. The Queen knows this, but she knows we cannot please everybody. If we stumble, hideous things may happen. Yet we must not be faint-hearted and bashful either, so Her Majesty says, but our old habits are not so easily shaken off, and all the young nobles of the present day are, on their side, only indulgent pleasure-seekers. . . .

Lady Izumi Shikibu corresponds charmingly, but her behavior is improper indeed. She writes with grace and ease and with a flashing wit. There is fragrance even in her smallest words. Her poems are attractive, but they are only improvisations which drop from her mouth spontaneously. Every one of them has some interesting point, and she is acquainted with ancient literature also, but she is not like a true artist who is filled with the genuine spirit of poetry. Yet I think even she cannot presume to pass judgment on the poems of others. . . .

Lady Sei Shonagon.[1] A very proud person. She values herself highly, and scatters her Chinese writings all about. Yet should we study her closely, we should find that she is still imperfect. She tries to be exceptional, but naturally persons of that sort give offence. She is piling up trouble for her future. One who is too richly gifted, who indulges too much in emotion, even when

1. Author of another famous literary work descriptive of court life—*The Pillow Book of Sei Shonagon.*

she ought to be reserved, and cannot turn aside from anything she is interested in, in spite of herself will lose self-control. How can such a vain and reckless person end her days happily!

[Here there is a sudden change from the court to her own home.]

Having no excellence within myself, I have passed my days without making any special impression on any one. Especially the fact that I have no man who will look out for my future makes me comfortless. I do not wish to bury myself in dreariness. Is it because of my worldly mind that I feel lonely? On moonlight nights in autumn, when I am hopelessly sad, I often go out on the balcony and gaze dreamily at the moon. It makes me think of days gone by. People say that it is dangerous to look at the moon in solitude, but something impels me, and sitting a little withdrawn I muse there. In the wind-cooled evening I play on the koto, though others may not care to hear it. I fear that my playing betrays the sorrow which becomes more intense, and I become disgusted with myself—so foolish and miserable am I.

My room is ugly, blackened by smoke. I play on a thirteen or six-stringed koto, but I neglect to take away the bridges even in rainy weather, and I lean it up against the wall between the cabinet and the door jamb. On either side of the koto stands a lute [Japanese *biwa*]. A pair of big bookcases have in them all the books they can hold. In one of them are placed old poems and romances. They are the homes of worms which come frightening us when we turn the pages, so none ever wish to read them. As to the other cabinet, since the person[2] who placed his own books there no hand has touched it. When I am bored to death I take out one or two of them; then my maids gather around me and say: "Your life will not be favored with old age if you do such a thing! Why do you read Chinese? Formerly even the reading of [Buddhist] Sutras was not encouraged for women." They rebuke me in the shade [i.e. behind my back]. I have heard of it and have wished to say, "It is far from certain that he who does no forbidden thing enjoys a long life," but it would be a lack of reserve to say it to the maids. Our deeds vary

2. Her husband, who had died seven years previously (in 1001).

with our age and deeds vary with the individual. Some are proud to read books, others look over old cast-away writings because they are bored with having nothing to do. It would not be becoming for such a one to chatter away about religious thoughts, noisily shaking a rosary. I feel this, and before my women keep myself from doing what otherwise I could do easily. But after all, when I was among the ladies of the court I did not say what I wanted to say either, for it is useless to talk with those who do not understand one and troublesome to talk with those who criticize from a feeling of superiority. Especially one-sided persons are troublesome. Few are accomplished in many arts and most cling narrowly to their own opinion.

Pretty and coy, shrinking from sight, unsociable, proud, fond of romance, vain and poetic, looking down upon others with a jealous eye—such is the opinion of those who do not know me, but after seeing me they say, "You are wonderfully gentle to meet with; I cannot identify you with that imagined one. . . ."

There is a lady, Saemon Naishi, who unreasonably cherished hatred of me. I was not at first aware of it, but later heard of much criticism of me in my absence. Once the King was listening to a reading of my "*Genji Monogatari*," and said, "She is gifted, she must have read the Chronicle of Japan." This lady heard of it, and unreflectingly spread abroad among the courtiers the idea that I am very proud of my learning, giving me the name of "The Japanese Chronicle lady"—it is laughable, indeed! I am reserved even before the maids of my own house; how then should I show my learning in court? When my elder brother Shikibu Jo was a boy he was taught to read the Chinese classics. I listened, sitting beside him, and learned wonderfully fast, though he was sometimes slow and forgot. Father, who was devoted to study, regretted that I had not been a son, but I heard people saying that it is not beautiful even for a man to be proud of his learning, and after that I did not write so much as the figure one in Chinese. I grew clumsy with my writing brush. For a long time I did not care for the books I had already read. Thus I was ashamed to think how others would hate me on hearing what Lady Saemon said, and I assumed an air of not being able to read the characters written on the royal screen. But the Queen made me read to her the poetical works of Li T'ai Po,[3] and as she wished to learn them I have been teaching her since the summer of two years ago the second and third volumes of that collection very secretly when none were present. Her Majesty and I tried to conceal it, but His Majesty the King and the Lord Prime Minister finding it out, the latter presented to the Queen many poetical books which he had had copied. I think that bitter Saemon does not know it yet. If she did, how she would criticize me! . . .

3. The eighth-century Chinese lyric poet, Li Po.

Introduction to the No Drama

The Japanese No drama ("No" means "accomplishment") is a highly stylized art form combining the elements of lyric drama, song, dance, and mimicry. As a distinct genre it was created in the late fourteenth century by the Shinto priest Kan'ami (1334-84) and his son Seami (1363-1443), who wrote and acted in their own works. Among the antecedents of the No theater in Japan were the formal Chinese-style dances given at the imperial court, the opera-form called *Dengaku* in which the actors alternately sang and recited, the charades performed in Shinto temples, and popular danced ballads. Though by the seventeenth century No had become largely an upper-class diversion, it seems not to have been so originally. The plays were given in Shinto temples as part of the religious ritual; or noblemen might sponsor out-of-door performances, to which the public was invited.

The action of a No play generally revolves around some incident of Japanese history or mythology, often interpreted according to the notions of popular Buddhism. The language is poetry or the formal upper-class prose of the fourteenth century, interspersed by quotations from Chinese poems or Buddhist hymns. The principal character in the play is also the dancer or "doer" (*shite*); a subordinate character or "assistant" (*waki*) explains the action. Each of these two may have one or several "adjuncts" (*tsure*). A chorus of between eight and twelve persons sings during the dances, comments upon the events of the play, and sometimes engages in dialogue with the actors. The stage is open on three sides and almost devoid of scenery; but the actors wear highly elaborate costumes and (in some cases) masks which are themselves minor works of art. The lines of the play are chanted to the rhythmic accompaniment of flute and percussion instruments. Action is elegant and restrained; emotion is suggested through postures and gestures.

The No play "Kiyotsune," by Seami, is built around an incident occurring near the end of the war between the Heike (Taira) and the Genji (Minamoto). Kiyotsune was a leader of the Heike forces and a grandson of that Kiyomori who had established Heike supremacy in Japan in 1160. Prior to the opening of the play, the Heike had suffered a series of military reverses which drove them back into the northern corner of Kyushu. Finding themselves near the shrine of the war-god Hachiman at Usa, the leaders asked the god for a prophecy. When Hachiman replied that the Heike cause was hopeless, Kiyotsune resolved to ensure his future bliss in the Western Paradise by throwing himself on Buddha's mercy. Calling out the name of Amida, he jumped into the sea and drowned himself.

SEAMI: FROM THE NO PLAY "KIYOTSUNE"*

AWAZU (*waki*)
Crossing the surges of the eightfold sea,
I must return to where the Court
Stands within its nine gates.

AWAZU I am a retainer of the late Kiyotsune, Lieutenant-General of the Left Wing of the Imperial Bodyguard. Awazu is my name. My late master was defeated in the battles in Kyushu, and since his retreat to Heian was cut off, he probably preferred to take his own life rather than perish at the hands

Nippon Gakujutsu Shinkokai, *Japanese Noh Drama*, Tokyo: Charles E. Tuttle Co., Inc., 1955, I, 61-73. Reprinted by permission of Charles E. Tuttle Co.

* By far the greater part of this play has been reprinted here. But for reasons of space, certain purely lyrical passages and repetitive stanzas have been omitted.

of the common soldiery no better than wayside weeds. So, late one moonlit night, he plunged from his boat into the sea off the coast of Yanagi.[1] Later, when searching the boat, I found a lock of hair he had left behind him as a keepsake. Having undeservedly escaped with my life, I am now carrying this keepsake to his wife in Heian.[2]

Grieving at my unhappy fate,
My sleeves are drenched with tears,
As in disguise my journey I pursue.

Travelling in haste, I have quickly reached Heian.

AWAZU A visitor is announcing his arrival. It is Awazu just come from Kyushu. Please announce him.

WIFE (*tsure*) What? Is it you, Awazu? You need not be announced. Pray enter. What message do you bring me from my lord?

AWAZU A message I am loath to deliver to my lady.

WIFE A message you are loath to deliver? Has my lord perchance renounced the world?[3]

AWAZU No, he has not renounced the world.

WIFE I have heard he has come safely through the recent battles in Kyushu.

AWAZU Yes, my lady, he has come safely through the recent battles in Kyushu. But since his way to Heian was cut off, my lord thought to put an end to his own life rather than lose it at the hands of nameless soldiery no better than wayside weeds. While we were off the coast of Yanagi in Buzen Province, late one moonlit night, he leapt overboard and was drowned.

WIFE What! You mean he cast himself into the sea?

Never can I forgive him such an end!
Had he in battle perished or died of illness,

1. Town on the eastern coast of Buzen province, Kyushu.
2. Kiyotsune's wife had lived in seclusion at Heian ever since 1183, when the Heike abandoned the city to the Genji.
3. Ie., taken the vows of a Buddhist monk.

I could resign myself to fate;
But that he himself should seek a watery grave
Proves all his vows were lying words.
Oh! Woe is me,
Naught's left in this world
Save my vain rancour against my lord!

CHORUS How dream-like now appear our wedded joys!
Through all these troubled years[4]
I've hid from prying eyes—
My sobs voiceless as the rustle of *susuki* grass[5]
Swayed by autumn winds
In the hedge round my dwelling.
From whom need I to-day conceal my grief?
Like to the cuckoo
Crying until the moon-beams
Grow pale in the dawn sky,
Freely and openly I'll weep!

AWAZU Later I searched the boat and found this lock of my lord's hair left you as a keepsake. Pray gaze on it and soothe your grieving heart.

WIFE Is this the raven lock of my late lord?
My eyes are blinded,
My spirit longs for its release
And ever stronger grows my yearning.

CHORUS As she repeats these lines,
The keepsake she returns and seeks her couch.
All through the night, tears of longing fall,
The while she prays that he may come to her
If but in dream.

The GHOST OF KIYOTSUNE, *who has appeared during the last chorus, advances.*

KIYOTSUNE (*shite*) 'Tis said: "The sage is dream-free"[6]
Yet for whom is life reality?

4. I.e., the three years since the Heike had left Heian.
5. A wild grass found throughout Japan, which reaches a height of five or six feet.
6. This quotation is traceable to the Chinese Taoist Chuang Tzu.

Past griefs are truly but illusion
And present sadness but a dream;
Which, like drifting cloud or running water,
Do pass away, leaving no trace.
O poor frail self that clings unto this world!
O thou whom I once loved!
Kiyotsune is here!

WIFE O wondrous marvel!
I see Kiyotsune by my pillow,
And yet I know that he has drowned himself.
How then can I behold him save in dream?
Though but a dream,
Yet I am thankful to see his form once more.
But since, defying heaven's decree,
You brought your life to an untimely end,
You've proved yourself untrue
And bred resentment in my breast.

KIYOTSUNE Though you reproach me for my deed,
You too are not unworthy of reproach.
Why did you spurn the keepsake I left to ease your pain?

WIFE No! No! Why I did so
Is set forth in a poem
Which scarce conveys
How deep the sight of it did stir me.

KIYOTSUNE Unless you had grown weary of my love, you should have treasured the gift I took such care to leave you.

WIFE You mistake my reason:
You meant the keepsake as a comfort,
But as I look upon that lock
My mind becomes unruly like my hair.

KIYOTSUNE Since you have spurned my gift and rendered vain my thoughtful care, I cannot forgive your cruelty.

WIFE Nor I your wilful death.

KIYOTSUNE One taunts the other with reproaches,

WIFE The other tauntingly replies.

KIYOTSUNE The keepsake is a source of woe.
WIFE And a lock of hair
CHORUS Becomes for us a source of strife.

KIYOTSUNE Listen while I tell you what befell me in the days gone by, and forget your grievance.
Hearken to me!
We chanced to learn
The foe was marching through Kyushu
Against our castle in Yamaga.[7]
Dismayed, in haste we took to barges,
Plying our oars the long night through,
And reached Yanagi in Buzen Province.
CHORUS Where, as its name bespeaks,
An avenue of willows lines the sea-front;
Here rude buildings were put up
To house the Imperial Court.
KIYOTSUNE Then we were told
The Emperor would invoke Hachiman at Usa Shrine;
CHORUS Thither a store of gold and silver
And countless precious gifts,
And seven steeds sacred to the god,
Were brought as offerings to the Lord of War.[8]
WIFE Though you may think I still reproach you,
Was it not a rash and foolish deed
To cast away your life before the time,
While yet you knew not
The fate awaiting the Emperor and the Heike clan?
KIYOTSUNE Truly you would be right,
Had not the sacred oracle declared
Our cause past hope.
But pray, hear me to the end!
CHORUS How while the Emperor and his court

7. In Chikuzen province, where a local lord had given them refuge.
8. Hachiman, the war-god.

Were keeping vigil at the shrine,
Offering up prayers and making vows,
Behind the curtain of brocade
That hangs before the holy place,
A voice divine proclaimed,—
KIYOTSUNE "No power hath the God of Usa
To change man's hateful fate on earth!
What serves it then to urge Him further?"

KIYOTSUNE Alas! Gods and Buddhas
CHORUS Both forsake our cause.
All confidence and spirit lost,
Like a rumbling cart
The Emperor we follow to his quarters.
O woeful sight!
Meanwhile we learn
The foe is marching into Nagato Province.[9]
Once more we embark,
Wretched indeed our plight!
Now as I ponder deeply
Wherefore Hachiman's fateful words
Run ever in my head,
I, Kiyotsune, call to mind
That in the head of an upright man
God dwells.[10]
Possessed by that single thought,
KIYOTSUNE I feel 'twould be but foolishness
To save the dew-drop of my foredoomed life,
CHORUS As though it could endure.
Rather than trust to any boat
Floating like seaweed to and fro,
A prey to endless sorrow,
Like to a water-fowl I'll dive into the sea,

9. In southwest Honshu, directly across the Inland Sea from the Heike encampment in northern Kyushu.
10. The god Hachiman supposedly had vowed always to protect and guide a just man.

And so end my life.
Keeping my own counsel
I stand and wait upon the bow-planks
While the autumn moon
Grows pale in the dawning sky.
Perish I must like surf upon the shore.
Our life is but a travail
And I can quit this world without regret.
Others may deem my deed stark mad;
Well, let them judge me as they will!
The moon descends the western sky,
I'll follow her to the Western Paradise.
Namu Amida Butsu![11] Receive my spirit!
Thus praying, overboard I leap
And sink down to the oozy bottom of the sea.
So pitifully ends my woeful life!

WIFE Hearing your tale, my mind is mazed;
Sobs shake me and hot tears fall.
O tragic ending to our wedded life!
KIYOTSUNE How true the saying,
"Once fallen in the pit
The selfsame grievous lot awaits all men."
KIYOTSUNE Where'er I turn in the world of demons,
CHORUS The trees are foes,
Arrows the falling rain,
Sharp swords strew the ground,
The hills are iron castles,
The clouds are battle-pennants,
Enemies thrust with their proud blades,
Hate flashing in their eyes.
Here all is strife:
Anger and lust, greed and ignorance
Strive against the Holy Way.
Now the foes advance in waves,
Now like the ebbing tide retreat.
The battles of Shikoku and Kyushu

11. This is the standard invocation to the Buddha Amida.

Endlessly are fought again
Till, now at last, these torments cease.
Relying utterly upon the barque of Holy Law,
The dying Kiyotsune uttered the tenfold prayer:
Kiyotsune, the Pure-hearted
Now enters the Western Paradise.
Praised be Amida!